ALAN ROGERS SELECTED SITES IN

EUROPE

Celebrating 50 years of inspiring campers, caravanners and motorhomers since 1968

Compiled by: Alan Rogers Travel Ltd

Editorial
Editor: Robin Fearn
Associate Editor: Russell Wheldon, Russet Marketing

Production
Production Manager: Robert Baker
Visual Design and Layout: Ben Tully

Advertising
UK Sales Manager: Jo Smethurst
European Sales Manager: Tolga Dervish
European Sales Agency: Servicios Turísticos Heinze Latzke S.A.

Alan Rogers Travel
Chief Operating Officer: Chris Newey
Finance Manager: Alison Harris
IT Manager: Roland Greenstreet

Published by: Alan Rogers Travel Ltd,
Spelmonden Old Oast, Goudhurst, Kent TN17 1HE
www.alanrogers.com

50th edition - February 2018
ISBN 978-1-909057-90-6

Printed in Great Britain by Stephens & George Print Group

Stay in touch alanrogers.com/signup

facebook.com/
alanrogerstravel

twitter.com/
alanrogers

plus.google.com/
+alanrogers

CONTENTS

WELCOME

TO THE 50TH ANNIVERSARY EDITION

Alan Rogers Guides were first published 50 years ago. Since Alan Rogers published the first campsite guide that bore his name, the nature of European campsites has changed immeasurably.

Back in 1968 many campsites, though well established, were still works in progress having been converted from farms and orchards in the post-war years. Of course, there were fewer to choose from than today and the quality levels varied hugely.

Over the 50 years since the first edition of the Alan Rogers guide, the quality of most campsites has evolved in leaps and bounds. In terms of today's facilities, infrastructure, technology and accommodation types there is very little comparison with what was on offer half a century ago.

Since 1968 we at Alan Rogers have developed longstanding relationships with many campsites. We have worked with different generations of campsite owners and shared with many of them the trials and tribulations along the way. Typically, campsite owners are a hardy breed, passionate about their campsite and ever keen to show it and their region off to every visitor.

The Alan Rogers guides have always aimed to celebrate the variety, recognise the quality and salute the unique (check out our annual awards on pages 10-11). So read on and find the perfect campsite for your next holiday, whatever type of campsite that may be.

Whether you're an old hand in terms of camping and caravanning or are contemplating your first trip, a regular Alan Rogers reader or a new convert, we wish you well in your travels and some pleasurable 'armchair touring' in the meantime!

The Alan Rogers Team

ALAN ROGERS
1919 - 2000

ALAN ROGERS

IN SEARCH OF THE BEST

There are many thousands of campsites across Europe of varying quality: this guide contains impartially written reports on over 400, including many of the very finest, in 16 countries. Are there more? Yes, of course, and in countries not included in this book. Online at alanrogers.com you'll find details of many more - over 8,000 campsites.

Put simply, a guide like this can never be exhaustive. We have had to make difficult editorial decisions with the aim of providing you with a selection of the best, rather than information on all – in short, a more selective approach.

We are mindful that people want different things from their choice of campsite so we try to include a range of campsite 'styles' to cater for a wide variety of preferences: from those seeking a small peaceful campsite in the heart of the countryside, to visitors looking for an 'all singing, all dancing' site in a popular seaside resort.

Those with more specific interests, such as sporting facilities, cultural events or historical attractions, are also catered for. The size of the site, whether it's part of a chain or privately owned, should make no difference in terms of quality. The key is that it should be 'fit for purpose' in order to shine and stand out.

If a campsite can identify and understand what kind of campsite it sets out to be, and who it wants to attract, then it can enhance its kerb appeal by developing with that in mind.

By way of example, a lakeside campsite with credentials as a serious windsurfing centre should probably offer equipment for hire, secure storage for customers' own kit, courses and tuition, meteorological feeds and so on.

A campsite in the heart of the Loire Valley might offer guided excursions to local châteaux, weekly tastings of regional wine and cheese, suggested walking or cycling itineraries to local châteaux with entry discounts and so on.

Whatever style of campsite you're seeking, we hope you'll find some inspiration here.

On-site information including accommodation count, pitch count, GPS coordinates, Postcode and campsite address.

Campsite Name

A description of the site in which we try to give an idea of its general features – its size, its situation, its strengths and its weaknesses. This section should provide a picture of the site itself with reference to the facilities that are provided and if they impact on its appearance or character. We include details on approximate pitch numbers, electricity (with amperage), hardstandings etc. in this section as pitch design, planning and terracing affects the site's overall appearance. Similarly we include reference to pitches used for caravan holiday homes, chalets, and the like.

Lists more specific information on the site's facilities and amenities and, where available, the dates when these facilities are open (if not for the whole season).

Campsite contact information

Opening dates

Below we list 'ideal for' themes. These features include dogs allowed, open all year, family friendly, naturist etc.

 Beach nearby

 Dogs allowed

Open all year

 Fishing

 Watersports

 Golf

This is a QR code. You can scan it with your smartphone and it will take you directly to the campsite listing on our website. Download a QR code app for your phone and Try it!

HOW TO USE

THIS GUIDE

The layout of this 2018 guide is slightly different from previous editions. We still aim to provide comprehensive information, written in plain English in an easy to use format, but a few words of explanation regarding the content may be helpful.

Toilet blocks: Typically, toilet blocks will be equipped with WCs, washbasins with hot and cold water and hot shower cubicles. They will have all necessary shelves, hooks, plugs and mirrors. There will be a chemical toilet disposal point and the campsite will provide water and waste water drainage points and bin areas.

Shop: Basic or fully supplied, and opening dates.

Bars, restaurants, takeaway facilities and entertainment: We try hard to supply opening and closing dates (if other than the campsite opening dates) and to identify if there are discos or other entertainment.

Swimming pools: These might vary from a simple, conventional swimming pool to an elaborate complex with multiple pools and waterslides. Opening dates, charges and levels of supervision are provided where we have been notified. There is a regulation whereby Bermuda shorts may not be worn in swimming pools (for health and hygiene reasons). It is worth ensuring that you do take 'proper' swimming trunks with you.

Leisure facilities: For example, playing fields, bicycle hire, organised activities and entertainment.

Dogs: If dogs are not accepted or restrictions apply, we state it here. If planning to take a dog, or other pet, we recommend you check in advance.

Opening dates: Campsites can, and sometimes do, alter these dates before the start of the season, often for good reasons. If you intend to visit shortly after a published opening date, or shortly before the closing date, it is wise to check that it will actually be open at the time required. Similarly some sites operate a restricted service during the low season, only opening some of their facilities (e.g. swimming pools) during the main season. Again if you are at all doubtful it is wise to check.

Sometimes, campsite amenities may be dependent on there being enough customers on site to justify their opening. Some campsites may not be fully ready by their stated opening dates – grass may not all be cut or perhaps only limited sanitary facilities open. At the end of the season they also tend to close down some facilities and generally wind things down.

We usually give an overview of the pitches, including an approximate quantity. This figure may vary year on year so is rarely absolute.

2017 AWARDS

BY ALAN ROGERS & CAMC

For over 50 years, the Alan Rogers guides have been providing campers, caravanners and motorhomers with impartial information about the best campsites in the UK and Europe. No other guide offers the level of detail and quality assessment found in ours.

In 2016 we joined forces with The Caravan & Motorhome Club to present the joint CAMC & Alan Rogers Awards for the very first time.

Our awards have a broad scope and before committing to our winners, we carefully consider more than 2,000 campsites featured in the Alan Rogers guides and The Caravan & Motorhome Club 'Venture Abroad' program, taking into account comments from our site assessors, our head office team and, of course, our members & readers.

For the 2017 awards there were nine categories, each with a winner and a highly commended runner-up.

PROGRESS AWARD 2017

This award reflects the hard work and commitment undertaken by particular site owners to improve and upgrade their site.

Winner	**FR85150**	**Camping Resort La Yole**	**France**	**p109**
Runner-up	**BE0670**	**Camping Parc la Clusure**	**Belgium**	**p39**

WELCOME AWARD 2017

This award takes account of sites offering a particularly friendly welcome and maintaining a friendly ambience throughout readers' holidays.

Winner	**FR17470**	**Le Domaine d'Oléron**	**France**	**p118**
Runner-up	**NL5600**	**Vakantiepark Delftse Hout**	**Netherlands**	**p324**

INNOVATION AWARD 2017

Our Innovation Award acknowledges campsites with creative and original concepts, possibly with features which are unique, and cannot therefore be found elsewhere. We have identified innovation both in campsite amenities and also in rentable accommodation.

Winner	**FR30290**	**Domaine de Massereau**	**France**	**p164**
Runner-up	**IT62030**	**Caravan Park Sexten**	**Italy**	**p277**

SEASIDE AWARD 2017

This award is made for sites which we feel are particularly suitable for a really excellent seaside holiday.

Winner	ES80350	Camping l'Amfora	Spain	p381
Runner-up	FR40060	Camping Club Eurosol	France	p160

COUNTRY AWARD 2017

This award contrasts with our seaside award and acknowledges sites which are attractively located in delightful, rural locations.

Winner	FR14090	Camping Le Brévedent	France	p77
Runner-up	SV4200	Camping Bled	Slovenia	p375

ALL YEAR AWARD 2017

This award acknowledges sites which are open all year round.

Winner	ES89640	Camping El Molino de Cabuérniga	Spain	p428
Runner-up	PO8130	Orbitur Guincho	Portugal	p357

FAMILY SITE AWARD 2017

Many sites claim to be family friendly but this award acknowledges the sites we feel to be the very best in this respect.

Winner	FR49010	Domaine de la Brèche	France	p96
Runner-up	IT62580	Azur Camping Rio Vantone	Italy	p274

SMALL CAMPSITE AWARD 2017

This award acknowledges excellent small campsites (fewer than 150 pitches) which offer a friendly welcome and top quality amenities throughout the season to their guests.

Winner	FR37030	Camping le Moulin Fort	France	p99
Runner-up	NL6565	Camping Den Driesch	Netherlands	p330

VIDEO AWARD 2017

This award reflects sites which have invested signifficantly in innovative video content and production.

Winner	IR9150	River Valley Caravan & Camping Park	Ireland	p256
Runner-up	DE38330	Camping LuxOase	Germany	p194

AUSTRIA

Austria is primarily known for two contrasting attractions: the capital Vienna with its cathedral, wine bars and musical events, and the skiing and hiking resorts of the Alps. It is an ideal place to visit all year round, for the Easter markets, winter sports and the many cultural and historical attractions, as well as the breathtaking scenery.

The charming Tirol region in the west of Austria is easily accessible, and popular with tourists who flock to its ski resorts in winter. In the summer months it is transformed into a verdant landscape of picturesque valleys dotted with wild flowers, a paradise for walkers.

Situated in the centre are the Lake District, and Salzburg, city of Mozart, with its wealth of gardens and palaces. Vienna's iconic ferris wheel is a must for taking in the beautiful parks and architecture from 200 ft.

The neighbouring provinces of Lower Austria, Burgenland and Styria, land of vineyards, mountains and farmland are off the tourist routes, but provide good walking territory. Further south, the Carinthia region enjoys a mild, sunny climate and is dominated by crystal clear lakes and soaring mountains, yet has plenty of opportunities for winter sports.

Language: German
Capital: Vienna
Currency: Euro (€)
Time Zone: Central European Time (GMT/UTC plus one hour)
Telephone Country Code: 00 33
Tourist Office: www.austria.info/uk

Say Hello
'guten tag' (goo-ten tahk)

Say Goodbye
'Auf Wiedersehen' (owf vee-der-say-en)

Public Holidays
New Year; Epiphany; Easter Mon; Labour Day; Ascension; Whit Mon; Corpus Christi; Assumption 15 Aug; National Day 26 Oct; All Saints 1 Nov; Immaculate Conception 8 Dec; Christmas 25, 26 Dec.

Motoring
Visitors using Austrian motorways and 'A' roads must display a Motorway Vignette on their vehicle as they enter Austria. Failure to have one will mean a heavy, on-the-spot fine. Vignettes are obtained at all major border crossings into Austria and at larger petrol stations. All vehicles above 3.5 tonnes maximum permitted laden weight are required to use a small device called the 'GO Box.'

1 accommodations
98 pitches
GPS: 46.95785, 11.011933
Post Code: A-6450

Sölden, Tirol

Camping Sölden

www.alanrogers.com/au0053
info@camping-soelden.com
052 542 6270
www.camping-soelden.com

Open (Touring Pitches):
All year excl. 15 April - 22 June and 23 September - 11 October.

Camping Sölden is a beautifully planned, family run site located deep within the Ötztaler Alps, and open for both summer and winter seasons. Pitches are arranged on grassy terraces and are all equipped with electricity (10A, Europlug), as well as TV and telephone connections. A number of heated wooden barrels are available for rent. The site boasts an excellent spa/wellness centre with a Finnish sauna, steam bath, infra-red cabin and comfortable relaxation room, all free to campers during the winter season. Other amenities include an excellent 85 sq.m. indoor climbing wall.

Superb sanitary facilities within the main building have some individual cabins and facilities for children and disabled visitors. Motorcaravan services. Washing machines and dryers. Dog shower. Camping essentials sold. Fresh bread. Restaurant, pizzeria and takeaway. Spa and wellness centre. Library/TV room. Play area. Ski and bicycle storage. Accommodation to rent. Fishing. WiFi over most of site (charged).

Ideal For...

 Dogs

 Fishing

 Golf

 Play Area

 Disabled Facilities

 Pets Accepted

Scan me for more information.

5 accommodations
80 pitches
GPS: 47.27563, 10.98619
Post Code: A-6422

Stams, Tirol

www.alanrogers.com/au0056
info@camping-eichenwald.at
052 636 159
www.camping-eichenwald.at

Open (Touring Pitches):
All year.

Camping Eichenwald

Camping Eichenwald is a small rural campsite in the Inn Valley area of the Tirol, 40 km. west of Innsbruck. The site lies on the outskirts of the small village of Stams, less than 3 km. from the A12 motorway. Although the site lies on a hillside, there are around 100 touring pitches set on attractive, level terraces, most with wonderful views over the valley and mountains. Some are open, others are in light woodland offering more shade. They are neither marked nor numbered, adding to the relaxed ambience of the site. Most have 16A electricity, metered in the winter.

High quality toilet facilities suitable for both summer and winter. Baby room. Wet room for disabled campers. Laundry facilities. Drying room. Shop for essentials. Bistro bar/restaurant with terrace and family/TV room. Pizzeria (1/5-30/9). Small heated swimming pool with sunbathing terrace (summer). Play areas. Organised family entertainment including local folklore evenings. E-bicycle hire. WiFi over most of site (free from 2016).

Ideal For...

 Beach

 Dogs

Year Round Camping

 Fishing

 Watersports

 Golf

Scan me for more information.

18 accommodations
205 pitches
GPS: 47.23755, 11.34201
Post Code: A-6161

Natters, Tirol

Ferienparadies Natterer See

www.alanrogers.com/au0060
info@natterersee.com
051 254 6732
www.natterersee.com

Open (Touring Pitches):
All year.

In a quiet location arranged around two lakes and set amidst beautiful alpine scenery, this site, founded in 1930, is renowned as one of Austria's top sites. Over the last few years many improvements have been carried out and pride of place goes to the award-winning, multifunctional building at the entrance to the site. This contains all the facilities expected of a top site, including a special section for children, private bathrooms to rent and also a dog bath. The reception, shop and café/bar/bistro are on the ground floor and on the upper floor is a panoramic lounge and cinema. Almost all of the generous pitches are for tourers. They are terraced, set on gravel/grass, and have electricity; many have water and drainage. Most offer a splendid view of the mountains.

Large sanitary block with underfloor heating, private cabins, and facilities for children & disabled visitors. Laundry facilities. Motorcaravan services. Fridge box hire. Bar. Restaurant and takeaway (at least one open all year). Pizzeria. Playgrounds. Children's activity programme. Child minding (seasonal). Sports field. Archery. Youth room with games, pool and billiards. TV room with Sky. Open-air cinema. Mountain bike hire (July/Aug). Aquapark (seasonal). Surf bikes & pedaloes. Canoes & mini sailboats (charged). Daily entertainment programme (seasonal). Dogs are not accepted from July/August. WiFi (charged).

Ideal For...

 Kids

 Beach

 Dogs

Year Round Camping

 Fishing

 Walking

Scan me for more information.

10 accommodations
130 pitches
GPS: 47.46196, 11.90713
Post Code: A-6233

Kramsach, Tirol

Camping Seehof

www.alanrogers.com/au0065
info@camping-seehof.com
053 376 3541
www.camping-seehof.com

Open (Touring Pitches):
All year.

Camping Seehof is a family run site and excellent in every respect. It is situated in a marvellous sunny and peaceful location on the eastern shores of the Reintalersee. The site's comfortable restaurant has a terrace with lake and mountain views and serves local dishes as well as homemade cakes and ice cream. The site is in two areas: a small one next to the lake is ideal for sunbathing, the other larger one adjoins the excellent sanitary block. There are 170 pitches, 130 of which are for touring (20 tent pitches), served by good access roads and with 16A electricity (Europlug) and TV points; 100 pitches are fully serviced, with more being upgraded every year.

The sanitary facilities are first class and include ten bathrooms to rent for private use. Baby room. Facilities for disabled visitors. Dog shower. Washing machine and dryer. Ski room. Motorcaravan services. Small shop. Good value restaurant. Playground. Bicycle hire. Fishing. WiFi over site (charged). Apartments to rent. Renovated fitness and play rooms.

Ideal For...

 Beach

 Dogs

Year Round Camping

 Fishing

 Watersports

 Walking

Scan me for more information.

40 accommodations
300 pitches
GPS: 47.2838, 12.81694
Post Code: A-5671

Bruck an der Glocknerstraße, Salzburg

Sportcamp Woferlgut

www.alanrogers.com/au0180
info@sportcamp.at
065 457 3030
www.sportcamp.at

Open (Touring Pitches):
All year.

Sportcamp Woferlgut, a family run site, is one of the very best in Austria. It lies in the village of Bruck lies at the northern end of the Großglocknerstrasse spectacular mountain road in the Hohe Tauern National Park, near the Zeller See. Surrounded by mountains, the site is quite flat with pleasant views. The 520 level, grass pitches (300 for touring units) are marked out by shrubs and each has 16A metered electricity (Europlug), water, drainage, cable TV socket and gas point. A high grass bank separates the site from the road. At the site's own lake, popular for swimming and sunbathing, is a new adventure timber ropeway and another playground. A free activity and entertainment programme is provided all year round, but especially during the summer.

Three modern sanitary blocks (the newest in a class of its own) have excellent facilities including private cabins, underfloor heating and music. Washing machines and dryers. Facilities for disabled visitors. Family bathrooms for hire (some with bathtubs). Motorcaravan services. Well stocked shop. Bar, restaurant and takeaway. Small, heated outdoor pool and children's pool (1/5-15/10). TV rooms. New gym. Three playgrounds, indoor play room and children's cinema. Fun train. Adventure rope walkway. Tennis. Bicycle hire. Watersports and lake swimming. Pony rides. New crazy golf course. WiFi over site (charged).

Ideal For...

 Kids

 Beach

 Dogs

 Year Round Camping

 Fishing

 Watersports

Scan me for more information.

10 accommodations
200 pitches
GPS: 47.57427, 12.70602
Post Code: A-5092

St Martin bei Lofer, Salzburg

Park Grubhof

www.alanrogers.com/au0265
home@grubhof.com
065 888 237
www.grubhof.com

Open (Touring Pitches):
All year excl. November.

Park Grubhof is a beautifully laid out, level and spacious site set in the former riding and hunting park of the 14th-century Schloss Grubhof. The 200 touring pitches, all with 12-16A electricity, have been carefully divided into separate areas for different types of visitor – dog owners, young people, families and groups, and a quiet area. There are 167 very large pitches (at least 120 sq.m), all with electricity, water and drainage, many along the bank of the Saalach river. Although new, the central building has been built in traditional Tirolean style using, in part, materials hundreds of years old reclaimed from old farmhouses. The result is most attractive. On the ground floor you will find reception, a cosy café/bar, a restaurant and a small shop, and on the first floor, a deluxe sauna, beauty and wellness suite, two apartments and a relaxation room.

Three attractive, modern sanitary units constructed of wood and glass provide excellent facilities. Large family bathrooms (free with certain pitches, to rent in winter). Washing machine, dryer and drying gallery. Gym upstairs (€ 5 membership). Recreation and conference room and a small library. Saunas, steam bath and massage. Ski and canoe storage room. Motorcaravan services. Luxury dog shower. Shop, restaurant and bar. Adventure-style playground. Youth room. Playroom. Watersports. Cabins to rent. Hotel and B&B accommodation. WiFi throughout (charged).

Ideal For...

 Beach

 Dogs

 Fishing

 Watersports

 Walking

 Golf

Scan me for more information.

36 accommodations
540 pitches
GPS: 46.77151, 13.64918
Post Code: A-9873

Döbriach, Carinthia

www.alanrogers.com/au0480
info@burgstaller.co.at
042 467 774
www.burgstaller.co.at

Open (Touring Pitches):
27 March - 1 November.

Campingpark Burgstaller

This is a large site in a beautiful location. It is busy, family oriented with a sociable atmosphere, particularly in the restaurant in the evenings. The 590 pitches (540 for tourers) are on flat, well drained grass, backing onto hedges on either side of access roads. They vary in size (45-120 sq.m) and access to some can be tricky. Special pitches are set aside for motorcaravans. The entrance is directly opposite the park leading to the swimming pool, which campers have free access to and where there is free WiFi. Many organised activities, including games & competitions. This site can become crowded in the school holidays. Good English is spoken.

Three good quality toilet blocks include washbasins in cabins, facilities for children & disabled visitors, dishwashers and underfloor heating for cool weather. Seven private rooms to rent (3 with jacuzzi baths). Motorcaravan services. Bar. Restaurant with terrace & shop (seasonal). Bowling alley. Disco (July/Aug). TV room. Sauna and solarium. Two play areas. Bathing and boating on lake. Special entrance rate for lake attractions. Fishing. Bicycle hire. Mountain bike area. Riding. Comprehensive entertainment programmes. Covered stage and outdoor arena for church services (in German) and folk and modern music concerts. WiFi over site (charged).

Ideal For...

Kids

Beach

Dogs

Fishing

Watersports

Golf

Scan me for more information.

10 accommodations
212 pitches
GPS: 46.949724, 13.509606
Post Code: A-9854

Malta, Carinthia

Camping Maltatal

www.alanrogers.com/au0490
info@maltacamp.at
047 332 34
www.camping-maltatal.at

Open (Touring Pitches):
27 April 2018 - 8 October 2018

Situated between two national parks in a valley between the mountains, this family run, four-hectare site offers spectacular views over the surrounding area, especially from the pool which is over 300 sq.m. with a grassy sunbathing area and is open to all (at extra cost). There are 220 grass pitches on narrow terraces (70-100 sq.m) and mostly in rows on either side of narrow access roads. Numbered and marked, some separated with low hedges, all have electricity and 160 have water and drainage.

Two toilet blocks, including one excellent new one, have about half the washbasins in cabins and ten family washrooms. Facilities for babies and children. Laundry facilities. Motorcaravan services. Fridge hire. Shop. Bar. Restaurant. Heated outdoor swimming pool (30/5-01/9). Sauna. Playground. Bicycle hire. Entertainment programme and many walks and excursions. WiFi over site (free). Gas. Electric barbecues are not permitted.

Ideal For...

 Dogs

 Fishing

 Golf

 Play Area

 Disabled Facilities

 Pets Accepted

Scan me for more information.

35 accommodations
429 pitches
GPS: 46.66371, 13.9748
Post Code: A-9570

Ossiach, Carinthia

Camping Ossiacher See

www.alanrogers.com/au0460
martinz@camping.at
042 434 36
www.terrassen.camping.at/en

Open (Touring Pitches):
1 May - 1 October.

Terrassen Camping Ossiacher See is a gently terraced site, protected by rising hills with lovely views across the lake to the mountains beyond. Trees, flowers, hedges and bushes abound, adding atmosphere to this neat and tidy site. The 429 level pitches, all with electricity, are in rows on the level grass terraces separated by hard roads and some divided by hedges. A separate area (40-50 pitches) is provided for campers with dogs. Good English is spoken.

Five well maintained sanitary blocks are heated in cool weather, some with washbasins in cabins. Ten family washrooms (charged), baby rooms and facilities for disabled campers. Laundry facilities. Motorcaravan services. Restaurant (15/5-15/9). Well stocked supermarket. ATM. High season entertainment programme. Beach volleyball. Trampoline. Playgrounds, games rooms and disco courtyard. Water-skiing and windsurfing schools and boats for hire. Tennis. Bicycle and moped hire. Fishing. Riding.

Ideal For...

 Beach

 Dogs

 Fishing

 Watersports

 Golf

 Play Area

Scan me for more information.

2 accommodations
100 pitches
GPS: 48.31078, 16.328119
Post Code: A-3400

Klosterneuburg, Lower Austria

www.alanrogers.com/au0320
campklosterneuburg@oeamtc.at
022 432 5877
www.campingklosterneuburg.at

Open (Touring Pitches):
19 March - 6 November.

Donaupark Klosterneuburg

Klosterneuburg lies just to the north of Vienna on the Danube. It is outside the city boundary, away from the noise and bustle of the famous city but only minutes away by train. Owned and run by the Austrian Motor Club (OAMTC), this site is in a park-like situation, surrounded by trees but with little shade. The 100 pitches are on the small side. However, all are accessed from hard roads and all have 6A electricity. Alongside the site is Happyland, an amusement park which also has a large swimming pool (discounts for campers).

Two modern sanitary units, one at reception and the other by the pitches (may be under pressure when busy). Facilities for disabled visitors. Motorcaravan services. Washing machines and dryer. Electric cooking rings. Freezer for ice packs. Restaurant/snack bar incl. small shop for basics (1/5-31/10). Play area. Bicycle hire. WiFi (free).

Ideal For...

 Beach

 Dogs

 Golf

 Play Area

 Disabled Facilities

 Pets Accepted

Scan me for more information.

70 pitches
GPS: 47.87965, 13.52444
Post Code: A-4865

Nussdorf am Attersee, Upper Austria

Seecamping Gruber

www.alanrogers.com/au0345
office@camping-gruber.at
076 668 0450
www.camping-gruber.at

Open (Touring Pitches):
15 April - 15 October.

The Attersee is the largest of a group of lakes just to the east of Salzburg, in the very attractive Salzkammergut area. Seecamping Gruber is a small, often crowded site halfway up the western side of the lake. There are 160 individual pitches, with an increasing number of seasonal units taking the larger pitches. There are some 70 pitches for tourers, all with 16A electricity and many with shade. Pitches tend to be small to medium size and the access roads are narrow making entrance and exit difficult.

Modern sanitary facilities, now with a children's area, offer some private cabins, washing machine and dryer, good unit for disabled visitors, and baby room. Bar, restaurant, shop and takeaway (all 15/4-15/10). TV room. Play area. Swimming, paddling pools, sauna, solarium and gym (all 1/5-30/9). Fishing. Bicycle hire. WiFi over site (free). Accommodation to rent.

Ideal For...

 Beach

 Dogs

 Fishing

 Watersports

 Golf

 Play Area

Scan me for more information.

2 accommodations
115 pitches
GPS: 47.170147, 9.807677
Post Code: A-6714

Nüziders bei Bludenz, Vorarlberg

www.alanrogers.com/au0232
sonnencamp@aon.at
055 526 4035
www.camping-sonnenberg.com

Open (Touring Pitches):
29 April - 3 October.

Camping Sonnenberg

A friendly welcome awaits at this well equipped, family run site delightfully located at the junction of five Alpine valleys. From this hillside site there are magnificent, ever-changing views along and across the mountains. Very easily reached from the A14 autobahn and located on the outskirts of a large village with all facilities, the site is not only ideal as a stopover but also as a base from which to tour in this spectacular alpine region. All of the 115 generously sized, terraced pitches have 13A electricity, 60 are fully serviced and most are hard enough for motorcaravans. Two terraces for caravans are car free with a separate car parking area.

A superb new building contains high quality facilities. On the lower floor are WCs, spacious hot showers, and washbasins (some in cubicles), and a baby room. No facilities for disabled visitors. Drying room, laundry and dishwashing room upstairs. Motorcaravan services. Small shop (1/5-3/10). Gas supplies. TV and cinema room with tourist information. Playground. Only one dog per unit is allowed. WiFi over site (charged). Two chalets to rent.

Ideal For...

 Dogs

 Fishing

 Golf

 Play Area

 Pets Accepted

Scan me for more information.

BELGIUM

A small country divided into three regions, Flanders in the north, Wallonia in the south and Brussels the capital. Belgium is rich in scenic countryside, culture and history, notably the great forest of Ardennes, the historic cities of Bruges and Gent, and the western coastline with its sandy beaches.

Brussels is at the very heart of Europe and is a must-see destination with its heady mix of shops, nightlife, exhibitions and festivals - a multicultural and multilingual city that is a focal point of art, fashion and culture.

In the French-speaking region of Wallonia lies the mountainous Ardennes, home to picturesque villages rich in tradition and folklore. It is a favourite of nature-lovers and walkers who enjoy exploring its many castles and forts. The safe, sandy beaches on the west coast run for forty miles. Bruges is Europe's best preserved medieval city, criss-crossed by willow-lined canals, where tiny cobbled streets open onto pretty squares. After visiting the many museums and art galleries, why not sample some of the delicious chocolate for which the city is famous for.

Language: There are three official languages. French is spoken in the south, Flemish in the north, and German in the eastern provinces.
Capital: Brussels
Currency: Euro (€)
Time Zone: Central European Time (GMT/UTC plus one hour)
Telephone Country Code: 00 32
Tourist Office: www.belgiumtheplaceto.be

Public Holidays
New Year's Day; Easter Mon; Labour Day; Ascension; Whit Monday; Flemish Day 11 July; National Day 21 July; Assumption 15 Aug; French Day 27 Sept; All Saints 1, 2 Nov; Armistice Day 11 Nov; King's Birthday 15 Nov; Christmas 25, 26 Dec.

Motoring
For cars with a caravan or trailer, motorways are toll free except for the Liefenshoek Tunnel in Antwerp. Maximum permitted overall length of vehicle/trailer or caravan combination is 18 m. Blue Zone parking areas exist in Brussels, Ostend, Bruges, Liège, Antwerp and Gent. Parking discs can be obtained from police stations, garages, and some shops.

34 accommodations
469 pitches
GPS: 51.12965, 2.77222
Post Code: B-8620

West Flanders, Flanders

Kompas Nieuwpoort

www.alanrogers.com/be0550
nieuwpoort@kompascamping.be
058 236 037
www.kompascamping.be

Open (Touring Pitches):
28 March - 12 November.

Not far from Dunkerque and Calais and convenient for the A18 motorway, this large, well equipped and well run site with 1056 pitches caters particularly for families. There are many amenities including a heated pool complex, a range of sporting activities, play areas and a children's farm. The 469 touring pitches, all with 10A electricity, are in regular rows on flat grass in various parts of the site; 120 also have a water point and waste water drainage. With many seasonal units and caravan holiday homes, the site becomes full during Belgian holidays and in July and August.

Five modern, clean and well maintained toilet blocks include washbasins in cubicles, controllable showers and excellent facilities for families, young children and disabled visitors. Dishwashing and laundry rooms. Washing machines and dryers. Motorcaravan services. Supermarket, bakery, restaurant, takeaway and café/bar (all w/ends low season, otherwise daily). Swimming pools (heated and supervised) with slide, paddling pool and pool games (17/5-14/9). Bicycle hire. Tennis. Extensive adventure playgrounds. Multisports court. Entertainment programme in July/Aug. WiFi throughout (charged).

Ideal For...

 Beach

 Dogs

 Fishing

 Watersports

 Walking

 Golf

Scan me for more information.

45 accommodations
137 pitches
GPS: 51.18448, 3.10445
Post Code: B-8490

West Flanders, Flanders

Recreatiepark Klein Strand

www.alanrogers.com/be0555
info@kleinstrand.be
050 811 440
www.kleinstrand.be

Open (Touring Pitches):
All year.

In a convenient location just off the A10 motorway and close to Bruges, this site is in two distinct areas divided by an access road. The main part of the site offers a lake with a marked off swimming area, a sandy beach, water slides and boating (no fishing). The touring section has 137 large pitches on flat grass separated by well trimmed hedges; all have electricity and access to water and drainage. Some leisure facilities for children are provided on this part of the site, along with a spacious bar and snack bar with takeaway (seasonal). The main site with all the privately owned mobile homes is closer to the lake, so has most of the amenities. These include the main reception building, restaurants, bar, minimarket, and sports facilities.

Single modern, heated, toilet block includes good sized showers (charged) and vanity style washbasins. Baby room. Basic facilities for disabled campers. Washing machines and dryer. Additional toilet facilities with washbasins in cubicles are located behind the touring field reception building (open July/Aug). Motorcaravan services. Bar and snack bar. Play area. Fun pool for small children. In main park: European and Chinese restaurants, bar and snack bar, takeaways (all year). Shop (Easter-end Aug). Tennis courts and sports field. Water ski school; water ski shows (Sundays in July/Aug). Bicycle hire. WiFi throughout (free).

Ideal For...

 Kids

 Beach

 Dogs

Year Round Camping

 Fishing

 Watersports

Scan me for more information.

26 accommodations
486 pitches
GPS: 51.28908, 4.85508
Post Code: B-2275

Antwerp, Flanders

www.alanrogers.com/be0655
info@lilsebergen.be
014 557 901
www.delilsebergen.be

Open (Touring Pitches):
1 April - 31 December

Camping De Lilse Bergen

This attractive, quietly located holiday site has 486 shady pitches, of which 233 (all with 10A Europlug electricity) are for touring units. Set on sandy soil among pine trees and rhododendrons and arranged around a large lake, the site has a Mediterranean feel. It is well fenced, with a night guard and comprehensive, well labelled fire-fighting equipment. Cars are parked away from units. The site is really child friendly with each access road labelled with a different animal symbol to enable children to find their own unit easily. An entertainment programme is organised in high season.

Two of the six heated toilet blocks are new. Some washbasins in cubicles and good hot showers (on payment). Well equipped baby rooms. Facilities for disabled campers. Laundry. Barrier keys can be charged up with units for operating showers, washing machine etc. First aid post. Motorcaravan services. Takeaway (Easter-30/9). Bar and well stocked shop (Easter-01/07 and 01/09-15/9: 10am-12h and weekends; July and August: 10am-6pm). Tennis. Minigolf. Boules. Climbing wall. Playground, trampolines and skateboard ramp. Pedalos, kayaks and bicycles for hire. Children's electric cars and pedal kart tracks (charged for). Free WiFi over site.

Ideal For...

 Kids

 Beach

 Dogs

 Golf

 Play Area

 Disabled Facilities

Scan me for more information.

12 accommodations
71 pitches
GPS: 51.35757, 4.95896
Post Code: B-2300

Antwerp, Flanders

Camping Baalse Hei

www.alanrogers.com/be0660
info@baalsehei.be
014 448 470
www.baalsehei.be

Open (Touring Pitches):
16 January - 15 December.

The Campine is an area covering three quarters of the Province of Antwerp, noted for its nature reserves, pine forests, meadows and streams and is ideal for walking and cycling, while Turnhout itself is an interesting old town. Baalse Hei, a long established, friendly site, has 469 pitches including a separate touring area of 71 large grass pitches (all with 16A electricity, TV connections and shared water point), thoughtfully developed with trees and bushes. Cars are parked away from, but near the pitches. Large motorcaravans can be accommodated (phone first to check availability). There is also accommodation to rent.

Three toilet blocks provide hot showers on payment (€ 0.50), some washbasins in cabins and facilities for disabled visitors. Dishwashing (hot water € 0.20). Launderette. Motorcaravan services. Shop (1/4-30/9). Café/restaurant (daily 1/4-30/9, w/ends only other times, closed 16/11-25/1). Breakfast served in high season. Club/TV room. Lake swimming. Fishing. Tennis. Boules. Volleyball. Basketball. Adventure play area. Bicycle hire. English is spoken. Overnight pitches for vehicles under 3.5t. In low season reception opens for limited hours (14.00-17.00). WiFi throughout (free).

Ideal For...

 Beach

 Dogs

 Fishing

 Watersports

 Walking

 Play Area

Scan me for more information.

24 accommodations
244 pitches
GPS: 51.17343, 5.53902
Post Code: B-3950

Limburg, Flanders

Goolderheide Vakantiepark

www.alanrogers.com/be0760
info@goolderheide.be
089 469 640
www.goolderheide.be

Open (Touring Pitches):
25 March - 30 September.

A large family holiday site with 900 individual pitches, Goolderheide has been owned and operated by the same family for many years and has an excellent pool complex and playgrounds. There are many seasonal and rental units, plus around 250 touring pitches with 6/10/16A electricity, all in a forest setting. The pitches are of variable size and access roads are quite narrow. The outdoor pool complex has two large pools (one of Olympic size), a slide and a paddling pool. There is also a fishing lake, and a lake with a small sandy beach. An enormous area is devoted to a comprehensive play area with a vast range of equipment.

Four sanitary buildings provide an ample supply of WCs and washbasins in cabins, but rather fewer preset showers. Family facilities. Two en-suite units for disabled visitors (key access). Laundry facilities. Dishwasher. Shop, bar and takeaway (daily in July/Aug, w/ends and public holidays in low season). Takeaway. Swimming pools. Tennis. Fishing. Boules. Minigolf. Play area and assault course. Extensive programme of activities (July/Aug).

Ideal For...

 Beach

 Dogs

 Fishing

 Walking

 Play Area

 Disabled Facilities

Scan me for more information.

2 accommodations
60 pitches
GPS: 51.0583, 5.6288
Post Code: B-3680

Limburg, Flanders

Camping Zavelbos

www.alanrogers.com/be0792
receptie@zavelbos.com
089 758 146
www.limburgcampings.be

Open (Touring Pitches):
All year.

Camping Zavelbos lies between woodland and moorland in a nature park of 2,000 hectares. It is a pleasant spot for nature lovers and those who love peace and quiet. There are many cycling and walking routes to enjoy in this beautiful region, alternatively you can simply relax in the peaceful campsite grounds complete with a large fishpond. There is no swimming pool but guests have free use of the pool complex at Wilhelm Tell Holiday Park (6 km). The 60 touring pitches (100-120 sq.m) all have 16A electricity (Europlug) and water. Bungalows and chalets are available to rent.

New sanitary facilities include family bathrooms, baths with jacuzzi and jet stream (key access € 50 deposit). Provision for disabled visitors. Laundry facilities. Dog shower. Motorcaravan services. Bar and snack bar. Tavern. Fishpond. Playground. Boules. Bicycle hire and free recharging of electric bikes. Free WiFi over site. No charcoal barbecues.

Ideal For...

 Dogs

 Year Round Camping

 Fishing

 Walking

 Golf

 Play Area

Scan me for more information.

15 accommodations
45 pitches
GPS: 51.05367, 3.97982
Post Code: B-9240

East Flanders, Flanders

Camping Groenpark

www.alanrogers.com/be0615
groenpark@scarlet.be
093 679 071
www.campinggroenpark.be/en/

Open (Touring Pitches):
1 March - 3 November.

Camping Groenpark is a popular wooded campsite in the heart of the Scheldt region of eastern Flanders. Between Antwerp and Ghent, it is only 10 minutes walk from a lake and close to the Donkmeer, the second largest lake in Flanders. There are 78 pitches, of which 55 good sized, level, grass pitches are for touring and access is good for large units. The pitches are naturally laid out in glades between the trees, some shady, some sunny and all have 16A electricity. There is an area especially for motorcaravans and a large, quiet open camping meadow. The site has large shower rooms, popular with families and a giant central barbecue area.

One large, modern toilet block at entrance and a smaller block on site with cabins containing toilet, shower and washbasin. Family shower room. Washing machine and dryer. Motorcaravan services. No shop, bar or meals but the town is only 500 m. TV room. Play area. WiFi on part of site (charged).

Ideal For...

 Beach

 Dogs

 Fishing

 Watersports

 Play Area

 Pets Accepted

Scan me for more information.

13 accommodations
109 pitches
GPS: 49.944925, 5.011002
Post Code: B-5555

Namur, Wallonia

www.alanrogers.com/be0713
info@3sources.be
061 730 051
www.3sources.be/

Open (Touring Pitches):
All year.

Camping les 3 Sources

Les 3 Sources can be found between the pilgrimage village of Beauraing and Bouillon. The campsite is run by a Dutch family and is well located for exploring the Belgian Ardennes. The site boasts a number of springs, three of which feed some large ponds, which are well stocked with carp and other coarse fish. Fishing is possible but you are asked to return your catch to the water. The site extends over 2.5 hectares and has 150 pitches. A number of these are occupied by seasonal units, or by mobile homes and chalets.

The sanitary building has modern fittings, heating and air conditioning. Play area. Three fishing ponds (small charge). Bar (selling snacks). Activity and entertainment programme. Accommodation to rent.

Ideal For...

 Beach

 Dogs

Year Round Camping

 Fishing

 Watersports

 Golf

Scan me for more information.

22 accommodations
55 pitches
GPS: 50.11128, 5.13376
Post Code: B-5580

Namur, Wallonia

Camping Le Roptai

www.alanrogers.com/be0850
info@leroptai.be
084 388 319
www.leroptai.be

Open (Touring Pitches):
1 February - 31 December.

This family site in the heart of the Ardennes, within easy reach of Dinant and Namur, was established in 1932. In a rural wooded setting with its own adventure playground in the trees, it is a good site for an active holiday, especially in high season when there is a weekly programme including rock climbing, abseiling, mountain biking and potholing. There are 55 good sized, grassy, touring pitches on sloping ground, most with 6A electricity. A programme of activities is organised for adults and children in high season.

Sanitary facilities below reception include an excellent suite for babies and disabled visitors. Five other blocks of varying styles are kept clean and offer basic facilities. Shop (1/7-31/8). Bar/snack bar with takeaway (1/7-31/8). Swimming pool and paddling pool (1/7-31/8). Play area. Activity programme (July/Aug). Bicycle hire. WiFi over part of site (charged). Mobile homes for rent.

Ideal For...

 Dogs

 Golf

 Play Area

 Disabled Facilities

 Pets Accepted

 Bar on Site

Scan me for more information.

15 accommodations
120 pitches
GPS: 50.41203, 5.95317
Post Code: B-4970

Liège, Wallonia

www.alanrogers.com/be0740
fb220447@skynet.be
080 863 075
www.eaurouge.eu

Open (Touring Pitches):
All year.

Camping l'Eau Rouge

A popular, lively and attractively situated site, l'Eau Rouge is in a sheltered valley close to Spa and the Grand Prix circuit. There are 140 grassy pitches of 110 sq.m. on sloping ground either side of a central road (speed bumps) - 120 for touring units, 80 with 10A electricity (70 with water and waste water), the remainder for static units. The main building houses the busy reception, shop, bar and the main sanitary facilities. There are plenty of sporting activities in the area including skiing and luge in winter. The site is close to the motor race circuit at Spa-Francorchamps and is within walking distance for the fit. The site's Dutch owners have completed a five year programme upgrading the infrastructure and have other ideas in the pipeline.

A brand new environmentally friendly toilet block has showers (on payment), private cubicles, and facilities for babies and children. Motorcaravan services. Washing machine. Shop. Baker calls daily at 08.30 (in season). Takeaway (in summer). Bar. Boules. Archery (free lessons in high season). Playground. Entertainment in season. WiFi over part of site (charged). Max. 2 dogs.

Ideal For...

 Beach

 Dogs

Year Round Camping

 Fishing

 Play Area

 Disabled Facilities

Scan me for more information.

9 accommodations
80 pitches
GPS: 50.32103, 5.81857
Post Code: B-4990

Liège, Wallonia

Camping Gossaimont

www.alanrogers.com/be0701
info@gossaimont.be
080 31 98 22
www.gossaimont.be

Open (Touring Pitches):
All year.

Located in beautiful countryside on the southern slope of one of the Belgian Ardennes' highest hills, this relaxing site of 295 pitches has direct access to the forest for hikers and cyclists. Under the new ownership of the Floreal group, there is a warm welcome from the managers. The 133 spacious touring pitches are set alongside mature trees and all have 10A electricity. Mobile homes and tents can be rented from April to October. An indoor games room, a cosy café, and outdoor playgrounds for young children are provided. The campsite is open over the winter season, when sledging and snowman building are popular. There is a ski slope just 4 km. away and its café has a welcoming log fire.

Three heated toilet blocks are well spaced around the site. Facilities for disabled visitors in two blocks. Motorcaravan service point. Laundry. Shop, bar and café (all year). Play areas. Games room. Pétanque. Accommodation for rent. WiFi on part of site (charged).

Ideal For...

 Dogs

 Year Round Camping

 Fishing

 Play Area

 Disabled Facilities

 Pets Accepted

Scan me for more information.

142 accommodations
276 pitches
GPS: 50.09647, 5.2857
Post Code: B-6927

Luxembourg, Wallonia

Camping Parc la Clusure

www.alanrogers.com/be0670
info@parclaclusure.be
084 360 050

Open (Touring Pitches):
All year.

A friendly and very well run site, Parc la Clusure is highly recommended. Set in a river valley in the lovely wooded uplands of the Ardennes, known as the l'Homme Valley touring area, the site has 469 large, marked, grassy pitches (276 for touring). All have access to electricity, cable TV and water taps and are mostly in avenues off a central, tarmac road. There is some noise from the nearby railway. There is a very pleasant riverside walk; the river is shallow in summer and popular with children (caution in winter). The site's heated swimming pool and children's pool have a pool-side bar and terrace.

Three excellent sanitary units, one heated in winter, include some washbasins in cubicles, facilities for babies and children. Facilities for disabled campers. Motorcaravan services. Well stocked shop, bar, restaurant, snack bar and takeaway (25/3-6/11). Swimming pools (30/4-18/9). Bicycle hire. Tennis. New playgrounds. Organised activity programme including canoeing, archery, abseiling, mountain biking and climbing (summer). Caving. Fishing (licence essential). WiFi over site (free). Barrier card deposit (€ 20). Max. 1 dog in July/Aug.

Ideal For...

 Kids

 Beach

 Dogs

Year Round Camping

 Fishing

 Golf

Scan me for more information.

3 accommodations
151 pitches
GPS: 50.33081, 5.90202
Post Code: B-6698

Luxembourg, Wallonia

Camping Les Neufs Prés

www.alanrogers.com/be0522
info@vielsalm-campings.be
080 216882
www.vielsalm-camping.be

Open (Touring Pitches):
1 April - 30 September.

Camping les Neufs Prés is a well kept, open, grassy municipal site in the Ardennes region of Belgium, close to the borders with Germany, Holland and Luxembourg. It lies on the banks of the small River Salm, to which there is direct access and it is only 1 km. north of the small town of Grand-Halleux. The site is spacious and offers 200 level pitches with 140 for touring and ten specially for motorcaravans. Mature trees give some pitches good shade and most have 10A electricity. For part of the high season there is a bar/snack bar, heated swimming pool and family entertainment.

Older style, heated sanitary blocks include hot showers (charged). Bar and snackbar. Large heated outdoor pool and paddling pool (July/Aug; charged). Large playground including zip wire. Games/ TV room. Minigolf. Table tennis. Tennis. Multisports court. Boules. Family entertainment (mid July/mid Aug). Bicycle hire. Communal barbecue area. Fishing. WiFi (charged).

Ideal For...

 Beach

 Dogs

 Fishing

 Golf

 Play Area

 Pets Accepted

Scan me for more information.

17 accommodations
110 pitches
GPS: 49.723073, 5.25625
Post Code: B-6820

Luxembourg, Wallonia

www.alanrogers.com/be0714
info@campingdelasemois.com
061 312 187
www.campingdelasemois.be

Open (Touring Pitches):
25 March - 4 September.

Camping de la Semois

La Semois is an attractive family site, located on the banks of the Semois river in the south of the Belgian Ardennes. This is a tranquil spot and an ideal base for walking, mountain biking and canoeing. The 110 touring pitches are grassy with good shade, but not always level. They are unmarked, but all have 10A electricity. Motorised vehicles are parked at the site entrance to create a tranquil and safe environment. A shallow brook runs through the site and forms a popular play area for children, along with a well equipped playground. The site is most suited to tents and small motorcaravans as the entry road is narrow and steep.

Three sanitary buildings. Covered dishwashing area with hot water. Shop and bar (7/7-27/8). Café/snack bar (July/Aug). Canoe hire. Play area. Children's farm. Games room. Activity programme. Accommodation to rent. Free WiFi in bar area.

Ideal For...

 Kids

 Beach

 Dogs

 Fishing

 Watersports

 Play Area

Scan me for more information.

CROATIA

Croatia has developed into a lively and friendly tourist destination, while retaining the unspoilt beauty and character of its coastal ports, traditional towns and tiny islands with their secluded coves. Its rich history is reflected in its Baroque architecture, traditional festivals and two UNESCO World Heritage sites.

The most developed tourist regions in Croatia include the peninsula of Istria, where you will find the preserved Roman amphitheatre in Pula, the beautiful town of Rovinj with cobbled streets, and Umag, with a busy marina and charming old town.

The coast is dotted with islands, making it a mecca for watersports enthusiasts. Further south, in the province of Dalmatia, Split is Croatia's second largest city. It is home to the impressive Diolectian's Palace and a starting point for ferry trips to the islands of Brac, Hvar, Vis and Korcula, with their lively fishing villages and pristine beaches. The old walled city of Dubrovnik is 150 km. south. In the summer it hosts a lively festival, be sure to visit the numerous historical sights and the newly restored cable car to the top of Mount Srd.

Language: Croatian
Capital: Zagreb
Currency: Kuna (Kn)
Time Zone: Central European Time (GMT/UTC plus one hour)
Telephone Country Code: 00 385
Tourist Office: www.croatia.hr

Say Hello
Bok (bohk)

Say Goodbye
Doviđenja (doh-vee-JEH-nyah)

Public Holidays
New Year's Day; Epiphany 6 Jan; Good Friday; Easter Monday; Labour Day 1 May; Parliament Day 30 May; Day of Anti-Fascist Victory 22 June; Statehood Day 25 June; Thanksgiving Day 5 Aug; Assumption 15 Aug; Independence Day 8 Oct; All Saints 1 Nov; Christmas 25, 26 Dec.

Motoring
Croatia is proceeding with a vast road improvement programme. There are still some roads which leave a lot to be desired but things have improved dramatically. Roads along the coast can become congested in summer and queues are possible at border crossings. Tolls: some motorways, bridges and tunnels. Cars towing a caravan or trailer must carry two warning triangles. It is illegal to overtake military convoys.

48 accommodations
730 pitches
GPS: 45.142117, 13.602267
Post Code: HR-52450

Vrsar, Istria

www.alanrogers.com/cr6725
info@maistra.hr
052 426 500
www.campingrovinjvrsar.com/campsites/porto_sole_vrsar

Open (Touring Pitches):
All year.

Camping Porto Sole

Located near the pretty town of Vrsar and its charming marina, Porto Sole is a spacious and comfortable campsite with a long water frontage and two tiny bays that provide rocky swimming areas. The site has good facilities, including a large and attractive first floor swimming pool and sunbathing area above the shopping arcade, restaurant, pizzeria and pub. There are 730 grassy touring pitches, most in front of the reception area. They are reasonably level and fairly open with 6-10A electricity but have hardly any views of the sea. In a separate area, there are a few pitches for tourers set on terraces looking out over a small bay.

The five toilet blocks (one refurbished in 2014) have mostly British style WCs and are very clean and well maintained. Facilities for children and disabled visitors. Washing machines and dryers. Large well stocked supermarket (1/5-15/9). Small shopping centre. Pub. Pizzeria. Formal and informal restaurants. Swimming pools (1/5-29/9). Massage. Miniclub. Play area. Boules. Tennis. Minigolf. Entertainment in season. Scuba diving courses. Boat launching. WiFi throughout (free).

Ideal For...

 Beach

 Dogs

 Year Round Camping

 Fishing

 Watersports

 Play Area

Scan me for more information.

229 accommodations
1771 pitches
GPS: 45.16522, 13.60723
Post Code: HR-52450

Vrsar, Istria

Camping Valkanela

www.alanrogers.com/cr6727
valkanela@maistra.hr
052 406 640
www.campingrovinjvrsar.com/Campsites/Valkanela_Vrsar

Open (Touring Pitches):
22 April - 2 October.

Camping Valkanela is located in a beautiful green bay, right on the Adriatic Sea, between the villages of Vrsar and Funtana. It offers 1,771 touring pitches, all with 10A electricity. Pitches near the beach are numbered, have shade from mature trees and are slightly sloping towards the sea. Those towards the back of the site are on open fields without much shade and are not marked or numbered. Unfortunately, the number of pitches has increased dramatically over the years, many are occupied by seasonal campers and statics of every description and these parts of the site are not very attractive.

Fifteen toilet blocks of varying styles and ages provide toilets, open style washbasins and controllable hot showers. Child size toilets, washbasins and showers. Bathroom (free). Facilities for disabled visitors. Laundry with sinks and washing machines. Dog showers. Two supermarkets. Fish market (08.00-14.00). Souvenir shops and newspaper kiosk. Bars and restaurants with dance floor and stage (22/4-2/10). Pâtisserie. Tennis. Minigolf. Fishing (with permit). Bicycle hire. Games room. Marina with boat launching. Boat and pedalo hire. Disco outside entrance. Daily entertainment programme for children up to 12 yrs. Excursions organised. Two dedicated dog areas. WiFi on part of site (free).

Ideal For...

 Beach

 Dogs

 Fishing

 Watersports

 Play Area

 Disabled Facilities

Scan me for more information.

194 accommodations
1806 pitches
GPS: 45.06286, 13.67489
Post Code: HR-52210

Rovinj, Istria

Camping Polari

www.alanrogers.com/cr6732
polari@maistra.hr
052 801 501
www.campingrovinjvrsar.com/Campsites/Polari_Rovinj

Open (Touring Pitches):
22 April - 2 October.

This 60-hectare site has excellent facilities and includes an area of 12 hectares to the left of the main site designated for naturist campers. Most parts of the site have good shade cover provided by mature trees. There are 1,806 level pitches for touring units on grass/gravel, terraced in places; many have open views over the sea to the islands. All have access to 10A electricity. An impressive swimming pool complex is child friendly with large paddling areas. The ancient town of Rovinj is well worth a visit and is best reached via the 4.5 km. coastal cycle path or by bus from the campsite.

The sanitary facilities are well maintained with plenty of hot water. Washing machines and dryers. Motorcaravan services. Bar, snack bar and takeaway (all season). Pool bar. Two restaurants. Aquapark with slide (15/5-15/9). Tennis. Minigolf. Children's entertainment with all major European languages spoken. Bicycle hire. Watersports. Windsurfing school. Trampoline. Miniclub. Games room. Live music (June-Sept). WiFi on part of site (free).

Ideal For...

 Kids

 Beach

 Dogs

 Fishing

 Watersports

 Play Area

Scan me for more information.

500 pitches
GPS: 45.05432, 13.68568
Post Code: HR-52210

Rovinj, Istria

www.alanrogers.com/cr6733
info@maistra.hr
052 803 700
www.campingrovinjvrsar.com/campsites/vestar_rovinj

Open (Touring Pitches):
22 April - 25 September.

Camping Vestar

Camping Vestar is a quiet site just 5 km. from the historic harbour town of Rovinj and is one of the rare sites in Croatia with a partly sandy beach. Right behind the beach is a large area, attractively landscaped with young trees and shrubs, with grass for sunbathing. The site has 650 large pitches, of which 500 are for touring units, all with 6/10A electricity (the rest being taken by seasonal units and 60 pitches for tour operators). It is largely wooded with good shade and from the bottom row of pitches there are views of the sea. Pitching is on two separate fields, one for free camping, the other with numbered pitches.

Six modern and one refurbished toilet blocks with British style toilets, open washbasins and controllable hot showers. Child size facilities. Baby rooms. Family bathroom. Facilities for disabled visitors. Laundry service. Fridge box hire. Motorcaravan services. Shop. Three bars. Two restaurants. Large swimming pool. Playground. Fishing. Boat and pedalo hire. Miniclub (5-11 yrs). Excursions. Internet access in reception. WiFi (free).

Ideal For...

 Beach

 Dogs

 Fishing

 Watersports

 Play Area

 Disabled Facilities

Scan me for more information.

550 pitches
GPS: 44.95043, 15.64114
Post Code: HR-47245

Rakovica, Central

Camping Korana

www.alanrogers.com/cr6650
info@np-plitvicka-jezera.hr
053 751 888
www.np-plitvicka-jezera.hr

Open (Touring Pitches):
1 April - 31 October.

This is the perfect site for a visit to the Plitvice Lakes National Park (over 100 sq.km), deservedly one of Croatia's most famous attractions with its waterfalls, vegetation and lakes. This 35-hectare site has a large, park-like environment and 550 unmarked pitches. Tourers can choose between the tarmac hardstandings close to the entrance and open grass plots with spectacular views towards the rear of the site. All have 16A electricity. The site has a good information centre and planning a visit to the park is well worthwhile. We took Tour E, down the waterfalls, which takes two and a half hours.

The well maintained toilet blocks include facilities for disabled visitors. Washing machines. Motorcaravan services. Large restaurant. Shop is opened in the morning and afternoon and a dedicated information office with details about the National Park is open all day. No charcoal barbecues. WiFi (free in information office). 47 furnished cabins for hire.

Ideal For...

 Beach

 Dogs

 Fishing

 Disabled Facilities

 Pets Accepted

 Bar on Site

Scan me for more information.

187 accommodations
952 pitches
GPS: 44.96346, 14.39747
Post Code: HR-51557

Cres, Kvarner

Camping Kovacine

www.alanrogers.com/cr6765
campkovacine@kovacine.com
051 573 150
www.camp-kovacine.com/en

Open (Touring Pitches):
19 March - 16 October.

Camping Kovacine is located on a peninsula on the beautiful Kvarner island of Cres, just 2 km. from the town of the same name. The site has just under 1,000 pitches for touring units, most with 16A electricity (from renewable sources) and a water supply. On sloping ground, partially shaded by mature olive and pine trees, pitching is on the large, open spaces between the trees. From the waterside pitches there are far reaching views over the sea to the coast beyond. Kovacine is partly an FKK (naturist) site, which is quite common in Croatia, and has a pleasant atmosphere. The site has its own beach (Blue Flag), part concrete, part pebbles, and a jetty for mooring boats and fishing.

Seven modern, well maintained toilet blocks (water heated by solar power) with open plan washbasins (some cabins for ladies) and free hot showers. Private family bathrooms for hire. Facilities for disabled visitors and children. Laundry sinks and washing machine. Motorcaravan services. Electric car/scooter charging point. Car wash. Mini-marina and boat crane. Supermarket. Bar. Restaurant and pizzeria (May-16/10). Playground. Daily children's club. Evening shows with live music. Boat launching. Fishing. Diving centre. Motorboat hire. WiFi (free). Airport transfers.

Ideal For...

 Kids

 Beach

 Dogs

 Fishing

 Watersports

 Play Area

Scan me for more information.

5 accommodations
247 pitches
GPS: 45.02440, 14.59280
Post Code: HR-51500

Krk, Kvarner

Camping Krk

www.alanrogers.com/cr6758
camping@valamar.com
051 221 351
www.camping-adriatic.com/camping-krk-politin

This is an excellent, attractive and well maintained site in a secluded hillside setting with views over the sea and close to the centre of Krk. On arrival you are assured of a good welcome from the staff, who speak good English. There are 361 clearly defined and well spaced out touring pitches, mostly on level sandy terraces, all with 10A electricity and ranging in size from 70-120 sq.m. Of these, 130 plots are fully serviced and include 96 with satellite TV connection. There are also 55 seasonal pitches that do not impinge on the touring units.

Two excellent sanitary blocks are clean and well decorated and provide hot showers. Facilities for disabled visitors. Laundry facilities. Restaurant, bar and shop (all 1/5-30/9). Tennis. Playground. Activity programme for children. Fishing. Boat launching. Sailing. New, spacious mobile homes for rent. Payphones at reception. Outdoor pool. Children's pool. Saunas. Free WiFi to most of site.

Open (Touring Pitches):
April - September.

Ideal For...

 Beach

 Dogs

 Fishing

 Watersports

 Play Area

 Disabled Facilities

Scan me for more information.

53 accommodations
272 pitches
GPS: 43.50333, 16.5275
Post Code: HR-21311

Split, Dalmatia

www.alanrogers.com/cr6855
camping.split@gmail.com
021 325 426
www.campingsplit.com

Open (Touring Pitches):
All year.

Camping Stobrec Split

Camping Stobrec is ideally located for those visiting Croatia and travelling down the coastal road or visiting the old town of Split – a must! The site has 272 touring pitches on a small peninsula, all with 10/16A electricity and some with water connections also. Some 37 of these are in a separate area reserved for tents. From the level pitches, which have ample shade from trees, there are views over the sandy beach and across the bay. Set on top of rocks at the point of the peninsula is a small, comfortable restaurant with terrace and wonderful views – an ideal place for a quiet drink or evening meal.

Three sanitary blocks include free hot water, controllable showers and some washbasins in cabins. Facilities for disabled visitors (key) and children. Laundry facilities. Motorcaravan services. Beach bars and restaurant. Supermarket at entrance. Play area. Children's club and entertainment programme (15/6-15/9). Bicycle hire. Fishing. Internet access and WiFi throughout (free).

Ideal For...

 Beach

 Dogs

Year Round Camping

 Golf

 Play Area

 Disabled Facilities

Scan me for more information.

300 pitches
GPS: 42.661883, 18.07135
Post Code: HR-20000

Dubrovnik, Dalmatia

Camping Solitudo

www.alanrogers.com/cr6890
camping-dubrovnik@valamar.com
020 448 686
www.camping-adriatic.com/solitudo-camp-dubrovnik

Open (Touring Pitches):
3 April - 31 October.

Solitudo is located on the north side of Dubrovnik. There are 21 mobile homes and 300 pitches for touring units, all with 10-16A electricity and 30 with water, arranged on four large fields that are opened according to demand. Field D is mainly used for tents and pitches here are small. Field A has pitches of up to 120 sq.m. and takes many motorcaravans (long leads required) and from some pitches here there are beautiful views of the mountains and the impressive Dr. Franjo Tudman Bridge. All pitches are numbered, some are on terraces and most are shaded by a variety of mature trees.

Two attractively decorated, clean and modern sanitary blocks have British style toilets, open washbasins and controllable, hot showers. Good facilities for disabled visitors. Laundry. Motorcaravan services. Shop. Attached restaurant/bar. Snack bar. Tennis. Minigolf. Fishing. Bicycle hire. Beach with pedalo, beach chair, kayak and jet ski hire. Excursions organised to the Elafiti Islands. WiFi (free).

Ideal For...

 Beach

 Dogs

 Watersports

 Play Area

 Disabled Facilities

 Pets Accepted

Scan me for more information.

2 accommodations
75 pitches
GPS: 42.983167, 17.205582
Post Code: HR-20250

Orebić, Dalmatia

Camping Lavanda

www.alanrogers.com/cr6877
info@lavanda-camping.com
020 454 484
www.lavanda-camping.com

Open (Touring Pitches):
15 April - 31 October.

Located at the foot of St. Elijah mountain Camping Lavanda opened in June 2017 following 5 years of construction. Originally a wine farm, this delightful campsite is set minutes from the small town of Orebić on Croatia's Pelješac peninsula. The campsite enjoys breathtaking views of the surrounding coast. The site is conveniently located just 2 hours drive from Dubrovnik, it's also a beautiful drive from Split (further north) where you will cross briefly over the Bosnian border. Enjoy one of the 70 large pitches or a luxury mobile home on the terraced landscaped ground, or pitch your own tent on one of the 5 specially created hard level pitches occupying their own area. All caravan and camper pitches are from 60 to 110m2 with electricity and water, so experiencing nature at it's finest has never been so easy. After relaxing on one of the 3 beaches (family, naturist or dog friendly), you can enjoy fine Mediterranean cuisine in the à la carte restaurant and beach bar Lavanda.

Two exceptionally clean sanitary blocks are equipped with showers, private washing cubicles, facilities for babies and children and disabled persons. Washing machines and dryers. Bar, restaurant and takeaway. 3 Beaches (main/family, dog friendly and naturist/FKK. Internet access WiFi (free of charge). Plan for outdoor swimming pool in 2018.

Ideal For...

 Naturist

 Kids

 Beach

 Watersports

 Walking

 Disabled Facilities

Scan me for more information.

DENMARK

Denmark offers a diverse landscape all within a relatively short distance. The countryside is green and varied with flat plains, rolling hills, fertile farmland, many lakes and fjords, wild moors and long beaches, interspersed with pretty villages and towns.

It is the easiest of the Scandinavian countries to visit, and distances are short so it is easy to combine the faster pace of the city with the tranquillity of the countryside and the beaches. It comprises the peninsula of Jutland and the larger islands of Zeeland and Funen, in addition to hundreds of smaller islands, many uninhabited.

Zeeland is home to the climate-friendly capital city, Copenhagen, with its relaxing waterside cafés, vibrant nightlife, Michelin star restaurants and the stunning Frederiksborg castle. Funen is Denmark's second largest island, linked to Zeeland by the Great Belt Bridge.

Known as the Garden of Denmark, its gentle landscape is dotted with orchards and pretty thatched, half-timbered houses. It also has plenty of safe, sandy beaches. Jutland's flat terrain makes it ideal for cycling and its long beaches are popular with windsurfers. It's also home to one of the most popular attractions in Denmark, Legoland, and the oldest town in Scandinavia, Ribe.

Language: Danish
Capital: Copenhagen
Currency: Danish Krone (DKK)
Time Zone: Central European Time (GMT/UTC plus one hour)
Telephone Country Code: 00 45
Tourist Office: www.visitdenmark.com

Say Hello
Hallo (halo)

Say Goodbye
Farvel (favel)

Public Holidays
New Year's Day, Three Kings Day 6 Jan; April Fool's Day 1 April; Maundy Thursday; Good Friday; Easter Monday; Queen's Birthday 16 April; Flag Day 18 April; Ascension; Whit Mon; Constitution Day 5 Jun; Valdemars 15 June; Mortens Day 11 Nov; Christmas 24-26; New Year's Eve

Motoring
Driving is easy with generally quiet roads. Driving is on the right. Do not drink and drive. Dipped headlights are compulsory at all times. Strong measures are taken against unauthorised parking on the beach, with on-the-spot fines.

45 accommodations
475 pitches
GPS: 55.67115, 12.433783
Post Code: DK-2610

Sjælland, Islands

DCU Camping Absalon

www.alanrogers.com/dk2252
absalon@dcu.dk
36 41 06 00
www.dcu.dk/campingplads/dcu-copenhagen-camp-absalon

Open (Touring Pitches):
All year.

This site was named after the founder of Copenhagen, Bishop Absalon who, after the Viking Age, defeated the Wends on Rügen and beheaded the false God Svantevit. The site is on the edge of Copenhagen with good traffic connections to the inner city by bus and train (timetables available from reception). Absalon has 475 pitches (all for tourers) with 13A electricity on pitches that vary in size (70-100 sq.m). On the older fields, pitches are partly separated by mature trees which provide some shade, whilst the newer areas are open. To the back of the site is a large tent field and there are 31 hardstandings for motorcaravans.

Two sanitary blocks (one old, one more modern, cleaning variable) with basic facilities. Washbasins in cabins and controllable hot showers (free). Family showers. Facilities for disabled visitors. Laundry. Basic kitchen. Motorcaravan services. Basic playground. Shop. Dining room with TV. Takeaway.

Ideal For...

Year Round Camping

Play Area

Disabled Facilities

Scan me for more information.

34 accommodations
275 pitches
GPS: 55.19287, 10.80530
Post Code: DK-5874

Fyn, Islands

Bøsøre Strand Feriepark

www.alanrogers.com/dk2210
info@bosore.dk
62 25 11 45
www.bosore.dk

Open (Touring Pitches):
27 March - 19 October.

A themed holiday site on the eastern coast of Fyn, the tales of Hans Christian Andersen are evident in the design of the indoor pool complex, the minigolf course and the main outdoor play area. The former has two pools on different levels, two hot tubs and a sauna and features characters from the stories; the latter has a fairytale castle with a moat as its centrepiece. There are 350 pitches in total (some up to 150 sq.m), and with only 25 seasonal units there should always be room for touring units out of the main season. All have 10A electricity, there are 124 multi-serviced pitches and 20 hardstandings.

Sanitary facilities provide all the usual facilities plus some family bathrooms, special section for children, baby rooms and facilities for disabled campers. They could be stretched in high season. Basic wellness facility. Laundry. Motorcaravan services. Shop, bar/ restaurant, pizzeria, takeaway (all open all season). Kitchen (water charged). Solarium. Indoor pool complex. Games and TV rooms. Indoor playroom for toddlers. Playground with moat. Animal farm. Internet access and WiFi (charged). Bicycle hire. Entertainment (main season). Boat launching with jetty. Communal barbecue.

Ideal For...

 Kids

 Beach

 Dogs

 Fishing

 Watersports

 Golf

Scan me for more information.

27 accommodations
496 pitches
GPS: 57.61611, 10.27908
Post Code: DK-9982

Nordjylland, Jutland

Skiveren Camping

www.alanrogers.com/dk2165
info@skiveren.dk
98 93 22 00
www.skiveren.dk

Open (Touring Pitches):
27 March - 30 September.

This high quality, friendly, family run seaside site is adjacent to a beautiful, long sandy beach. Skiveren Camping has 595 pitches (496 for tourers), all with 10/16A electricity and generally separated into named areas. A number of pitches are fully serviced, and chalets are available to rent. Around the site are different varieties of low spruce and fir which give the site a pleasing appearance and atmosphere. All of the amenities are of a very high standard and there is something to suit campers of all ages. A horse and cart can take campers for rides around the site, which has an excellent supermarket and restaurant (high season).

Three toilet blocks include free family showers and private facilities with shower, toilet and basin to rent (DKK 40-70). Facilities for disabled visitors. Laundry. Campers' kitchens. Motorcaravan services. Car and caravan wash (charged). Supermarket. Strand Café for meals, drinks and takeaway (27/3-15/9). Outdoor pool (17/5-1/9) with paddling pool. Whirlpool and sauna. Playground with area for toddlers. Excellent new large indoor play hall. Multisports court. Tennis. Wellness centre. Gym. Games room with machines and wide screen TV. 2 large screens for video games. Bicycle hire. Minigolf (charged). Fishing. Horse and cart rides. Children's club daily (from 16.00, July/Aug) and entertainment. Live music and dancing.

Ideal For...

 Beach

 Dogs

 Fishing

 Watersports

 Golf

 Play Area

Scan me for more information.

6 accommodations
100 pitches
GPS: 57.46788, 10.17861
Post Code: DK-9870

Nordjylland, Jutland

A35 Sindal Camping

www.alanrogers.com/dk2371
info@sindal-camping.dk
98 93 65 30
www.sindal-camping.dk

Open (Touring Pitches):
All year.

Situated in Northern Jutland, 40 kilometres from Skagen and with easy access to the North Sea coast, Sindal Camping has 175 large (100-150 sq.m) pitches, 100 for touring, with 13-16A electricity hook-ups (metered). They are separated by bushes and well sheltered. Ten new motorcaravan pitches (no electricity) are in a separate area. Luxury caravans and fully equipped cabins are available to rent. The town is less than a five minute drive away and has a few shops, but another 10 kilometres will bring you to Hjørring, one of Denmark's oldest towns, which hosts a number of cultural events and has a growing commercial centre.

Three heated sanitary blocks with hot showers, washbasins in cubicles, family rooms and facilities for disabled visitors. Washing machine. Motorcaravan services. Shop. Solar-heated swimming pool (10/6-30/8). Minigolf. Beach volleyball. Pétanque. Pavilion tent. Evening entertainment (music, folk dancing, bonfires). Pet goats. Well equipped playgrounds. Excursions and canoe tours arranged. No charcoal barbecues. WiFi (charged).

Ideal For...

Beach

Dogs

Year Round Camping

Fishing

Watersports

Golf

Scan me for more information.

14 accommodations
250 pitches
GPS: 57.32075, 9.67753
Post Code: DK-9480

Nordjylland, Jutland

www.alanrogers.com/dk2175
info@gronhoj-strand-camping.dk
98 88 44 33
www.gronhoj-strand-camping.dk

Open (Touring Pitches):
18 March - 18 September.

Grønhøj Strand Camping

Grønhøj Strand Camping is a large site of 500 pitches (100-150 sq.m), of which 250 are for tourers. They are arranged in small enclosures of 10-12 units, surrounded by trees and tall hedges, all with 13A electricity (long leads may be necessary). Despite this being a large site, the layout is such that it gives the feeling of camping on a small site in the country. There are two camping areas where dogs are not permitted, plus a separate field for tents. Although not as modern as some sites, all the facilities are very good, clean and well maintained. The kitchen for campers is an excellent addition. There are three play areas around the site, and the main attraction is one of the finest bathing beaches in Europe which is just 700 m. away.

Four good, clean sanitary facilities include some washbasins in cabins, and controllable hot showers (DKK 5). Family shower rooms. Baby room. Campers' kitchen. Sauna (charged). Basic facilities for disabled visitors. Washing machine and dryer. Motorcaravan services. Shop (fresh bread daily). Solarium. Animal park. Playground. Football field. 10-pin bowling. Minigolf. TV/ games room. Free WiFi.

Ideal For...

 Beach

 Dogs

 Fishing

 Golf

 Play Area

 Disabled Facilities

Scan me for more information.

350 pitches
GPS: 57.278461, 9.661118
Post Code: DK-9493

Nordjylland, Jutland

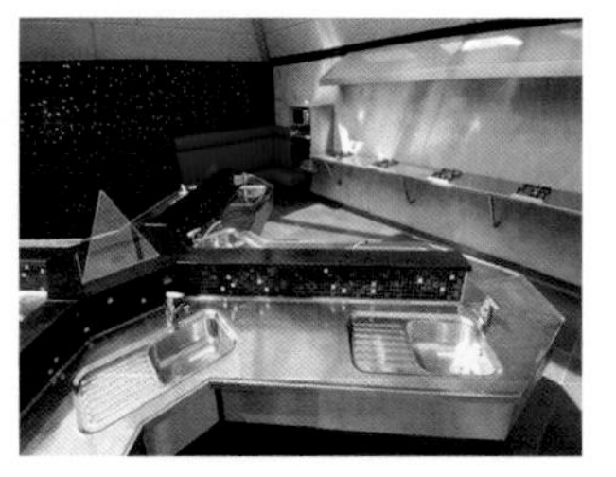

Jambo Vesterhav

www.alanrogers.com/dk2160
info@jambo.dk
98 88 16 66
www.jambo.dk

Open (Touring Pitches):
8 April - 16 October.

Jambo Vesterhav is reported to be one of the best sites in Denmark and the sanitary facilities here are certainly some of the best we have seen. It offers 350 attractive, level pitches, landscaped with a variety of bushes. Of these, 200 are fully serviced. Some pitches also have TV connections and private Internet point. There are some newer fields to the rear of the site with very limited shade. With children in mind, the on-site facilities include a huge play castle, sports hall, outdoor pool with slide and imaginative minigolf. Member of Leading Campings group.

Three superb toilet blocks with card operated hot showers and washbasins in cabins. Good facilities for children with baby room. Family showers. Facilities for disabled visitors. Shop. Bar/restaurant. Snack bar. Ice cream bar. Outdoor pool with slide and jacuzzi. Sauna. Sports hall. Large play castle. Indoor play room. Games room. Minigolf. Full entertainment programme in high season.

Ideal For...

 Beach

 Dogs

 Fishing

 Play Area

 Disabled Facilities

 Pets Accepted

Scan me for more information.

50 accommodations
50 pitches
GPS: 57.10904, 8.66757
Post Code: DK-7730

Nordjylland, Jutland

www.alanrogers.com/dk2362
info@hanstholm-camping.dk
97 96 51 98
www.hanstholm-camping.dk

Open (Touring Pitches):
All year.

Hanstholm Camping

Hanstholm Camping is a naturally laid out, all year campsite in Denmark's last wilderness area. It is close to the Thy National Park, Denmark's first and largest park, where red deer roam. The site is built on a 40 m. sand dune and is only five minutes' walk from the North Sea beach. It is well sheltered by pine, beech and oak trees. There are 50 pitches, including about 370 undelineated, slightly uneven places for touring units, all with 13A electricity, water and drain. There is a choice between quiet pitches overlooking the sea to enjoy the wonderful sunrises and sunsets, or close to all the campsite activities. A cycle path runs between the site and the beach.

Two sanitary blocks with all necessary facilities including those for families and disabled campers. Restaurant, grill and takeaway (1/6-31/8). Small shop with bakery. Outdoor pool complex (1/4-1/10, heated from 1/5) with water park containing a large slide and a paddling pool and play area. Two playgrounds. Tennis. Boules. Minigolf. Multisports court. Bicycle hire. Riding. Fishing. Excellent weekly entertainment programme. Excursions. Internet café. WiFi over site (free).

Ideal For...

 Beach

 Dogs

Year Round Camping

 Fishing

 Watersports

 Golf

Scan me for more information.

300 pitches
GPS: 55.34101, 8.76647
Post Code: DK-6760

Ribe, Jutland

Ribe Camping

www.alanrogers.com/dk2402
info@ribecamping.dk
75 41 07 77
www.ribecamping.dk

Open (Touring Pitches):
All year.

Ribe Camping, open all year, lies close to Ribe, Denmark's oldest and best preserved city. This modern well-appointed campsite has 420 pitches with 300 level, grassy pitches for touring, some with shade and all with 10A electricity. Thirty-six large super pitches are fully serviced. There is a special area for motorcaravans and one pitch is on a turntable allowing the unit to always face the sun. The modern facilities including kitchen and dining areas are kept very clean. There is a large heated pool complex with a children's play area and large toboggans.

Good quality, well-appointed heated toilet block with facilities for children and campers with disabilities (charge for showers). Motorcaravan services. Kitchen/dining area. Bar/snack bar. Shop (1/5-1/10). Heated pool complex with children's area and toboggans (1/6-1/9). Play area. Bonfire pit. Petting zoo. Dog bath. TV/games room. Organised excursions. WiFi throughout (charged).

Ideal For...

 Beach

 Dogs

Year Round Camping

 Fishing

 Watersports

 Golf

Scan me for more information.

13 accommodations
193 pitches
GPS: 55.51302, 8.38778
Post Code: DK-6710

Ribe, Jutland

Esbjerg Camping

www.alanrogers.com/dk2015
info@esbjergcamping.dk
75 15 88 22
www.esbjergcamping.dk

Open (Touring Pitches):
All year.

Owned and run by Britta and Peter Andersen, this superb site is in the northeast of Esbjerg and is a great starting point from which to tour the city with its harbour, museums and sea water aquarium. It is also convenient for those arriving on the ferry from Harwich (16 hours). From the attractive, tree lined drive, gravel lanes lead to large fields with well mown grass and good services. The site has 193 pitches for touring visitors (some with hardstanding) and there are 30 seasonal places. The pitches are split into groups of five or ten by mature trees that provide some shade.

Two very clean toilet blocks with free hot showers. Special, brightly coloured section for children and family shower rooms (for hire). Excellent facilities for disabled visitors. Baby room. Laundry. Campers' kitchen. Motorcaravan services. Basics from reception (bread to order). Outdoor pool (15x10 m) with slide, waterfall, flume and paddling pool (1/6-1/9). Two new playgrounds. Animal farm. Giant chess. Minigolf. WiFi. TV room with library.

Ideal For...

Beach

Dogs

Year Round Camping

Fishing

Watersports

Golf

Scan me for more information.

19 accommodations
200 pitches
GPS: 55.73614, 9.41777
Post Code: DK-7300

Vejle, Jutland

Fårup Sø Camping

www.alanrogers.com/dk2048
mail@fscamp.dk
75 87 13 44
www.fscamp.dk

Open (Touring Pitches):
28 March - 12 September.

Fårup Sø Camping is a friendly and welcoming family run site next to the beautiful Fårup Lake, a good location for visiting some of Denmark's best known attractions such as Legoland and the Lion Park. There are 250 grassy pitches, mostly on terraces (from top to bottom the height difference is 53 m). Some have beautiful views of the Fårup Lake. There are 200 pitches for touring units, all with 16A electricity, and some tent pitches without electricity. A heated swimming pool (min. 25°C), a whirlpool (free of charge) and an indoor play area for children are popular, as are the available activities, many associated with the lake.

One modern and one older toilet block have British style toilets, washbasins in cabins and controllable hot showers (charged). Family shower rooms. Baby room. Facilities for disabled visitors. Laundry. Campers' kitchen. Motorcaravan services. Shop (bread to order). Heated swimming pool and whirlpool. Indoor play area. Playgrounds. Lake with fishing, watersports and Viking ship. Three play areas. Activities for children (high season). WiFi (charged).

Ideal For...

 Beach

 Dogs

 Fishing

 Watersports

 Golf

 Play Area

Scan me for more information.

FRANCE

From the hot sunny climate of the Mediterranean to the more northerly and cooler regions of Normandy and Brittany, with the châteaux of the Loire and the lush valleys of the Dordogne, and the mountain ranges of the Alps, France offers holidaymakers a huge choice of destinations to suit all tastes.

France boasts every type of landscape imaginable, ranging from the wooded valleys of the Dordogne to the volcanic uplands of the Massif Central, the rocky coast of Brittany to the lavender-covered hills of Provence and snow-capped peaks of the Alps. The diversity of these regions is reflected in the local customs, cuisine, architecture and dialect.

Many rural villages hold festivals to celebrate the local saints and you can also find museums devoted to the rural arts and crafts of the regions. France has a rich cultural heritage with a wealth of festivals, churches, châteaux, museums and historical monuments to visit. The varied landscape and climate ensure many opportunities for outdoor pursuits from hiking and cycling, wind- and sand-surfing on the coast and rock climbing and skiing in the mountains. And no trip to France is complete without sampling the local food and wine.

Language: French
Capital: Paris
Currency: Euro (€)
Time Zone: Central European Time (GMT/UTC plus one hour)
Telephone Country Code: 00 33
Tourist Office: www.franceguide.com

Say Hello
Bonjour (bohn-ZHOOR)

Say Goodbye
Au revoir (oh ruh-VWAHR)

Public Holidays
New Year; Easter Mon; Labour Day; VE Day 8 May; Ascension; Whit Mon; Bastille Day 14 July; Assumption 15 Aug; All Saints 1 Nov; Armistice Day 11 Nov; Christmas Day.

Motoring
France has a comprehensive road system from motorways (Autoroutes), Routes Nationales (N roads), Routes Départmentales (D roads) down to purely local C class roads. Tolls are payable on the autoroute network which is extensive but expensive, and also on certain bridges.

60 accommodations
196 pitches
GPS: 47.79337, -3.80049
Post Code: F-29920

Finistère, Brittany

Camping le Raguénès-Plage

www.alanrogers.com/fr29090
leraguenesplage@orange.fr
02 98 06 80 69
www.camping-le-raguenes-plage.com

Open (Touring Pitches):
9 April - 30 September.

Mme. Guyader and her family will ensure you receive a warm welcome on arrival at this well kept and pleasant site. Camping International Le Raguénès-Plage is an attractive and well laid out campsite with many shrubs and trees. The 196 pitches are a good size, flat and grassy, separated by trees and hedges. All have electricity (10/15A), water and drainage. The site is used by tour operators (51 pitches) and has 60 mobile homes of its own. A pool complex complete with heated indoor pool and water toboggan is a key feature and is close to the friendly bar, restaurant, shop and takeaway.

Two clean, well maintained sanitary blocks include British and Turkish style toilets, washbasins in cabins, baby baths and facilities for disabled visitors. Laundry room. Motorcaravan services. Small shop, restaurant, bar and takeaway (all 1/5-14/9). Reading and TV room. Heated indoor and outdoor pools with sun terrace and paddling pool. Sauna (charged). Bicycle hire. Play areas. Games room. Large variety of activities organised in July/ Aug. Internet access. WiFi throughout (charged).

Ideal For...

 Beach

 Dogs

 Fishing

 Watersports

 Play Area

 Disabled Facilities

Scan me for more information.

353 accommodations
121 pitches
GPS: 48.65807, -3.92833
Post Code: F-29660

Finistère, Brittany

Camping les Mouettes

www.alanrogers.com/fr29000
contact@les-mouettes.com
02 98 67 02 46
www.yellohvillage.co.uk/camping/les_mouettes

Open (Touring Pitches):
1 April - 11 September.

Yelloh! Village Camping Les Mouettes is a sheltered site on the edge of an attractive bay, with access to the sea at the front of the site. In a wooded setting with many attractive trees and shrubs, the 474 pitches include 121 for touring units, all with electricity, water and drainage. The remainder are taken by tour operators and by 353 mobile homes and chalets to rent. At the centre of the 'village' are shops, a bar, a restaurant, an entertainment stage, sports facilities and an impressive heated pool complex with swimming, paddling and water slide pools, plus a 'Tropical river', jacuzzi and sauna. There is also an excellent indoor swimming pool.

Two clean sanitary blocks include controllable showers and washbasins in cabins. In the main block there are showers with washbasins and delightful rooms for children and babies. Facilities for disabled visitors. Laundry. Shop (limited hours outside the main season). Takeaway. Bar with TV. Restaurant/pizzeria/grill. Heated pool complex indoor (all season) and outdoor. Beauty salon. Games rooms (special one for under 5s). Play area. Half-court tennis. Minigolf. Bicycle hire. Entertainment all season. Large units should phone first. WiFi throughout (charged).

Ideal For...

 Beach

 Dogs

Fishing

 Watersports

 Golf

 Play Area

Scan me for more information.

27 accommodations
156 pitches
GPS: 47.97685, -4.11102
Post Code: F-29000

Finistère, Brittany

Domaine de Lanniron

www.alanrogers.com/fr29050
contact@lanniron.com
02 98 90 62 02
www.camping-lanniron.com

Open (Touring Pitches):
28 March - 15 November.

Castel Camping du Domaine de Lanniron is a beautiful and peaceful family site set in ten acres of a 17th-century, 38-hectare country estate on the banks of the Odet river, formerly the home of the Bishops of Quimper. The site has 199 grassy pitches (156 for touring units) of three types varying in size, services and price. They are on flat ground, laid out in rows alongside access roads with shrubs and bushes providing separation. All have electricity and 88 have three services. The original outbuildings have been attractively converted around a walled courtyard. Used by tour operators (30 pitches).

Excellent heated block in the courtyard and second modern block serving the top areas of the site. Facilities for disabled visitors and babies. Washing machines and dryers. Motorcaravan services. Shop & Bar (Seasonal). Gas supplies. Restaurant and takeaway (open daily). Swimming and paddling pool. Aquapark with waterfall, Balnéo, spa, jacuzzi, fountains and water slides. Small play area. Tennis. Minigolf. Golf course (9 holes), driving range, two putting greens, training bunker and pitching area (weekly package available). Fishing. Archery. Bicycle hire. Reading, games and billiards rooms. TV/video room. Karaoke. Outdoor activities. Large room for indoor activities. Pony rides and tree climbing (high season). Internet access and WiFi throughout (charged).

Ideal For...

 Beach

 Dogs

 Fishing

 Watersports

 Golf

 Play Area

Scan me for more information.

54 accommodations
183 pitches
GPS: 48.40120, -2.31736
Post Code: F-22270

Côtes d`Armor, Brittany

Camping Au Bocage du Lac

www.alanrogers.com/fr22200
contact@campinglacbretagne.com
02 96 31 60 16
www.camping-location-bretagne.com

Open (Touring Pitches):
1 April - 5 October.

This well kept former municipal site has been continually updated over the past few years by the current owners, M. and Mme. Rivière. It is on the edge of a small village beside a 172-acre lake, 800 metres from the pretty historic village of Jugon les Lacs and a short drive from the sea. It offers 183 large touring pitches, most with electrical connections, set on gently sloping grass and divided by shrubs and bushes, with mature trees providing shade. Just over 50 wooden chalets and mobile homes are interspersed with the touring pitches. On-site facilities include an excellent swimming pool complex with both heated outdoor and covered pools with children's sections and sunbathing patio. There is also an extensive play area and numerous activities for all to enjoy - especially the children.

Two sanitary blocks are equipped with showers, private washing cubicles and facilities for babies. Washing machines and dryers. Well stocked shop. Bar. Restaurant and takeaway. Heated outdoor pools. Indoor pool with 5 slides, changing rooms. Extensive activity and entertainment programmes (during school holidays). Riding. Canoe trips. Fishing. Internet access and WiFi (free spot).

Ideal For...

 Kids

 Fishing

 Golf

 Play Area

 Disabled Facilities

 Bar on Site

Scan me for more information.

60 accommodations
156 pitches
GPS: 47.59675, -3.06162
Post Code: F-56340

Morbihan, Brittany

Le Moulin de Kermaux

www.alanrogers.com/fr56090
contact@camping-moulinkermaux.com
02 97 52 15 90
www.camping-moulinkermaux.com

Open (Touring Pitches):
14 April - 22 September

Only 100 m. from the famous Carnac megaliths, Camping Le Moulin de Kermaux is an excellent base from which to see these ancient stones with their ever changing mood, colour and profile. Family run, the site has 156 pitches, 45 for touring units; all have 10/15A electricity and 35 have water and drainage. They are mostly separated by hedges and have many mature trees offering welcome shade. The compact nature of the site offers a safe environment for parents and children of all ages. There is an aquatic complex with heated indoor and outdoor pools and a separate toboggan pool. This is a well run, quiet and immaculately kept site.

The modern, fully equipped, heated sanitary block has washbasins in cabins. Facilities for disabled visitors. Baby room. Laundry facilities. Motorcaravan services. Shop (July/Aug). Bar with satellite TV. Takeaway (July/Aug). Swimming and paddling pools. Sauna and jacuzzi. Adventure playground. Minigolf. Organised activities (July/Aug). Bicycle hire. WiFi all over the campsite (charged).

Ideal For...

 Beach

 Dogs

 Fishing

 Watersports

 Play Area

 Disabled Facilities

Scan me for more information.

180 accommodations
167 pitches
GPS: 47.61419, -2.92596
Post Code: F-56870

Morbihan, Brittany

www.alanrogers.com/fr56130
info@camping-baden.com
02 97 57 02 06
www.camping-baden.com

Open (Touring Pitches):
2 April - 2 November.

Camping Mané Guernehué

Located close to the Morbihan gulf, Mané Guernehué is a smart, modern site with excellent amenities, including an equestrian centre, and a variety of pitches. Some are terraced beneath pine trees, others in a former orchard with delightful views of the surrounding countryside. The 377 pitches are generally large, 210 being occupied by mobile homes and chalets. Most pitches have 10A electricity and a few also have water and drainage. Many are level but a few, particularly in the centre of the site, slope to varying degrees. An impressive indoor pool complex has been added to the existing complex of outdoor pools and there is an equally impressive new spa and wellness facility.

Three modern toilet blocks include washbasins in cabins. Facilities for disabled visitors. Washing machines and dryers. Small shop, bar and takeaway (2/4-30/9). Heated outdoor pool with slides (2/4-30/9). Heated indoor pool (all season), water slide. Spa complex. Fishing. Minigolf. Equestrian centre and pony trekking. Fitness room. Teenagers' room with games and TV. Play area. Tree top adventure area. Varied entertainment programme in high season, based around a large purpose built hall. Mobile homes to rent. WiFi (charged).

Ideal For...

 Beach

 Dogs

 Fishing

 Watersports

 Golf

 Play Area

Scan me for more information.

18 accommodations
70 pitches
GPS: 48.382199, -1.835054
Post Code: F-35190

Ille-et-Vilaine, Brittany

Domaine du Logis

www.alanrogers.com/fr35080
domainedulogis@wanadoo.fr
02 99 45 25 45
www.domainedulogis.com

Open (Touring Pitches):
30 March - 5 October.

Camping le Domaine du Logis is an attractive rural site with enthusiastic owners, set in the grounds of an old château. The site's upgraded modern facilities are housed in traditional converted barns and farm buildings, which are well maintained and equipped. There is a total of 203 pitches, 85 of which are for touring units. The grass pitches are level, of a generous size and divided by mature hedges and trees. All have 10A electricity connections, water and drainage. This site would appeal to most age groups, with plenty to offer the active, including a fitness room with a good range of modern equipment and a sauna for those who prefer to relax, or perhaps enjoy a quiet day's fishing by the lake.

One comfortable toilet block with washbasins and showers. Toilet and shower for disabled visitors. Laundry facilities. Bar with Sky TV. Restaurant and takeaway (1/7-29/8). Outdoor swimming pool and whirlpool (1/5-30/9). Fitness and games rooms. Sauna. BMX circuit. Bicycle hire. Lake fishing. Unfenced play areas. Club for children (high season). WiFi throughout (free).

Ideal For...

- Kids
- Beach
- Dogs
- Fishing
- Walking
- Golf

Scan me for more information.

61 accommodations
230 pitches
GPS: 49.66715, -1.48704
Post Code: F-50330

Manche, Normandy

www.alanrogers.com/fr50070
welcome@anse-du-brick.com
02 33 54 33 57
www.anse-du-brick.com

Open (Touring Pitches):
30 March - 15 September

Camping l'Anse du Brick

A friendly, family site, Castel Camping Caravaning l'Anse du Brick overlooks a picturesque bay on the northern tip of the Cotentin Peninsula, eight kilometres east of Cherbourg port. This quality site makes a pleasant night halt or an ideal longer stay destination for those not wishing to travel too far. Its pleasing location offers direct access to a small sandy beach and a woodland walk. This is a mature, terraced site with magnificent views from certain pitches. Tarmac roads lead to the 117 touring pitches (all with 10A electricity) which are level, separated and mostly well shaded by many trees, bushes and shrubs.

New sanitary facilities are kept spotlessly clean and are well maintained. Washbasins mainly in cubicles and pushbutton showers. Provision for children, families and disabled visitors. Laundry area. Possibility of private sanitary on the pitch. Motorcaravan services. Shop (all season), restaurant and bar/ pizzeria. Heated swimming pools (indoor all season, outdoor from 1/5). Tennis. Play area. Organised entertainment in season. Miniclub (6-12 yrs). Bicycle and kayak hire. WiFi throughout (charged).

Ideal For...

 Beach

 Dogs

 Fishing

 Watersports

 Golf

 Play Area

Scan me for more information.

57 accommodations
162 pitches
GPS: 48.79778, -1.52498
Post Code: F-50380

Manche, Normandy

Château de Lez Eaux

www.alanrogers.com/fr50030
bonjour@lez-eaux.com
02 33 51 66 09
www.lez-eaux.com

Open (Touring Pitches):
1 April - 17 September.

Set in the grounds of a château, Castel Camping le Château de Lez Eaux lies in a rural situation just off the main route south, under two hours from Cherbourg. Of the 250 pitches, 162 are for touring units, all with electricity (10A, Europlug) and 92 with water and drainage. Most of the pitches are of a very good size, partly separated by trees and shrubs on flat or slightly sloping, grassy ground overlooking Normandy farmland and a small fishing lake. The campsite offers several kinds of camping accommodation and pitch depending on your desires and needs - from treehouse to mobile-home with Jacuzzi, and chalet to camping pitches for tents, caravans and mobile homes. Activities are certainly not lacking and they include a covered water park with slides, paddling pool, swimming pools; games area, bouncy castles, fishing lake, tennis court and bike rental.

Three sanitary blocks (1 heated) are equipped with showers, private washing cubicles and facilities for babies. Washing machines and dryers. Shop. Bar. Takeaway. Fresh bakery in the morning. Covered water park (pool, slides, paddling pool) + 1 outdoor pool. Games areas and bouncy castles. Fishing lake. Football. Volleyball grounds. TV room and games room. Bicycle hire. Tennis court hire. Kids club during the summer. Summer activities: 2 concerts per week, local market, daily aquatonic.

Ideal For...

 Kids

 Beach

 Dogs

 Fishing

Watersports

Walking

Scan me for more information.

12 accommodations
109 pitches
GPS: 49.22525, 0.30438
Post Code: F-14130

Calvados, Normandy

Camping Le Brévedent

www.alanrogers.com/fr14090
contact@campinglebrevedent.com
02 31 64 72 88
www.campinglebrevedent.com

Open (Touring Pitches):
30 April - 17 September.

Castel Camping Le Brévedent is a well established, traditional site with 132 pitches (105 for touring units, 31 used by tour operators) set in the grounds of an elegant, 18th-century hunting pavilion. Pitches are either around the fishing lake in the lower gardens (level), or in the old orchard (gently sloping). All have 10A electricity. It is an excellent holiday destination within easy reach of the Channel ports and its peaceful, friendly environment makes it ideal for mature campers or families with younger children (note: the lake is unfenced). Reception provides a good selection of tourist information and English is spoken.

Three toilet blocks include washbasins in cubicles and facilities for disabled visitors. One has been refurbished with spacious en-suite cubicles (shower, washbasin and baby bath) and a second is due to be replaced for 2016. Laundry facilities. Kitchen for mothers with babies. Motorcaravan services. Shop (baker delivers each morning). Bar in château open evenings. Restaurant (from 15/5). Takeaway (from 1/5). Café (July/Aug). Clubroom. TV and library. Heated swimming and paddling pools (unsupervised) (from 1/5). Playgrounds. Minigolf. Boules. Games room. Fishing. Canoeing. Bicycle and buggy hire. Organised excursions. Musical evenings and children's club (July/Aug). WiFi (free in café). Dogs are not accepted.

Ideal For...

 Beach

 Fishing

 Watersports

 Golf

 Play Area

 Disabled Facilities

Scan me for more information.

10 accommodations
178 pitches
GPS: 49.20974, 0.389792
Post Code: F-14590

Calvados, Normandy

Camping le Colombier

www.alanrogers.com/fr14050
chateau@camping-lecolombier.com
02 31 63 63 08
www.camping-lecolombier.com

Open (Touring Pitches):
1 May - 15 September.

Le Colombier is a real gem of a campsite, situated in the grounds of a Normandy château. Within the attractive, landscaped gardens there is a large, rectangular swimming pool and an impressive former dovecote now houses a cosy bar and library. There are no mobile homes or chalets here; all 178 pitches are dedicated to touring, most with electricity connections. They are large and marked out by trees at the corners, but with no dividing hedges. Reception is in a restored building and the staff are efficient and friendly. The site's main amenities are open all season. Camping Le Colombier was acquired by the Huttopia group just prior to the 2017 season and major investment is planned for the 2018 season.

Two toilet blocks include private cabins and a unit for disabled visitors. Motorcaravan services. Laundry facilities. Bar, shop, crêperie and takeaway. Occasional dinners (limited numbers) served in the château. Heated swimming pool (25x12 m). Tennis. Minigolf. Indoor and outdoor play area. Organised events all season. Internet point. Free WiFi on part of site.

Ideal For...

 Dogs

 Fishing

 Watersports

 Golf

 Play Area

 Disabled Facilities

Scan me for more information.

4 accommodations
160 pitches
GPS: 49.24299, -0.60588
Post Code: F-14740

Calvados, Normandy

www.alanrogers.com/fr14030
chateau.martragny@wanadoo.fr
02 31 80 21 40
www.chateau-martragny.com

Open (Touring Pitches):
23 May - 26 August.

Le Château de Martragny

Castel Camping le Château de Martragny is an attractive site in the parkland of a château. Close to D-Day beaches and Bayeux, it is also convenient for the ports of Caen and Cherbourg, and has the facilities and charm to encourage both long stays and stopovers. The pleasant lawns surrounding and approaching the château take 160 touring units, with electricity connections (10A, some longer leads required). Most pitches are divided by either a small hedge or a few trees. In contrast to the busyness of Bayeux, the de Chassey family ensure you can enjoy the peace and calm of their home when you enjoy a glass of wine in the lovely courtyard, surrounded by the warm ancient stonework.

Three sanitary blocks (one new) include washbasins in cabins, showers, sinks for dishwashing and laundry, and a baby room. Disabled visitors are well catered for. Good laundry. Shop. Bar, brasserie and takeaway (all season). Heated outdoor swimming pool (20x6 m) and paddling pool. Play areas. Tennis. Minigolf. Games and TV room. Fishing pond. Some family entertainment (July/Aug). WiFi over site (free).

Ideal For...

 Beach

 Dogs

 Fishing

 Watersports

 Golf

 Play Area

Scan me for more information.

98 accommodations
157 pitches
GPS: 49.3463, -0.7732
Post Code: F-14520

Calvados, Normandy

Camping Port'land

www.alanrogers.com/fr14150
info@camping-portland.fr
02 31 51 07 06
www.camping-portland.com

Open (Touring Pitches):
25 March - 5 November.

Camping Port'land, now a mature site, lies on the western edge of the delightful little resort of Port-en-Bessin, one of Normandy's busiest fishing ports. The 279 pitches are large and grassy with 156 for touring units, all with electricity (mainly 16A), water and waste water, and 35 with hardstandings. There are 98 mobile homes for rent. The camping area has been imaginatively landscaped, many pitches overlooking small fishing ponds. An attractive modern building houses the refurbished reception and a smart bar/restaurant with an interesting menu. A coastal path leads to the little town, which has a number of shops and waterfront bars and restaurants.

Main sanitary block is well maintain with controllable showers, washbasins in cubicles and an attractive baby room. En-suite unit for disabled campers. A second, more basic, block is open in high season. Heated swimming pool with paddling pool and retractable roof. Open-air pool with slides (July/Aug). Shop, bar, restaurant with takeaway (all open all season). Wood-fired pizza oven (July/Aug). Large TV and games room (1st floor with lift). Multisports pitch. Fishing. Play area. Free WiFi in main building.

Ideal For...

 Beach

 Dogs

 Fishing

 Watersports

 Golf

 Play Area

Scan me for more information.

7 accommodations
374 pitches
GPS: 49.268986, -0.255024
Post Code: F-14150

Calvados, Normandy

www.alanrogers.com/fr14260
contact@vacances-seasonova.com
02 31 97 12 66
www.vacances-seasonova.com/camping/camping-riva-bella

Open (Touring Pitches):
15 February - 15 December.

Camping Le Riva Bella

Camping Seasonova Le Riva Bella (formally known as Les Pommiers) is an attractive and well equipped municipal site which is very convenient for the Ouistreham ferry terminal. The site is located on the edge of the small town of Ouistreham alongside the large canal which passes Pegasus Bridge and leads to the city of Caen. There are 374 grassy pitches here, some are well shaded and others with a sunnier aspect. Most have electrical connections (6A) and around 20 pitches have been specially designated for motorcaravans with a special nightly rate. A supermarket can be found 800 m. from the site. A few small mobile homes are available to rent.

Basic but clean sanitary facilities include WCs and showers. Laundry facilities. Motorcaravan services. Play area. Tennis. Activities and entertainment in high season. Internet access. Mobile homes to rent.

Ideal For...

 Beach

 Dogs

 Fishing

 Watersports

 Golf

 Play Area

Scan me for more information.

17 accommodations
84 pitches
GPS: 49.43487, 0.82897
Post Code: F-76480

Seine-Maritime, Normandy

Camping de la Forêt

www.alanrogers.com/fr76130
info@campinglaforet.com
02 35 37 93 43
www.campinglaforet.com

Open (Touring Pitches):
1 April - 31 October.

This is a pleasant family site with a friendly, relaxed atmosphere. It has recently been taken over by the Commare family who have started a programme of improvements by adding a cover to the pool and rebuilding the main toilet block. The 110 grassy pitches (80 for tourers, all with 10A electricity) are attractively located in woodland. Most pitches have some shade at different times of the day. The nearby village of Jumièges, a short walk away, is surrounded on three sides by one of the huge bends of the River Seine - it is located in the Parc Naturel Régional des Boucles de la Seine.

The central toilet block has been rebuilt and fitted out to a high standard with washbasins in cubicles, and preset showers. A second, smaller block (refurbishment is planned) has toilets and open-style washbasins, baby room, facilities for disabled visitors and laundry facilities. Motorcaravan services. Shop (bread to order). Small swimming pool with retractable roof and paddling pool (both heated 1/6-15/9). Playground. Boules. Games room with TV. Outdoor fitness equipment. Bicycle hire. WiFi over site (charged). Chalets, mobile homes and two tents to rent.

Ideal For...

 Beach

 Dogs

 Fishing

 Watersports

 Golf

 Play Area

Scan me for more information.

24 accommodations
80 pitches
GPS: 50.0855, 1.71492
Post Code: F-80870

Somme, Picardy

Camping le Val de Trie

www.alanrogers.com/fr80060
raphael@camping-levaldetrie.fr
03 22 31 48 88
www.camping-levaldetrie.fr

Open (Touring Pitches):
25 March - 2 October.

Le Val de Trie is a natural countryside site in woodland, near a small village. The 80 numbered, grassy touring pitches are of a good size, divided by hedges and shrubs with mature trees providing good shade in most areas, and all have electricity (10A). Eleven also have water and waste water. It can be very quiet in April, June, September and October. If there is no-one on site, just choose a pitch or call at the farm to book in. This is maturing into a well managed site with modern facilities and a friendly, relaxed atmosphere. It is well situated for the coast and also the cities of Amiens and Abbeville. There are five new wooden chalets (including one for disabled visitors).

Two clean, recently renovated sanitary buildings include washbasins in cubicles, units for disabled visitors, babies and children. Laundry facilities. Microwave. Shop, bar with TV (all season), bread to order and butcher visits in season. Snack bar with takeaway (22/4-3/9). Room above bar for children. Covered heated swimming pool with jacuzzi (13/4-29/9). Outdoor pool for children (22/4-3/9). Bicycle hire. WiFi in bar area. Electric barbecues are not permitted.

Ideal For...

 Kids

 Beach

 Dogs

 Fishing

 Watersports

 Golf

Scan me for more information.

17 accommodations
42 pitches
GPS: 50.33645, 1.71285
Post Code: F-80120

Somme, Picardy

La Ferme des Aulnes

www.alanrogers.com/fr80070
contact@fermedesaulnes.com
03 22 29 22 69
www.fermedesaulnes.com

Open (Touring Pitches):
25 March - 1 November.

This peaceful site has been developed on the meadows of a small, 17th-century farm on the edge of Fresne and is lovingly cared for by its new enthusiastic owners, Marie and Denis Lefort, and their hard working team. Restored outbuildings house reception and the facilities, around a central courtyard that boasts a fine heated swimming pool. A new development includes a bar and entertainment room. Outside, facing the main gate, are large, level grass pitches for touring. There is also an area for tents. The remaining touring pitches are in the main complex, hedged and fairly level.

Both sanitary blocks are heated and include washbasins in cubicles, with a large cubicle for disabled visitors. Motorcaravan services. Shop, piano bar, restaurant and takeaway. TV room. Swimming pool (16x9 m; heated and with cover for cooler weather, all season). Jacuzzi and sauna. Fitness room. Aquagym. Balnéotherapy. Playground. Boules. Archery. Fishing. WiFi throughout (free). Shuttle service to stations and airports.

Ideal For...

 Beach

 Dogs

 Fishing

 Watersports

 Golf

 Play Area

Scan me for more information.

12 accommodations
146 pitches
GPS: 50.86632, 1.85698
Post Code: F-62340

Pas-de-Calais, Nord/Pas-de-Calais

Camping la Bien-Assise

www.alanrogers.com/fr62010
castels@bien-assise.com
03 21 35 20 77
www.camping-la-bien-assise.com

Open (Touring Pitches):
20 April - 15 September

Le Castel Camping de La Bien-Assise is a mature and well developed campsite, the history of la Bien-Assise goes back to the 1500s. There are 198 pitches here, including 4 with hardstanding, mainly set among mature trees with others on a newer field. Connected by surfaced and gravel roads and of a good size (up to 300 sq.m), shrubs and bushes divide most of the pitches. Being close to Calais, the Channel Tunnel exit and Boulogne, makes this a good stopping point en-route, but La Bien-Assise is well worth a longer stay. It is a very popular site which is also used by tour operators, but is well managed and there are no adverse effects.

Three well equipped toilet blocks provide many washbasins in cubicles, showers and baby rooms. Laundry facilities. The main block is in four sections, two unisex. Two motorcaravan service points. Shop. Restaurant. Bar/grill and takeaway (all from mid April). TV room. Pool complex (mid April-mid Sept) with toboggan, covered paddling pool and outdoor pool. Play areas. Minigolf. Tennis. Bicycle hire. WiFi (charged, but free with a drink in the bar).

Ideal For...

 Beach

 Dogs

 Fishing

 Watersports

 Golf

 Play Area

Scan me for more information.

18 accommodations
110 pitches
GPS: 50.81924, 2.17753
Post Code: F-62910

Pas-de-Calais, Nord/Pas-de-Calais

Château du Gandspette

www.alanrogers.com/fr62030
contact@chateau-gandspette.com
03 21 93 43 93
www.chateau-gandspette.com

Open (Touring Pitches):
1 April - 30 September.

This spacious, family run site is set in the grounds of a 19th-century château. It is conveniently situated for the Channel ports and tunnel, providing overnight accommodation together with a range of facilities for longer stays. There are 110 touring pitches, all with 6A electricity hook-ups and 21 with hardstanding. These are interspersed with 20 privately owned mobile homes and caravans with a further 18 for hire. Most pitches are delineated by trees and hedging. Mature trees form the perimeter of the site, through which there is access to woodland walks. Even when the site is busy, there is still a sense of space with large green areas kept free of caravans and tents.

Two sanitary blocks with some washbasins in cubicles. Good facilities for babies and disabled visitors. Laundry facilities. Motorcaravan services. Bar, grill restaurant and takeaway (all 1/5-15/9). Swimming pools (15/5-15/9). Playground. Multisports court. Tennis. Pétanque. Room for children. Entertainment in season. Electric barbecues are not permitted. WiFi over site (charged).

Ideal For...

 Beach

 Dogs

 Fishing

 Watersports

 Golf

 Play Area

Scan me for more information.

65 accommodations
225 pitches
GPS: 48.9399, 2.14589
Post Code: F-78600

Yvelines, Paris/Ile de France

Camping de Maisons-Laffitte

www.alanrogers.com/fr78010
vacances@sandaya.fr
04 11 32 90 00
www.sandaya.fr/camping/france/paris/maisons-laffitte

Open (Touring Pitches):
25 March - 5 November.

This site on the banks of the Seine, Camping International de Maisons-Laffitte is consistently busy, has multilingual, friendly reception staff and occupies a grassy, tree covered area bordering the river. There are 336 pitches, 111 occupied by mobile homes and tour operators, plus two areas dedicated to tents. Most pitches are separated by hedges, are of a good size with some overlooking the Seine (unfenced access), and all 225 touring pitches have electricity hook-ups (10A). The roads leading to the site are a little narrow so large vehicles need to take care. There is a frequent train service and occasional noise from aircraft.

Three sanitary blocks, two insulated for winter use and one more open (only used in July/Aug). Facilities are clean with constant supervision necessary due to volume of visitors. Provision for disabled visitors. Motorcaravan services. Self-service shop. Restaurant/bar. Takeaway food and pizzeria (all open all season). TV in restaurant. Football area. Fishing possible with licence. Internet point and WiFi throughout (charged).

Ideal For...

- Kids
- Dogs
- Fishing
- Golf
- Play Area
- Disabled Facilities

Scan me for more information.

64 accommodations
116 pitches
GPS: 48.62638, 1.84375
Post Code: F-78120

Yvelines, Paris/Ile de France

Camping à Rambouillet

www.alanrogers.com/fr78040
rambouillet@huttopia.com
01 30 41 07 34
europe.huttopia.com/site/camping-rambouillet

Open (Touring Pitches):
6 April - 6 November.

This pleasant site is part of the Huttopia group whose philosophy is to rediscover the camping spirit. It is in a peaceful forest location beside a lake, with good tarmac access roads and site lighting. The 116 touring pitches, 100 with electricity connections (10A), are set among the trees and in clearings. As a result, shade is plentiful and grass sparse. The main area is kept traffic-free but there is a section for motorcaravans and those who need or prefer to have their car with them. The result is a safe, child-friendly site. There is an Espace Nature with 40 large pitches for camping.

The heated sanitary block has controllable showers, some washbasins in cubicles and a number of more spacious family cubicles. Facilities for disabled visitors. Laundry facilities. Three outlying 'rondavels' each with two family rooms. Motorcaravan services. Small shop (all season) selling basics plus bar/ restaurant/takeaway with terrace (weekends in low season). Only electric barbecues allowed. Communal barbecue area. Games room with TV. Play area. Natural swimming pool (June-Sept, earlier if possible). Boules. Volleyball. Picnic area. Bicycle hire. Fishing. Family activities with a nature theme (July/Aug).

Ideal For...

 Kids

 Dogs

 Fishing

 Walking

 Golf

 Play Area

Scan me for more information.

6 accommodations
140 pitches
GPS: 48.75060, 2.89714
Post Code: F-77610

Seine-et-Marne, Paris/Ile de France

Caravaning des 4 Vents

www.alanrogers.com/fr77040
contact@caravaning-4vents.fr
01 64 07 41 11
www.caravaning-4vents.fr

Open (Touring Pitches):
20 March - 1 November.

This peaceful, pleasant site has been owned and run by the same family for over 50 years. There are around 200 pitches with a few permanent and seasonal units, however, there are 140 spacious grassy pitches for touring units, well separated by good hedges, all with 6A electricity and a water tap shared between two pitches. The whole site is very well cared for and landscaped with flowers and trees everywhere. This is a great family site with the swimming pool and games facilities located at the top end of the site so that campers are not disturbed.

Three sanitary units (two heated in cooler weather) provide washbasins (mainly in cubicles) and pushbutton showers. Facilities for disabled visitors. Laundry facilities. Motorcaravan services. Mobile snack bar and pizzeria (July/Aug, 16.00-23.00) and a baker (07.30-11.00). Well fenced but unsupervised, circular swimming pool (16 m. diameter; June-Sept). Playground. Games room. Volleyball. Boules court. WiFi on part of site (free).

Ideal For...

 Dogs

 Fishing

 Golf

 Play Area

 Disabled Facilities

 Pets Accepted

Scan me for more information.

26 accommodations
180 pitches
GPS: 47.87317, 5.38069
Post Code: F-52200

Haute-Marne, Champagne-Ardenne

Camping Lac de la Liez

www.alanrogers.com/fr52030
contact@camping-liez.fr
03 25 90 27 79
www.campingliez.com

Open (Touring Pitches):
1 April - 30 September.

Managed by the charming Baude family, this excellent lakeside site is near the city of Langres. Only twenty minutes from the A5/A31 junction, Camping Lac de la Liez provides an ideal spot for an overnight stop en route to the south of France. However, there is also a lot on offer for a longer stay. The site provides 180 fully serviced pitches, 16 with private sanitary units. Attractive terracing on the lower part of the site means that some have views of the 250-hectare lake with its sandy beach and small harbour where boats and pedaloes may be hired. Perfect for watersports, access to the lake is down steps and across quite a fast road.

Two older heated toilet blocks (one closed in low season) have all facilities including washbasins in cabins, controllable showers and facilities for babies and disabled campers. A more recent block has eight en-suite units along with 16 pitches with private sanitary facilities. Laundry facilities. Motorcaravan services. Shop (from 15/4). Bar and restaurant with takeaway (from 15/4). Indoor pool with spa and sauna. Heated outdoor pool with slide. Games room. Playground. Extensive games area. Tennis (free in low season). Bicycle hire. WiFi throughout (charged).

Ideal For...

 Beach

 Dogs

 Fishing

 Watersports

 Walking

 Golf

Scan me for more information.

20 accommodations
180 pitches
GPS: 48.26331, 4.34666
Post Code: F-10140

Aube, Champagne-Ardenne

Camping Le Lac d'Orient

www.alanrogers.com/fr10020
info@camping-lacdorient.com
03 25 40 61 85
www.camping-lacdorient.com

Open (Touring Pitches):
8 April - 23 September.

Le Lac d'Orient opened in 2009 equipped with a good range of leisure amenities and with an attractive rural location. The site can be found at the centre of the large Forêt d'Orient natural park and is just 100 m. from the Lac d'Orient which is ideal for all manner of watersports. Previously a small municipal site, it has been rebuilt and offers a modern restaurant, bar and takeaway as well as a heated indoor pool and outdoor swimming pools with slides, all in one complex with the reception and the shop. The 212 pitches here are large and are semi-shaded with mature trees.

One purpose built toilet block and one totally refurbished, both of a high standard. Facilities for disabled visitors and children. Laundry facilities. Restaurant, bar and takeaway (8/4-17/9). Shop (all season). Heated indoor pool (as site) and outdoor swimming pools with slides (13/5-10/9). Paddling pool with small slides. Play area. Multisports court. Max. one dog. WiFi (free for 30 mins every 6 hours).

Ideal For...

 Beach

 Dogs

 Fishing

 Watersports

 Play Area

 Disabled Facilities

Scan me for more information.

25 accommodations
64 pitches
GPS: 48.16826, 6.89025
Post Code: F-88430

Vosges, Lorraine

Clos de la Chaume

www.alanrogers.com/fr88120
info@camping-closdelachaume.com
03 29 50 76 76
www.camping-closdelachaume.co.uk

Open (Touring Pitches):
27 April - 20 September

Sites et Paysages Camping Au Clos de la Chaume is a pleasant site is within walking distance of the town, on level ground with a small stream. The friendly family owners, who are British and French, live on site and do their best to ensure campers have an enjoyable relaxing stay. There are 94 level grassy pitches of varying sizes and with varying amounts of sun and shade. All 64 touring pitches have electricity hook-ups (6/10A) and some are divided by shrubs and trees. The site carries the LPO (League for Bird Protection) label with over 30 species present. There is an attractive, well fenced, new swimming pool and an excellent small adventure-style playground. Wine tasting evenings are held in July and August.

Two modern sanitary blocks provide all the necessary facilities for families and disabled visitors. Childrens sanitary facilities. Laundry with washing machines and dryers. Motorcaravan services. Reception keeps basic supplies (June/Aug). New covered swimming pool (1/5-20/9). Play area. Games room with pool table and library. Boules. Volleyball. WiFi throughout (charged) and also a FREE WiFi limited zone.

Ideal For...

 Beach

 Dogs

 Fishing

 Watersports

 Golf

 Play Area

Scan me for more information.

81 accommodations
69 pitches
GPS: 48.33722, 7.28862
Post Code: F-67220

Bas-Rhin, Alsace

Camping Le Giessen

www.alanrogers.com/fr67070
giessen@campeole.com
03 88 58 98 14
www.campeole.com/etablissement/post/le-giessen-bassemberg

Open (Touring Pitches):
31 March - 1 October

Le Giessen is a member of the Campéole group and can be found at the foot of the Vosges mountains, with easy access to many of the best loved sights in Alsace. Although there is no pool on site, a large complex comprising indoor and outdoor pools with a water slide can be found adjacent to the site, with free admission for all campers. The 69 touring pitches here are grassy and of a good size, mostly with 6A electrical connections and some shaded by mature trees. A number of mobile homes and fully equipped tents are available to rent. A supplement is payable for twin-axle caravans.

Two toilet blocks with all facilities including controllable hot showers and facilities for disabled visitors. Laundry. Bar (May-Sept). Snack bar/takeaway (July/Aug). Motorcaravan service point. Play area. Multisports court. Activities and entertainment. Bicycle hire. Fishing. Mobile homes and equipped tents to rent. WiFi (charged).

Ideal For...

 Beach

 Dogs

 Fishing

 Play Area

 Disabled Facilities

 Pets Accepted

Scan me for more information.

30 accommodations
120 pitches
GPS: 48.07962, 7.38652
Post Code: F-68180

Haut-Rhin, Alsace

Camping de l'Ill Colmar

www.alanrogers.com/fr68110
nfo@campingdelill.fr
03 89 41 15 94
www.campingdelill.fr/en

Open (Touring Pitches):
23 March - 31 December.

Stretching alongside the Ill river in urban Colmar, this site has 150 unseparated pitches, 120 for touring, arranged on terraces. Due to the danger of flooding on the lowest terrace during the winter months, this part of the site is closed during that period. Despite some noise from the A35 motorway, this is a pleasant, well maintained setting with some shade from mature trees. All pitches have 10A electricity connections (Europlug, some pitches require long leads). The reception is comfortable and welcoming with English spoken. Rental accommodation includes wood and canvas tents and wooden lodges. A supplement is payable for twin-axle caravans.

One modern heated sanitary block next to the main building and two older blocks (one closed in low season). Washbasins in cubicles, hot showers and facilities for disabled visitors. Washing machine and dryer. Motorcaravan services. Bread to order at reception. Bar (all season). Restaurant and takeaway (May-Sept). New heated pool and paddling pool. Play area. Outdoor chess. TV room. Boules. Fishing. Bicycle hire. Barbecue hire. WiFi (free in TV lounge).

Ideal For...

- Kids
- Dogs
- Fishing
- Walking
- Golf
- Play Area

Scan me for more information.

48 accommodations
147 pitches
GPS: 48.575507, 7.71506
Post Code: F-67200

Bas-Rhin, Alsace

Camping de Strasbourg

www.alanrogers.com/fr67060
info@camping-strasbourg.com
03 88 30 19 96
www.camping-indigo.com/en/indigo-strasbourg

Open (Touring Pitches):
All year.

Reopened in July 2015 after a lengthy refurbishment, Camping Indigo Strasbourg is a beautifully designed and built, brand new city site in south-west Strasbourg. During the low season you pick your pitch but in high season and during the time of the Christmas market (when there may be snow!), reservations are advised as the site becomes full. There are currently 90 pitches with electricity connections (6-9A, Europlug). A new central lodge has been added, the sanitary facilities completely rebuilt and a modern café/restaurant opened on site. There is a bus stop 200 m. from the site and the city tram runs into town. The city centre is only 30 minutes' walk. This site is an ideal base from which to explore the city.

Two brand new, heated sanitary blocks with facilities for families and disabled visitors. Washing machines and dryer. Motorcaravan services. Bar, restaurant and takeaway (all 6/7-31/8). Outdoor heated swimming pool (30/4-18/9). Bicycle hire. Free WiFi on part of site. Wood and canvas tents and Romany-style caravans available to rent.

Ideal For...

 Kids

 Dogs

Year Round Camping

 Play Area

 Disabled Facilities

 Pets Accepted

Scan me for more information.

115 accommodations
135 pitches
GPS: 47.24731, -0.00048
Post Code: F-49730

Maine-et-Loire, Pays de la Loire

www.alanrogers.com/fr49010
contact@domainedelabreche.com
02 41 51 22 92
www.domainedelabreche.com

Open (Touring Pitches):
15 April - 10 September.

Domaine de la Brèche

The Saint Cast family developed Domaine de la Brèche with care and attention. The attractive site occupies a 24-hectare estate, 4 km. northeast of Saumur on the edge of the Loire behind the levees. There are 235 spacious, level, grass pitches, with 135 for touring, including ten premium pitches. Trees and bushes give some shade. All have electricity (some require long cables). Eighty have a water supply and drainage. The restaurant (open to the public), bar and terrace provide an attractive social base and are popular with British visitors. The pool complex includes a heated indoor pool, flumes and toboggans and a paddling pool.

Three modern toilet blocks with all necessary facilities including those for babies and disabled campers. Washing up sinks and laundry. Good shop and épicerie. Bar. Restaurant (open to public), pizzeria and takeaway. Outdoor swimming pool and heated indoor swimming pool, both open all season. Tennis. Multisports pitch. Go-karts. Minigolf. Bicycle hire. Games and TV rooms. Varied sporting and entertainment programme & kids club (01/7-31/8). Pony riding. Torch useful. WiFi throughout (charged).

Ideal For...

 Kids

 Dogs

 Fishing

 Watersports

 Golf

 Play Area

Scan me for more information.

207 accommodations
126 pitches
GPS: 47.23486, -2.16757
Post Code: F-44250

Loire-Atlantique, Pays de la Loire

www.alanrogers.com/fr44190
camping@lefief.com
02 40 27 23 86
www.lefief.com

Open (Touring Pitches):
31 March - 23 September

Camping le Fief

Sunêlia Le Fief welcomes all campers on large pitches of 100 m^2, partly shaded and bordered by lush, established vegetation, and would particularly suit if you are a family with young children or lively teenagers. Le Fief is a well established site only 900 m. from sandy beaches on the southern Brittany coast. It has a magnificent aquapark with outdoor and covered swimming pools, paddling pools, slides, river rapids, fountains, jets and more. The site has 126 pitches for touring units, all with 8A electricity and varying slightly in size and accessibility. There are also 205 mobile homes and chalets to rent and 40 privately owned units. An impressive Taos mobile home village includes a new Sunny Club for children.

Laundry facilities. Shop (25/05-24/09). Bar, restaurant and takeaway (all season) with terrace overlooking the pool complex. Heated outdoor pools (1/5-15/9). Covered pool (all season). Wellness centre. Play area. Tennis. Pétanque. Archery. Games room. Organised entertainment and activities (weekends April/June, daily July/Aug). Bicycle hire. WiFi over site (charged). 900m from the city centre and from the long sandy beach.

Ideal For...

 Kids

 Beach

 Dogs

 Fishing

 Watersports

 Walking

Scan me for more information.

5 accommodations
90 pitches
GPS: 48.10586, 0.34108
Post Code: F-72460

Sarthe, Pays de la Loire

Château de Chanteloup

www.alanrogers.com/fr72030
contact@chateaudechanteloup.com
02 43 27 51 07
www.chateau-de-chanteloup.com

Open (Touring Pitches):
29 May - 31 August.

This attractive and peaceful site, close to Le Mans, is situated in the park of a 19th-century château in the heart of the Sarthe countryside. There are 90 very large pitches all with 10A electricity, although long leads may be required in some places. Some pitches adjoin woodland, many are around the edges of the lawns and completely open, and a few overlook a small fishing lake. New premium pitches are also equipped with unlimited WiFi, furniture and parasol, barbecue and fridge. The pitches are unobtrusively marked out and this enhances the feeling of spaciousness around the old château.

All sanitary facilities are in the château outbuildings and are well maintained and kept very clean. Washbasins are in cabins. Baby facilities and good en-suite unit for disabled visitors. Laundry facilities. Small shop (12/6-30/8). Fresh bread daily. Takeaway and restaurant with covered outdoor seating (12/6-31/8). Bar and TV room. Outdoor swimming pool (heated July/Aug). Play area (parental supervision essential). Games room. Volleyball. Organised activities (high season). Rowing boat and fishing rods free to use on site lake. Bicycle hire. WiFi over site (charged).

Ideal For...

 Kids

 Dogs

 Fishing

 Watersports

 Golf

 Play Area

Scan me for more information.

130 pitches
GPS: 47.32735, 1.08936
Post Code: F-37150

Indre-et-Loire, Val de Loire

www.alanrogers.com/fr37030
lemoulinfort@wanadoo.fr
02 47 23 86 22
www.lemoulinfort.com

Open (Touring Pitches):
1 May - 30 September.

Camping le Moulin Fort

Camping le Moulin Fort is a tranquil, riverside site with British owners, John and Sarah Scarratt. The 130 pitches are enhanced by trees and shrubs offering plenty of shade and 110 pitches have electricity (6A). From the snack bar terrace adjacent to the restored mill building, a timber walkway over the mill race leads to the unheated swimming pool and paddling pools. The site is ideal for couples and families with young children, although the river is unfenced. There is occasional noise from trains passing on the opposite bank of the river.

Two toilet blocks with all the usual amenities are of a good standard and include washbasins in cubicles, baby baths and facilities for disabled visitors. Washing machines and dryer. Motorcaravan services. Shop (1/5-30/9). Bar, restaurant and takeaway (all 21/5-20/9, closed Wed. low season). Swimming pool (21/5-25/9). Excellent play area. Minigolf. Pétanque. Games room and TV. Library. Fishing. Bicycle hire. In high season regular family entertainment including wine tasting, quiz evenings, activities for children, light hearted games tournaments and live music events. WiFi in bar area (charged).

Ideal For...

 Beach

 Dogs

 Fishing

 Watersports

 Golf

 Play Area

Scan me for more information.

205 accommodations
394 pitches
GPS: 47.1487, 0.6548
Post Code: F-37800

Indre-et-Loire, Val de Loire

Camping Parc de Fierbois

www.alanrogers.com/fr37120
contact@fierbois.com
02 47 65 43 35
www.fierbois.com

Open (Touring Pitches):
28 April - 3 September.

Castel Camping Parc de Fierbois has a wide variety of accommodation to rent if you're not bringing your own caravan or tent. There's a range of Mobile homes, Chalets, Gîtes and Tree houses. The campsite provides plenty of opportunity for a restful family holiday, but there are many activities for everyone if you prefer to be more active. As well as a covered heated pool, you'll also find a water-park complex with toboggans, a children's club, adventure park, including archery and a skate park, and a good restaurant and bar. The region also has a rich heritage for you to discover including chateaux Villandry, Azay-le-Rideau and Chenonceau, as well as many famous vineyards.

Two sanitary blocks are equipped with showers, private washing cubicles and facilities for babies. Washing machines and dryers. Well stocked shop. Bar. Restaurant and takeaway. Heated indoor pool. Outdoor pool with waterslides. Activity and entertainment programmes (in July and August). Bicycle hire. Fishing. Adventure park in the trees. Internet access and WiFi (charged).

Ideal For...

 Kids

 Beach

 Dogs

 Fishing

 Walking

 Golf

Scan me for more information.

Villandry Castle and Gardens, Indre-et-Loire

320 accommodations
230 pitches
GPS: 47.54398, 2.19193
Post Code: F-41300

Loir-et-Cher, Val de Loire

Camping les Alicourts

www.alanrogers.com/fr41030
info@lesalicourts.com
02 54 88 63 34
www.lesalicourts.com

Open (Touring Pitches):
29 April - 4 September

A secluded holiday village set in the heart of the forest, with many sporting facilities and a super spa centre, Leading Camping les Alicourts Resort is midway between Orléans and Bourges, to the east of the A71. There are 550 pitches, 230 for touring and the remainder occupied by mobile homes and chalets. All pitches have 6A electricity connections and good provision for water, and most are 150 sq.m. (min. 100 sq.m). Locations vary from wooded to more open areas, thus giving a choice of amount of shade. All facilities are open all season and the leisure amenities are exceptional. A member of Leading Campings group.

Three modern sanitary blocks include some washbasins in cabins and baby bathrooms. Laundry facilities. Facilities for families and disabled visitors. Motorcaravan services. Shop. Boutique. Restaurant. Takeaway in bar with terrace. Pool complex. 7 water slides. Spa centre. Library. 7-hectare lake (fishing, bathing, canoes, pedaloes, cable-ski). 9-hole golf course. Adventure play area. Tennis. Minigolf. Boules. Roller skating/skateboarding (bring own equipment). Bicycle hire. Internet access and WiFi (charged).

Ideal For...

 Kids

 Beach

 Dogs

 Fishing

 Walking

 Golf

Scan me for more information.

15 accommodations
164 pitches
GPS: 47.4811, 1.450106
Post Code: F-41700

Loir-et-Cher, Val de Loire

www.alanrogers.com/fr41100
contact@camping-cheverny.com
02 54 79 90 01
www.camping-cheverny.com

Open (Touring Pitches):
31 March - 16 September.

Camping les Saules

Set in the heart of the château region, Sites et Paysages Camping les Saules has developed into a popular, friendly campsite run by a local family. The well renovated, traditional reception buildings in their lakeside setting give a very pleasant welcome. There are 164 good size, level pitches with 148 for touring units. All have shade from the many trees on the site, and 10A electricity connections (a few will require leads longer than 25 m), and there are ample water taps. A large, grassy field provides room for youngsters to play safely. There are many designated cycle paths and walking circuits in the area, often linking châteaux through attractive, sleepy countryside.

Two sanitary blocks with toilets, showers, washbasins in cubicles and facilities for disabled visitors. Laundry facilities. Motorcaravan services. Gas supplies. Shop, snack bar and takeaway (14/5-12/9). Restaurant (July/Aug). Bar. Heated swimming and paddling pools (1/4-17/9). TV/social room with toys, board games, books. Two play areas. Large grass area for ball games. Minigolf (free). Fishing. Bicycle hire. Internet and WiFi.

Ideal For...

 Kids

 Fishing

 Walking

 Golf

 Play Area

 Disabled Facilities

Scan me for more information.

100 accommodations
386 pitches
GPS: 46.9969, -2.2201
Post Code: F-85330

Noirmoutier-en-l'Ile, Vendée

Camping Noirmoutier

Located in woodland and on dunes along a two kilometre stretch of sandy beach, just east of the attractive little town of Noirmoutier on the island of the same name, this could be paradise for those who enjoy a simple campsite in a natural setting. On land belonging to France's forestry commission, this site is operated by Huttopia whose aim is to adapt to the environment rather than take it over. The 386 touring pitches, all with electricity (10A), are situated among the pine trees and accessed along tracks. Those on the sand dunes have fantastic views across the Baie de Bourgneuf. They cost a few euros extra – if you are lucky enough to get one. Some pitches may experience noise from a nearby bar.

Five unheated sanitary blocks provide preset showers and washbasins in cubicles. The central one is larger and more modern. Facilities for children and disabled visitors. Laundry. Motorcaravan services. Freezer service. Bread to order. Snack bar and takeaway (July/Aug). Picnic tables. New play area. Boules. Volleyball. Bicycle and canoe hire. Only electric barbecues allowed. Free WiFi over part of site.

www.alanrogers.com/fr85720
noirmoutier@huttopia.com
02 51 39 06 24
europe.huttopia.com/en/site/noirmoutier

Open (Touring Pitches):
6 April - 2 October.

Ideal For...

 Kids

 Beach

 Dogs

 Fishing

 Watersports

 Walking

Scan me for more information.

124 accommodations
294 pitches
GPS: 46.65273, -1.74987
Post Code: F-85150

Saint Julien-des-Landes, Vendée

Village de la Guyonnière

www.alanrogers.com/fr85260
info@laguyonniere.com
02 51 46 62 59
www.camping-guyonniere.com

Open (Touring Pitches):
22 April - 17 September.

Camping Village de la Guyonnière is a spacious (30 hectare) rural site. It is Dutch owned but English is spoken and all visitors are made very welcome. The pitches are arranged on ten different fields, each being reasonably level. There are around 300 mostly large pitches (225 sq.m) with a mix of sun and shade and large units are welcome. Some are open, others are separated by a tree and a few bushes. All have access to electricity connections (10A, Europlug) and 136 are occupied by mobile homes, chalets and glamping accommodation. The pool complex is fully heated and includes an outdoor pool with a wild water river and a heated indoor pool with a waterfall. Bar and restaurant facilities are housed in original farm buildings, attractively converted.

Five toilet blocks (two open in low season and recently upgraded) provide washbasins in cubicles and hot showers. Provision for children and disabled visitors. Laundry facilities. Motorcaravan service point. Shop, bar with TV and pool table, restaurant, pizzeria with takeaway (all season). Heated pool complex with outdoor pool (all season) and wild water river and covered pool (all season) with waterfall and disability lift. Paddling pool. Wellness facility. Play areas. Sand pit. Tennis. Multisports pitch. Bicycle hire. WiFi throughout (free).

Ideal For...

 Kids

 Fishing

 Watersports

 Golf

 Play Area

 Disabled Facilities

Scan me for more information.

53 accommodations
265 pitches
GPS: 46.6432, -1.71198
Post Code: F-85150

Saint Julien-des-Landes, Vendée

Château La Forêt

www.alanrogers.com/fr85820
camping@chateaulaforet.com
02 51 46 62 11
www.chateaulaforet.com

Open (Touring Pitches):
21 April - 4 September.

Set in the tranquil and beautiful natural parkland surrounding a 19th-century château, Yelloh! Village Château La Forêt is a lovely site with 266 large pitches, of which 161 are for touring units. There are also 60 units to rent and 45 pitches are occupied by tour operators. All are on grass and fully serviced including 10A electricity; some are in shady woodland and others, for sun worshippers, are more open. The camping area is only a small part of the 50-hectare estate, with a mix of woodland, open meadows and fishing lakes, all accessible to campers. The many outbuildings around the courtyard have been tastefully converted and include a bar and restaurant in the old stables.

Three sanitary blocks are newly refurbished and include washbasins in cubicles, with good provision for babies and disabled campers. No motorcaravan service point. Laundry facilities with washing machines and dryers. Shop, bar, small restaurant and takeaway. Two swimming pools (one outdoor, one heated and covered with children's pool and slide). Play area. Regular evening entertainment, children's clubs and disco (July/Aug). Large adventure playground (charged). Trampoline. Games room. Tennis. Boules. Fishing lakes. 6-hole golf course and minigolf. Canoeing trips. Bicycle hire. Free WiFi. Only gas barbecues permitted. No double-axle caravans accepted.

Ideal For...

 Kids

 Beach

 Dogs

 Fishing

 Walking

 Golf

Scan me for more information.

58 accommodations
151 pitches
GPS: 46.663648, -1.713395
Post Code: F-85150

Saint Julien-des-Landes, Vendée

Camping La Garangeoire

www.alanrogers.com/fr85040
info@garangeoire.com
02 51 46 65 39
www.garangeoire.com

Open (Touring Pitches):
2 May - 18 September.

Castel Camping La Garangeoire is a stunning campsite, situated some 15 km. inland, near the village of Saint Julien-des-Landes. Set in 200 hectares of parkland surrounding the small château of la Garangeoire, of which there is an outstanding view as you approach through the gates. With a spacious, relaxed atmosphere, the main camping areas are on either side of the old road which is edged with mature trees. The 357 pitches (151 for touring), all named rather than numbered, are individually hedged, some with shade. They are well spaced and are especially large (most 150-200 sq.m), 87 have electricity (16A, Europlug), 45 have water and drainage also, and four have a private WC facility.

Ample, first class sanitary facilities. All have washbasins in cabins and showers. Facilities for babies & disabled visitors. Laundry facilities. Motorcaravan services. Shop, full restaurant and takeaway with bars & terrace. Pool complex with heated, covered pool, water slides, fountains and a children's pool. Play field with play equipment. Football pitch. Games room. Tennis courts (charged July/Aug). Multisports court. Bicycle hire. Minigolf. Seasonal Archery and Riding. Fishing and boating. Bouncy castle. Trampolines. Children's club. Only gas barbecues allowed. Shuttle bus to beach. WiFi on part of site (free).

Ideal For...

 Beach

 Dogs

 Fishing

 Golf

 Play Area

 Disabled Facilities

Scan me for more information.

60 accommodations
170 pitches
GPS: 46.75659, -2.00792
Post Code: F-85160

Saint Jean-de-Monts, Vendée

Camping Resort La Yole

www.alanrogers.com/fr85150
contact@la-yole.com
02 51 58 67 17
www.la-yole.com

Open (Touring Pitches):
2 April - 25 September.

Camping Resort La Yole is an attractive and well run site, two kilometres from a sandy beach. It offers 369 pitches, of which 76 are occupied by tour operators and 133 mobile homes are either privately owned or available to rent. There are 170 touring pitches, most with shade and separated by bushes and trees. An area at the rear of the site is a little more open. All the pitches are of at least 100 sq.m. and have electricity (10A), water and drainage. The pool complex includes an attractive outdoor pool, a paddling pool, slide and an indoor heated pool with jacuzzi. An extension to the pool area is planned for 2016. There are also gym facilities and entertainment is organised in high season. This is a clean and tidy site, ideal for families with children and you will receive a helpful and friendly welcome.

Four toilet blocks (one heated in low season) include washbasins in cabins, hot showers and facilities for disabled visitors and babies. Laundry facilities. Shop (20/5-5/9). Bar with TV, restaurant and takeaway (2/4-7/9). Outdoor pool and paddling pool. Indoor heated pool with jacuzzi (all season). Gym centre. Play area (4-10 yrs). Tennis. Games room. Chidren's club. Bicycle hire. Entertainment in high season. WiFi on part of site (charged). Gas barbecues only. Communal barbecue area provided. Max. 1 dog.

Ideal For...

 Kids

 Beach

 Dogs

 Watersports

 Walking

 Golf

Scan me for more information.

150 accommodations
46 pitches
GPS: 46.47207, -1.72646
Post Code: F-85180

Le Château-d'Olonne, Vendée

www.alanrogers.com/fr85710
lebelair@cybelevacances.com
02 51 22 09 67
www.campingdubelair.com

Open (Touring Pitches):
2 April - 5 November.

Camping le Bel Air

Le Bel Air is a well established site close to the Vendée's largest resort, Les Sables-d'Olonne. It is now very much dedicated to mobile homes and chalets. Of its 286 pitches, just 46 are for touring – 40 on grass mostly with electricity (16A), water and drainage and a further six on concrete for motorcaravans. This is a very well equipped site with the focal point being a new and impressive pool complex including a large covered pool and separate outdoor pool.

Five well equipped small sanitary blocks with facilities for babies and disabled visitors. Laundry with washing machines and dryers. Motorcaravan services. Bar, snack bar, takeaway and shop. Heated outdoor pool with children's pool and waterslides (April-Sept). Heated indoor pool with sauna, spa and gym (all season). TV room. Games room. Multisports court. Playground. Bicycle hire. Activities in high season. Mobile homes and chalets for rent. Charcoal barbecues not permitted. WiFi throughout (charged).

Ideal For...

 Kids

 Beach

 Dogs

 Fishing

 Watersports

 Golf

Scan me for more information.

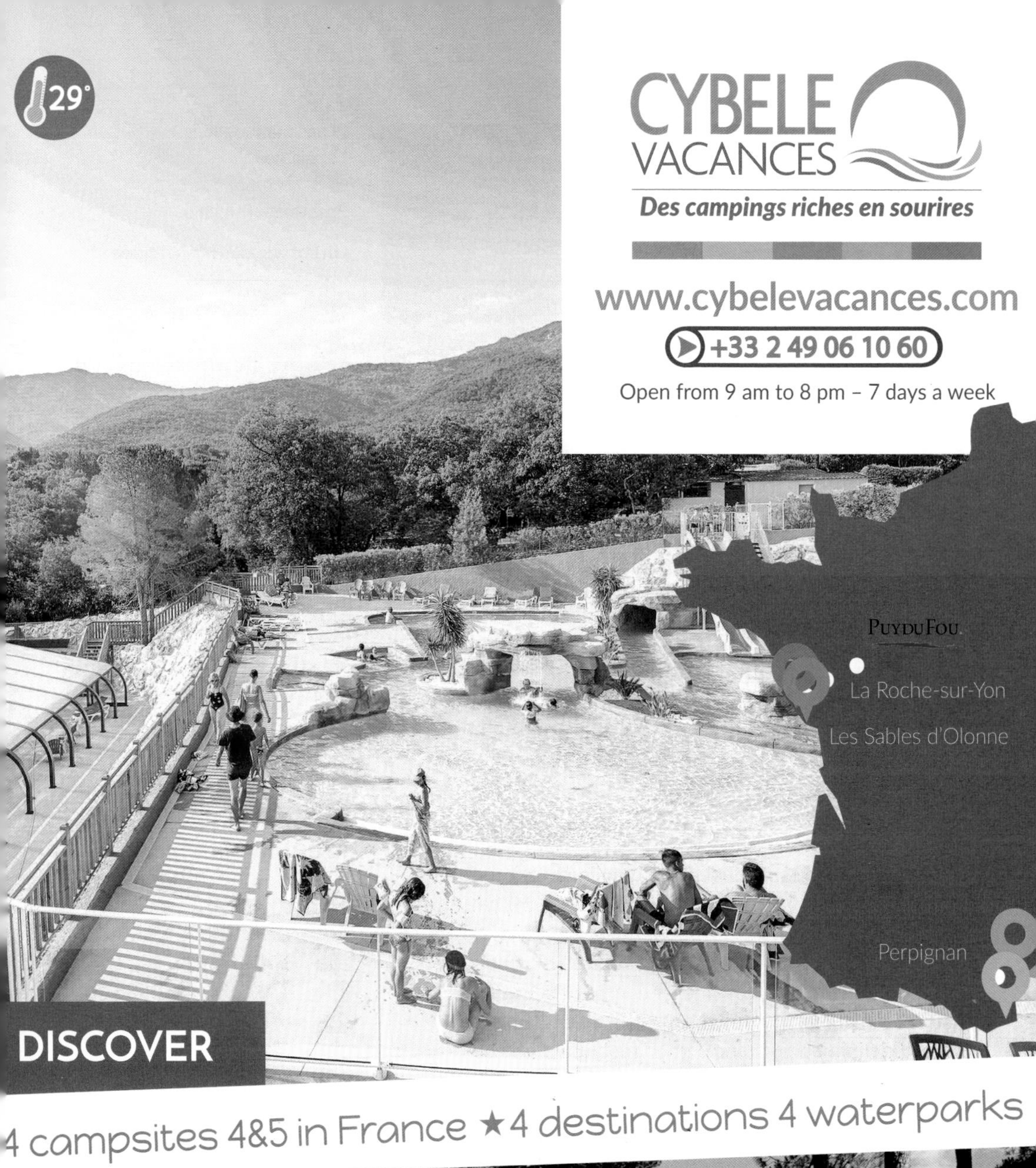
29°
CYBELE
VACANCES
Des campings riches en sourires
www.cybelevacances.com
+33 2 49 06 10 60
Open from 9 am to 8 pm – 7 days a week
PUYDUFOU
La Roche-sur-Yon
Les Sables d'Olonne
Perpignan
DISCOVER
4 campsites 4&5 in France ★4 destinations 4 waterparks

19 accommodations
130 pitches
GPS: 46.2055, -1.2555
Post Code: F-85360

La Tranche-sur-Mer, Vendée

Camping Baie d'Aunis

www.alanrogers.com/fr85870
info@camping-baiedaunis.com
02 51 27 47 36
www.camping-baiedaunis.com

Open (Touring Pitches):
20 April - 16 September

This very popular 2.5-hectare site has direct access to a sandy beach through a pedestrian gate (with key code) and across a car park. The town centre is also only 500 m. away. Shady and level, there are 130 touring pitches, all with 10A electricity. A good number of pitches are on a gravel base and a few are suitable only for smaller units. There are chalets and mobile homes (19) to rent. On-site amenities include a heated swimming pool and a good restaurant and bar. This is a popular seaside resort with 13 km. of good quality sandy beaches.

The main centrally located sanitary unit is large, good quality and very well appointed. A smaller unit at the far end of the site has been renovated to a high standard. British style WCs, washbasins in cubicles, provision for children and disabled campers. Laundry room at each block. Motorcaravan services. Bar/restaurant and takeaway (21/4-17/9). Outdoor heated swimming pool (10x20 m). Playground. Games room. TV room. Library. Multisports area. Dogs not accepted July/Aug or in rental accommodation. WiFi over site (free).

Ideal For...

 Beach

 Dogs

 Fishing

 Watersports

 Play Area

 Disabled Facilities

Scan me for more information.

50 accommodations
40 pitches
GPS: 46.81511, -1.77472
Post Code: F-85670

Saint Christophe-du-Ligneron, Vendée

Le Domaine de Bellevue

www.alanrogers.com/fr85385
contact@vendee-camping-bellevue.com
02 51 93 30 66
www.vendee-camping-bellevue.com

Open (Touring Pitches):
Year round.

Le Domaine de Bellevue is a family friendly site located in the northern Vendée, close to the town of Challans (famous for its market), and around 20 minutes from the broad, sandy beaches at Saint Gilles-Croix-de-Vie. There are 126 large (minimum 150 sq.m) pitches here, of which 40 are for tourers, 10 fully serviced with 16A electricity and dispersed around a large park, which has two generous fishing ponds (catch and release, and surrounded by a secured fence for the children) stocked with carp and other species. An entertainment programme runs during April, July and August and includes special activities for children. There is a range of mobile homes, chalets and bungalow-style tents for rent.

Three sanitary blocks with washbasins and showers in cubicles and facilities for children (ergonomic baby baths and a baby care space) and disabled visitors. Laundry. Snack/bar (April and July/Aug). Covered, heated swimming pool and children's covered paddled pool (1/4 - 1/11). Play area. Games room. Trampoline. Bouncy castle. Volleyball, Football ground, Pétanque pitch. Activity and entertainment programme (April and July/Aug). WiFi throughout (charged). Mobile homes and chalets for rent. Free Fishing (catch and release). Small animal farm.

Ideal For...

 Kids

 Beach

 Dogs

 Fishing

 Watersports

 Walking

Scan me for more information.

182 accommodations
180 pitches
GPS: 46.66622, -1.75528
Post Code: F-85220

La Chapelle-Hermier, Vendée

Camping le Pin Parasol

www.alanrogers.com/fr85680
contact@campingpinparasol.fr
02 51 34 64 72
www.campingpinparasol.fr

Open (Touring Pitches):
20 April - 16 September

Tucked away in the Vendée countryside, just 15 minutes' drive from the beach, this campsite enjoys a rural setting above the Lac du Jaunay, well away from the bustle of the coast. There are 184 good sized touring pitches, all with 10A electricity (Europlug) and 33 with water tap and drainage. Some have shade, others are in the open with maturing hedges and trees. The enthusiastic family owners are very hands-on and the facilities are of a high standard, most notably the entrance and reception building, and the pool area with its excellent indoor and outdoor pools, slides, flumes, jacuzzi, steam room and fitness suite. Fishing is well-catered for with direct access to the lake. You can buy your fishing licence, store equipment in a secure room, keep bait in a fridge at the site.

Four excellent toilet blocks (one heated) include hot showers, washbasins in cabins and facilities for babies and disabled visitors. Washing machines and dryers. Shop, Bar with terrace, Takeaway and Heated outdoor pool with paddling pool, slides and flumes (20/4/2018-16/9/2018). Indoor pool. Wellness centre and fitness equipment. Jacuzzi (free), hamman (charged). Play areas. Games room. Multisports pitch. Boules. Bicycle, canoe and pedalo hire. Entertainment in high season. Children's club. Fishing. Tennis. WiFi over site (charged). Internet boxes for hire giving access via your electric connection.

Ideal For...

 Kids

 Beach

 Dogs

 Fishing

 Watersports

 Walking

Scan me for more information.

97 accommodations
27 pitches
GPS: 46.21121, -1.5298
Post Code: F-17590

Charente-Maritime, Poitou-Charentes

Camping le Cormoran

www.alanrogers.com/fr17260
info@cormoran.com
05 46 29 46 04
www.cormoran.com

Open (Touring Pitches):
1 April - 25 September.

On the outskirts of Ars-en-Ré, le Cormoran offers a quiet rural holiday. There are 97 mobile homes, many for hire, and 27 pitches of varying sizes for touring units (all with 10A electricity). A lovely new bar/restaurant serves imaginative meals and takeaway dishes all season. Being just 500 m. from a sandy beach, close to the local oyster beds and with numerous cycle paths that include routes through a nature reserve, this campsite is popular with families of all ages.

The two toilet blocks provide excellent facilities for babies, young children and disabled visitors. Laundry. Motorcaravan services. Bar, restaurant and takeaway meals (all season). Heated swimming pool and terrace with paddling pools, spa pools and jacuzzi. Sauna and Hammam. Fitness centre. Tennis. Games room. Play areas and bouncy castle. Multisports court. Boules. Children's entertainment and family activities (July/Aug). Bicycle hire. No charcoal barbecues. WiFi throughout (free).

Ideal For...

 Kids

 Beach

 Dogs

 Fishing

 Watersports

 Golf

Scan me for more information.

400 accommodations
240 pitches
GPS: 45.81095, -1.06109
Post Code: F-17320

Charente-Maritime, Poitou-Charentes

Camping Séquoia Parc

www.alanrogers.com/fr17140
info@sequoiaparc.com
05 46 85 55 55
www.sequoiaparc.com

Open (Touring Pitches):
5 May - 5 September

Just 7 km from the beach (Marennes), this is a family campsite in the heart of the Charente-Maritime region. Séquoia Parc is set in the grounds of La Josephtrie, a château with beautifully restored outbuildings and courtyard area with a bar and restaurant. The pitches are between 120 &140m² with 6/10A electricity connections, separated by shrubs providing plenty of privacy. The site has mobile homes, chalets and fully equipped tents for up to 7 people. This is a popular site and reservations are necessary in high season. Children's clubs are free and run all season, with entertainment in high season. This site is a member of Leading Campings group.

Three spotless toilet blocks include units with washbasins and showers. Facilities for disabled visitors & children. Large laundry. Motorcaravan services. Supermarket with fresh bread. Restaurant/bar. Takeaway with wood oven pizzas. 2000 m² swimming pool complex with water slides, river and large paddling pool. Wellness & Fitness centre with indoor swimming pool, sauna, hammam and Jacuzzi. Massage rooms, spa treatments & fitness area with cardio & weight training equipment. Multisports pitch. Tennis. Games & TV rooms. Bicycle & pedal-go-kart hire. Entertainment/excursions in high season. Children's club & farm. Equestrian centre (seasonal). WiFi zones (charged).

Ideal For...

 Kids

 Beach

 Dogs

 Fishing

 Watersports

 Walking

Scan me for more information.

The Mairie in Saint-Just-Luzac - By Cobber17 - CC BY-SA 3.0

100 accommodations
60 pitches
GPS: 45.9674685, -1.3192605
Post Code: F-17190

Charente-Maritime, Poitou-Charentes

www.alanrogers.com/fr17470
info@chadotel.com
05 46 76 54 97
www.chadotel.com

Open (Touring Pitches):
6 April - 21 September.

Le Domaine d'Oléron

Camping le Domaine d'Oléron is a neat, well presented and well managed site where you will receive a warm and friendly welcome from Anneke and Freddy who speak excellent English. The site is set in a peaceful rural location between Saint Pierre and Saint Georges and is part of the Chadotel group. At present there are 172 pitches of which 60 are for touring units. The pitches are generously sized (100-150 sq.m) and are mostly sunny, level and easily accessible, all with 10A electricity. The site is just 3 km. from the beach and the Forest of Saumonards. The local port, shops and restaurants are also nearby.

Two modern sanitary blocks include facilities for disabled visitors and babies. Laundry facilities. Motorcaravan services. Snack bar and takeaway, bar with TV (all 15/5-10/9). Bread delivered daily. Swimming pool with slides (1/5-14/9). Adventure style play area. Six pétanque lanes. Bicycle hire. Organised entertainment two or three times a week in July/Aug. Gas barbecues only on pitches, communal areas for charcoal. WiFi over site (charged). Max. 1 dog per pitch.

Ideal For...

 Beach

 Dogs

 Fishing

 Watersports

 Golf

 Play Area

Scan me for more information.

107 accommodations
251 pitches
GPS: 45.583583, -0.986533
Post Code: F-17110

Charente-Maritime, Poitou-Charentes

www.alanrogers.com/fr17010
info@bois-soleil.com
05 46 05 05 94
www.bois-soleil.com

Open (Touring Pitches):
1 April - 8 October.

Camping Bois Soleil

Close to the sea, Bois Soleil is a large site in three parts, with serviced pitches for touring units and a few for tents. All the touring pitches are hedged and have electricity (10A), with water and drainage between two. The main part, Les Pins, is attractive with trees and shrubs providing shade. Opposite is La Mer with direct access to the beach, some areas with less shade and an area for tents. The third part, La Forêt, is for caravan holiday homes. It is best to book your preferred area as it can be full mid June to late August. Excellent private sanitary facilities are available to rent, either on your pitch or at a block (subject to availability).

Each area has one large and one small sanitary block. Heated block near reception. Cleaned twice daily, they include facilities for disabled visitors and babies. Launderette. Supermarket, bakery, beach shop (all 15/4-15/9). Restaurant, bar and takeaway (all 15/4-15/9). Swimming pool (heated 15/6-15/9). Steam room. Tennis. Play area. TV room and library. Internet terminal. WiFi throughout (charged). Charcoal and electric barbecues are not permitted. Dogs are not accepted 2/7-27/8.

Ideal For...

 Kids

 Beach

 Dogs

 Fishing

 Watersports

 Golf

Scan me for more information.

37 accommodations
132 pitches
GPS: 45.6598, 0.557667
Post Code: F-16220

Charente, Poitou-Charentes

Les Gorges du Chambon

www.alanrogers.com/fr16020
info@camping-gorgesduchambon.com
05 45 70 71 70
camping-gorgesduchambon.com

Open (Touring Pitches):
27 April - 15 September

Yelloh! Village les Gorges du Chambon is a wonderful site with 28 hectares of protected natural environment to be enjoyed in the rolling Perigord Vert countryside. Of 132 pitches, the 92 for touring are extremely generous in size (150 sq.m), some level, others on a gentle slope, and they enjoy a mixture of sunshine and shade. This spacious site offers fine walks through the woodlands and around the grounds. Flora and fauna are as nature intended. Here you can feel at peace and enjoy precious moments of quiet. There has been much work done with the ecology association.

Traditional style sanitary blocks include facilities for disabled visitors. Washing machine, dryer. Shop stocks regional produce and groceries. Bar, restaurant (all season). Takeaway (all season). New swimming pool (all season, heated with new slides for 2018), children's pool. Large play area. Games room, TV and library with English books. Pony riding and Yoga (July/Aug). Tennis. Minigolf. Volleyball. Multisports pitch. Bicycle hire. Beach, Fishing in the river. Canoe hire nearby. Organised activities July/Aug, children's club, youth disco. WiFi (charged).

Ideal For...

 Kids

 Beach

 Dogs

 Fishing

 Walking

 Golf

Scan me for more information.

26 accommodations
94 pitches
GPS: 46.31492, -0.60835
Post Code: F-79510

Deux-Sèvres, Poitou-Charentes

www.alanrogers.com/fr79040
accueil@camping-laveniseverte.fr
05 49 35 90 36
www.camping-laveniseverte.fr

Open (Touring Pitches):
1 April - 31 October.

Camping de la Venise Verte

Owners, Marie and Bruno, will be pleased to welcome you to their site on the edge of the Sèvre Nortaise and the Marais Poitevin, which is ideal for short or long stays. With canoe and bicycle hire on site you have no excuse for not exploring the local area. In the Deux-Sèvres, the department of discovery, so named because it has two rivers named Sèvre, the Noirtaise and Nantaise, the Venise Verte provides an excellent site. There are 120 flat pitches here with 94 used for touring units, the remainder occupied by 26 mobile homes. The pitches are of a good size, most with 10A electricity, water and drainage, and with some shade.

Modern toilet facilities are of a high standard with free showers. Facilities for disabled visitors. Washing machine and dryer. Motorcaravan services. Heated swimming pool (15/6-15/9). Play area. Bicycle hire. Boules area. Fishing. WiFi on part of site (free).

Ideal For...

 Dogs

 Fishing

 Watersports

 Play Area

 Disabled Facilities

 Pets Accepted

Scan me for more information.

30 accommodations
97 pitches
GPS: 46.885533, 0.586133
Post Code: F-86220

Vienne, Poitou-Charentes

www.alanrogers.com/fr86010
chateau@petit-trianon.fr
05 49 02 61 47
www.petit-trianon.fr

Open (Touring Pitches):
18 April - 11 September.

Camping le Petit Trianon

A family owned site, Castel Camping le Petit Trianon is situated halfway between Tours and Poitiers. It enjoys a countryside position within the lovely grounds of a small 18th-century château. Visitors to the site often return several times after their first visit for the calm and tranquil atmosphere here. There are 116 fairly open pitches, all with electricity (10A), set in seven hectares, which gives a real sense of spaciousness. Plants are well tended and shade is provided in parts by the many attractive trees. Access around the site is good and large units are accepted by prior arrangement.

The sanitary facilities include washbasins in cabins, some washbasin and shower units, baby baths, washing machines and dryer. Facilities for disabled visitors. Motorcaravan services. Shop. Snack bar. Takeaway. Heated swimming pool and paddling pool. Playground. Minigolf. Badminton, croquet, volleyball and boules. Satellite TV. Reading room. Children's club and entertainment (July/Aug). Bicycle hire. Bread making (July/Aug). Internet access. WiFi (charged). Caravan storage.

Ideal For...

 Dogs

 Fishing

 Watersports

 Play Area

 Disabled Facilities

 Pets Accepted

Scan me for more information.

45 accommodations
120 pitches
GPS: 46.65485, 4.94463
Post Code: F-71240

Saône-et-Loire, Burgundy

Château de l'Epervière

www.alanrogers.com/fr71070
info@domaine-eperviere.com
03 85 94 16 90
www.domaine-eperviere.com

Open (Touring Pitches):
1 April - 30 September.

Castel Camping Château de l'Epervière is a popular high quality site, peacefully situated in the wooded grounds of a 16th-century château, close to the A6 and near the village of Gigny-sur-Saône. It is within walking distance of the river where you can watch the cruise boats on their way to and from Châlon-sur-Saône. There are 160 pitches arranged over two areas separated by a small fishing lake, 120 are used for touring. All have 10A electricity, some are on hardstanding and 30 are fully serviced. Close to the château and fishing lake, the pitches are hedged and have shade from mature trees; whilst the area behind the lake has a more open aspect.

Two well equipped, very clean toilet blocks with all necessary facilities including those for babies and disabled campers. Washing machine/dryer. Motorcaravan services. Basic shop, takeaway and restaurant with good menu (all 26/4-30/9). Cellar with wine tasting. Converted barn with bar, large TV. Heated outdoor swimming pool and new heated paddling pool with slides (26/4-30/9) partly enclosed by old stone walls. Smaller indoor heated pool (all season). Play areas and open field. Fishing. Bicycle hire. Free WiFi in bar area.

Ideal For...

 Beach

 Dogs

 Fishing

 Watersports

 Golf

 Play Area

Scan me for more information.

9 accommodations
91 pitches
GPS: 46.78448, 4.87295
Post Code: F-71380

Saône-et-Loire, Burgundy

www.alanrogers.com/fr71140
campingchalon71@wanadoo.fr
03 85 48 26 86
www.camping-chalon.com

Open (Touring Pitches):
1 April - 30 September.

Du Pont de Bourgogne

Camping du Pont de Bourgogne is a well presented and cared for site, useful for an overnight stop or for a longer stay to explore the local area. It is close to the A6 autoroute, and the interesting market town of Châlon-sur-Saône is within 2 km. There are 100 mainly level pitches (90 sq.m) all with 10A Europlug, most on grass, but 30 have a gravel surface. They are separated by beech hedging and a variety of mature trees provide shade. Many pitches overlook the river, a good spot to watch the passing boats, and a cycle route runs alongside. Access is easy for large outfits.

Three sanitary blocks, two of which are superb modern buildings, are kept very clean and have high quality fittings including a children's bathroom, disabled bathroom and family shower. Motorcaravan services. Laundry facilities. No shop but essentials kept in the bar (bread to order). Modern bar/restaurant (July/Aug). Simple play area. Bicycle hire arranged. WiFi (free in bar). Chalets for rent, one adapted for disabled visitors.

Ideal For...

 Dogs

 Fishing

 Watersports

 Golf

 Play Area

 Disabled Facilities

Scan me for more information.

61 accommodations
149 pitches
GPS: 47.23661, 4.62810
Post Code: F-21320

Côte d`Or, Burgundy

Camping Lac de Panthier

www.alanrogers.com/fr21000
info@lac-de-panthier.com
03 80 49 21 94
www.lac-de-panthier.com

Open (Touring Pitches):
1 April - 30 September.

Camping Lac de Panthier is an attractively situated lakeside site in the Burgundy countryside. It is divided into two areas, one housing the reception, shop, restaurant, indoor pool and sauna. The other, larger area is 200 m. along the lakeside road and is where the other site activities take place and the outdoor pools can be found. Many of the pitches here have views across the countryside. The 210 pitches (149 for touring) all have 6A electricity and are mostly on gently sloping grass, although in parts there are shallow terraces. The restaurant and some pitches have views over the lake which offers many watersports and is popular with anglers. Used by tour operators.

Each area has two adequate unisex toilet blocks including provision for babies and disabled visitors. Shop, bar, restaurant and takeaway (all season). Games and TV rooms. Swimming pool, children's pool and slide (1/6-31/8). Indoor pool, sauna and gym. Fishing. Bicycle hire (including electric bikes with trailers for children) and canoe hire. Watersports. Entertainment and activities organised in high season and clubs for children and teenagers. WiFi throughout (charged). Trampoline. Electric barbecues are not permitted. Max. 1 dog.

Ideal For...

 Beach

 Dogs

 Fishing

 Watersports

 Golf

 Play Area

Scan me for more information.

30 accommodations
171 pitches
GPS: 47.00284, 5.663
Post Code: F-39380

Jura, Franche-Comté

www.alanrogers.com/fr39010
plageblanche@huttopia.com
03 84 37 69 63
europe.huttopia.com/en/site/la-plage-blanche

Open (Touring Pitches):
27 April - 25 September.

Camping la Plage Blanche

Huttopia La Plage Blanche is located in the Jura, by the rippling waters of the River Loue. This spacious eight-hectare site has 218 pitches (171 for touring, 40 of these on the riverbank). All are large, grassy and level with 10A electricity (Europlugs). This is a great site for family holidays with its children's activities and themed evenings in the bar/restaurant (DJ or live music) in high season. Other activities include kayaking, canoeing, fishing, fly fishing and woodland walks in the site's own wood. A number of distinctive safari style tents are available to rent.

Three sanitary blocks include showers, washbasins in cabins and facilities for babies and disabled campers. Launderette. Motorcaravan service area. Shop with basics. Bar/snack bar/pizzeria with terrace. Takeaway. Heated swimming and paddling pools (all season). Adults only spa with small pool, jacuzzi and sauna. Play area. Entertainment and activities for children and families. TV room. Library. Volleyball. Boules. River fishing and fishing lake. Woodland walks. Canoeing. WiFi (free).

Ideal For...

 Beach

 Dogs

 Fishing

 Golf

 Play Area

 Disabled Facilities

Scan me for more information.

2 accommodations
78 pitches
GPS: 45.93299, 1.29006
Post Code: F-87270

Haute-Vienne, Limousin

Le Château de Leychoisier

www.alanrogers.com/fr87020
contact@leychoisier.com
05 55 39 93 43
www.leychoisier.com

Open (Touring Pitches):
15 April - 20 September.

You will receive a warm welcome at the beautiful, family run site Castel Camping le Château de Leychoisier. It offers peace and quiet in superb surroundings. It is ideally situated for short or long stays being only 2 km. from the A20 and 10 km. north of Limoges. The large, slightly sloping and grassy pitches are in a parkland setting with many magnificent mature trees offering varying amounts of shade. The 78 touring pitches have 10A electricity and many have a tap. The small heated swimming pool with sunbathing area is accessed through the reception and bar, and the restaurant serves high quality, freshly prepared meals.

The sanitary block is very clean with separate provisions for disabled visitors. Some washbasins in cabins. Family bathroom. Washing machine and dryer. Basic grocery provisions (bread can be ordered daily). Restaurant, bar, TV room, small heated swimming pool with sunbathing area (all open all season). Lake. Fishing. Play area. Tennis and boules courts. Torch useful. WiFi (charged).

Ideal For...

 Dogs

 Fishing

 Watersports

 Golf

 Play Area

 Disabled Facilities

Scan me for more information.

30 accommodations
101 pitches
GPS: 45.2163, 4.2124
Post Code: F-43600

Haute-Loire, Auvergne

www.alanrogers.com/fr43030
camping@vaubarlet.com
04 71 66 64 95
www.vaubarlet.com

Open (Touring Pitches):
1 May - 30 September.

Camping de Vaubarlet

Expect a warm welcome at Sites et Paysages de Vaubarlet, a peaceful and spacious family run site. Located in a beautiful riverside setting, it has 131 marked, level, grassy, pitches, with those around the perimeter having shade (young trees and shrubs provide separation between the large pitches). The family has made great efforts to ensure all guests benefit equally from its facilities. There are 101 pitches, all with 16A electricity for touring units. The remaining places are occupied by site-owned tents and mobile homes including two fully equipped for disabled guests. Excellent facilities for guests with disabilities including an electric buggy, hoist to assist entry into the pool, and well equipped sanitary facilities.

Very good, clean toilet blocks include a baby room. Two family bathrooms are also suitable for disabled visitors. Washing machine, dryer. Small shop, bread. Bar, restaurant and takeaway (mid May-mid Sept). Attractive swimming pool, children's pool. Separate solarium. Boules. Extensive riverside grass games area. Playground. Activities in season include camp fire, music evenings, children's canoe lessons. Trout fishing. Birdwatching. WiFi (free).

Ideal For...

 Beach

 Dogs

 Fishing

 Watersports

 Golf

 Play Area

Scan me for more information.

121 accommodations
295 pitches
GPS: 45.56251, 2.93852
Post Code: F-63790

Puy-de-Dôme, Auvergne

Camping la Ribeyre

www.alanrogers.com/fr63050
info@laribeyre.com
04 73 88 64 29
www.laribeyre.com

Open (Touring Pitches):
28 April - 17 September.

At the heart of the Auvergne, only 35 km to the South of Clermont-Ferrand and 12 km from Besse St. Anastaise, the friendly Pommier family have put much care into the spacious Sunêlia la Ribeyre campsite. This unique 5 star campsite offers 464 level, grassy pitches, of which 295 are for tourers and 108 of these have electricity (6/10A). Electricity, water and drainage is available for 59 pitches. They also offer a wide range of mobile homes for rental. A superb large indoor/outdoor water park includes slides, toboggan and lazy river. A small man-made lake at one end of the campsite provides facilities for water sports. It is a great base for touring being only 1 km. from Murol, dominated by its ancient château, 6 km. from Saint Nectaire and about 20 km. from Le Mont Dore and Puy-de-Sancy, the highest peak in the area.

Five sanitary blocks are equipped with showers, private washing cubicles and facilities for babies. Washing machines and dryers. Bar. Snack bar. Large indoor/outdoor water park (heated July/Aug). TV. Games room. Tennis. Fishing. Lake swimming and canoeing. Many organised activities in high season. children's club (from 6 to 12 years) free in high season. WiFi (charged).

Ideal For...

 Kids

 Beach

 Dogs

 Fishing

 Watersports

 Walking

Scan me for more information.

25 accommodations
225 pitches
GPS: 44.39804, 4.39878
Post Code: F-07150

Ardèche, Rhône Alpes

Nature Parc l'Ardéchois

www.alanrogers.com/fr07120
ardechoiscamping@wanadoo.fr
04 75 88 06 63
www.ardechois-camping.com

Open (Touring Pitches):
1 April - 30 September.

Castel Camping Nature Parc l'Ardéchois is a very high quality, family run site within walking distance of Vallon-Pont-d'Arc. It borders the River Ardèche and canoe trips are run, professionally, direct from the site. This campsite is ideal for families with younger children seeking an active holiday. The facilities are comprehensive and the central toilet unit is of an extremely high standard. Of the 250 pitches, there are 225 for touring units, separated by trees and individual shrubs. All have electrical connections (6/10A) and with an additional charge, 125 larger pitches have full services (22 include a fridge, patio furniture, hammock and free WiFi). Forming a focal point are the bar and restaurant (excellent menus) with an attractive terrace and a takeaway service. A member of Leading Campings group.

Two very well equipped toilet blocks, one superb with everything working automatically. Facilities are of the highest standard, very clean and include good facilities for babies, children and disabled visitors. Laundry facilities. Four private bathrooms to hire. Well stocked shop. Excellent restaurant, bar and takeaway. Heated swimming pool and paddling pool (no Bermuda shorts). Massage. Gym. Tennis. Very good play area. Organised activities, canoe trips. Bicycle hire. Only gas barbecues are permitted. Communal barbecue area. WiFi throughout (charged).

Ideal For...

 Kids

 Beach

 Dogs

 Fishing

 Watersports

 Play Area

Scan me for more information.

In the old center of Vallon Pont d'Arc

38 accommodations
97 pitches
GPS: 44.40547, 4.37916
Post Code: F-07150

Ardèche, Rhône Alpes

Camping la Roubine

www.alanrogers.com/fr07310
roubine.ardeche@wanadoo.fr
04 75 88 04 56
www.camping-roubine.com

Open (Touring Pitches):
14 April - 9 September

This site on the bank of the Ardèche has been in the same family ownership for over 30 years. During this time there has been constant upgrading and it must now be considered one of the best sites in the area. There are 97 touring pitches, all with electricity (10A) and quite spacious. Well tended grass, trimmed hedging and mature trees and smart tarmac roads create a calm and well kept atmosphere. The proprietors, M. Moulin and Mme. Van Eck like to welcome their guests and are available to help during the day – they are rightly proud of their well run campsite.

Several small sanitary blocks include washbasins in cubicles. The main toilet block has showers, washbasins in vanity units, a baby bathroom, 2 childrens' bathrooms and facilities for disabled visitors. Laundry. Swimming pools, paddling pool and separate children's pool. Wellness centre. Tennis. Boules, Fishing. Barbecues only permitted on communal sites. River beach. WiFi throughout (charged).

Ideal For...

 Kids

 Beach

 Dogs

 Fishing

 Watersports

 Walking

Scan me for more information.

262 accommodations
410 pitches
GPS: 44.4447, 4.3663
Post Code: F-07120

Ardèche, Rhône Alpes

Aluna Vacances

www.alanrogers.com/fr07630
contact@alunavacances.fr
04 75 93 93 15
www.alunavacances.fr

Open (Touring Pitches):
30 March - 5 November

Nestled on the doorstep of the Ardèche Gorges, surrounded by nature and outdoor pursuits of all varieties; energetic ones such as rafting, cycling and swimming, and relaxing ones like walking, picnicking and exploring nature, camping at Sunêlia Aluna Vacances has something for all the family. This leafy site prides itself on its large 'closer to nature' pitches set on grass, some with hardstanding, measuring 100 to 120 sq.m. Electricity (10A) is available and there are four sanitary blocks throughout the site. There is rental accommodation on site as well as a new water park, both indoor and outdoor pools with many slides, a large restaurant with a terrace and bar, kid's club, a grocery store and a spa. Many sports are available during high season; football, tennis, volleyball, badminton, basketball, table tennis, jeu-de-boules, aquagym and dance, plus an outdoor fitness area.

Four sanitary blocks are equipped with showers, private washing cubicles and facilities for babies and disabled guests. Washing machines and dryers. Well stocked shop. Bar with TV. Restaurant and takeaway. Waterpark with heated outdoor pools, indoor pool and slides. Sports and kid's club (seasonal). Tennis & Volleyball court. Table tennis. Boules. Multisports field. Playground. Entertainment programmes. Some off site activities bookable on site (cycling, horse riding, canoeing). WiFi extra charges

Ideal For...

 Kids

 Beach

 Dogs

 Fishing

 Play Area

 Disabled Facilities

Scan me for more information.

30 accommodations
134 pitches
GPS: 44.431189, 4.32959
Post Code: F-07120

Ardèche, Rhône Alpes

Camping la Chapoulière

www.alanrogers.com/fr07410
camping@chapouliere.com
04 75 39 64 98
www.lachapouliere.com

Open (Touring Pitches):
24 March - 4 November

Camping la Chapoulière is a medium sized site, alongside the Ardèche river, some two kilometres south of Ruoms. Grassy banks allow easy access to the river with a deeper area for bathing. The site is in two areas: the upper level, above the pool, has chalets and touring pitches; the older, more established area is for touring pitches nearer the river, with some chalets/mobile homes close to the restaurant. Trees provide dappled shade. There are 13 4 fairly level touring pitches (no hedges) on sand and grass, all with 6/8A electricity. This site is a good choice for those who prefer to make their own entertainment, and many visitors return year after year, creating a lively community and a sociable atmosphere.

Modern and adequate sanitary blocks. Facilities for babies and disabled visitors in main block. Preset hot showers and some washbasins in cabins. Washing machine. Shop (June/Aug), bread to order all season. Bar (April-Sept). Restaurant (July/Aug and w/ends). Pizza takeaway. Heated swimming pool. Spa and fitness centre with Hammam and massage. Play area. Games room with large TV screen. Organised activities (July/Aug). Riding trips. River bathing. Fishing. Canoe trips. WiFi on most of site (free).

Ideal For...

 Beach

 Dogs

 Fishing

 Play Area

 Disabled Facilities

 Pets Accepted

Scan me for more information.

192 accommodations
87 pitches
GPS: 44.4141, 4.2729
Post Code: F-07120

Ardèche, Rhône Alpes

Le Ranc Davaine

www.alanrogers.com/fr07050
contact@rancdavaine.fr
04 75 39 60 55
www.camping-ranc-davaine.fr

Open (Touring Pitches):
4 April - 13 September

Sunêlia Le Ranc Davaine is a large, busy, family oriented site with direct access to the River Chassezac. There are 435 pitches with 87 for touring, all with electricity (10/16A) for which very long leads are required (some may cross roads). Most pitches are scattered between static caravan and tour operator pitches on fairly flat, stony ground under a variety of trees, some of which are quite low giving much needed shade. The site can get very busy for much of the season. A lively entertainment programme is aimed at young children and teenagers with an enclosed disco four nights a week until 03.00.

Three fully equipped, very clean and modern toilet blocks include facilities for disabled visitors. Washing machines, dryers. Large shop. Internet. Bar/restaurant, pizzeria, takeaway. Swimming pool, covered pool (heated), two small square pools, slide and water park (all facilities all season; no shorts allowed). Large play area. Tennis. Fishing nearby. Extensive activity and entertainment programme (July/Aug). Discos. Fitness area. Free WiFi on part of site.

Ideal For...

 Beach

 Dogs

 Fishing

 Walking

 Play Area

 Disabled Facilities

Scan me for more information.

19 accommodations
80 pitches
GPS: 44.99165, 4.56477
Post Code: F-07270

Ardèche, Rhône Alpes

Camping de Retourtour

www.alanrogers.com/fr07460
campingderetourtour@wanadoo.fr
04 75 06 40 71
www.campingderetourtour.com

Open (Touring Pitches):
1 April - 30 September.

This family run site is situated in the lesser known, but beautiful, northern Ardèche and you can be sure of a warm and friendly welcome here. Set in a wooded valley close to a tiny village below the ruins of a château, there are 130 good sized, level, grass pitches with 80 for touring (all with 4-13A electricity). Separated by hedges and mature trees, most have good shade. The town of Lamastre is often used as a stage for cycling events and has markets on Tuesdays and Saturdays. The site is close to the Doux river with a beautiful natural river swimming area within 150 m.

Three very clean, refurbished toilet blocks with hot showers, washbasins in cubicles, family shower room and facilities for disabled visitors. Washing machine. Motorcaravan services.. Small shop, bar (all season). Restaurant/takeaway (15/5-15/9). Good play area. Multisports area. Fitness room with covered patio for use in wet weather. Boules. Minigolf. Climbing. Fishing. Family entertainment (July/Aug). Bicycle hire. WiFi on part of site (charged). Only gas and electric barbecues are allowed. Mobile homes to rent.

Ideal For...

 Beach

 Dogs

 Fishing

 Play Area

 Disabled Facilities

 Pets Accepted

Scan me for more information.

56 accommodations
GPS: 44.434151, 4.410989
Post Code: F-07150

Ardèche, Rhône Alpes

www.alanrogers.com/fr07660
domainedesevenier@orange.fr
04 75 88 29 44
www.sevenier.net

Open (Touring Pitches):
30 March - 4 November.

Castel Domaine de Sévenier

Le Domaine de Sévenier is a modern, high quality chalet complex enjoying a hilltop location with fine panoramic views over the surrounding garrigue, a unique mix of oak trees, juniper, rosemary and thyme. There are no touring pitches at this site. Located 4 km. from Vallon-Pont-d'Arc and 800 m. from the pretty village of Lagorce, the domaine is an old winery which has been sensitively converted and offers accommodation in well appointed wooden chalets serving the needs of families, both large and small. Rest and relaxation is the theme here and the restaurant has a good reputation. On-site amenities include a swimming pool and a separate children's pool. The site has links to Nature Parc Camping de l'Ardèche and guests are welcome to enjoy the camping site's evening entertainment.

The sanitary block includes hot showers and provision has been made for disabled visitors. Washing machine. Shop. Bar. Restaurant. Outdoor heated swimming pool. Paddling pool. Activity programme. Play area. Minigolf. Bicycle hire. Fully equipped chalets to rent.

Ideal For...

 Dogs

 Fishing

 Walking

 Play Area

 Disabled Facilities

 Pets Accepted

Scan me for more information.

96 accommodations
400 pitches
GPS: 46.33972, 5.13592
Post Code: F-01340

Ain, Rhône Alpes

www.alanrogers.com/fr01010
contact@laplainetonique.com
04 74 30 80 52
www.laplainetonique.com

Open (Touring Pitches):
25 April - 2 September

Camping La Plaine Tonique

This excellent site, ideal for active families, belongs to a syndicate of several local villages. It is a very well maintained, large site with 560 marked and numbered pitches, 400 with 10A electricity, 96 accommodation and 70 seasonal pitches. The majority are of a good size, hedged and on flat grass, with shade in most parts. The site is spacious and broken up into sections by trees and hedges. One area has been allocated for eight teepees to rent, with cooking facilities. It is on the edge of an attractive 95 hectare lake with an adjacent public beach.

Very clean sanitary facilities are in ten blocks and include some washbasins in cabins, baby rooms and washing machines. Motorcaravan services. Restaurant, bar (all season), takeaway and shop (July/Aug) on site. Aquatic centre with five pools (free for campers, no Bermuda shorts). Indoor pool (all season) and outdoor pool (16/6-2/9). Watersports and fishing. Minigolf. Tennis. Play area. TV room. Bicycle hire. Fitness trail. WiFi. Chalets, mobile-homes, tepees and safari tents to rent.

Ideal For...

Kids

Beach

Fishing

Watersports

Walking

Play Area

Scan me for more information.

Montrevel-en-Bresse nr. Malafretaz - By Junkey83 - CC BY-SA 4.0

14 accommodations
178 pitches
GPS: 45.54115, 5.60778
Post Code: F-38490

Isère, Rhône Alpes

Camping le Coin Tranquille

www.alanrogers.com/fr38010
contact@coin-tranquille.com
04 76 32 13 48
www.coin-tranquille.com

Open (Touring Pitches):
1 April - 31 October.

Le Coin Tranquille is well placed for visits to the Savoie regions and the Alps. It is an attractive, well maintained site of 192 grass pitches (178 for touring units), all with 10A electricity. They are separated by neat hedges of hydrangea, flowering shrubs and a range of trees to make a lovely environment doubly enhanced by the rural aspect and marvellous views across to the mountains. This is a popular, family run site with friendly staff, making it a wonderful base for exploring the area. Set in the Dauphiny countryside north of Grenoble, le Coin Tranquille is truly a quiet corner, especially outside school holiday times, although it is still popular with families in high season.

The central well appointed sanitary block is well kept, heated in low season. Facilities for disabled visitors. Two smaller blocks provide facilities in high season. Busy shop. Excellent restaurant. Heated swimming pool and paddling pool (1/5-30/9; no Bermuda style shorts) with sunbathing areas. Play area. TV and games in bar. Quiet reading room. Weekly entertainment for children and adults (July/Aug) including live music (not discos). Bicycle hire (limited). WiFi near reception (free).

Ideal For...

- Kids
- Beach
- Dogs
- Fishing
- Walking
- Golf

Scan me for more information.

51 accommodations
101 pitches
GPS: 44.658534, 5.407172
Post Code: F-26310

Drôme, Rhône Alpes

Camping le Couriou

www.alanrogers.com/fr26340
contact@lecouriou.fr
04 75 21 33 23
www.drome-campings.fr

Open (Touring Pitches):
1 May - 15 September.

Le Couriou is a family run site in the beautiful Drôme countryside just south of Die. There are 131 stony/grassy, level pitches of varying sizes with 101 for touring (10A electricity). They are laid out on high terraces with superb views over the surrounding wooded hills; not ideal for those with walking difficulties. The pitches are separated by some shrubs and a variety of trees giving some shade. Though the site roads can be quite steep, access is not difficult for large outfits. It has a large pool complex, terraced bar and restaurant (all open to the public) with views across to the Vercors mountains.

Three adequate toilet blocks with facilities for babies and campers with disabilities. Washing machines/dryer. Shop, bar, restaurant/ takeaway (1/7-30/8, or sooner depending on demand). Four heated swimming pools, toboggans, paddling pool. Multisport area. Boules. No charcoal barbecues allowed on site. Communal barbecues available. WiFi on part of site (charged).

Ideal For...

 Dogs

 Fishing

 Play Area

 Disabled Facilities

 Pets Accepted

 Bar on Site

Scan me for more information.

22 accommodations
93 pitches
GPS: 46.1201, 6.10552
Post Code: F-74160

Haute-Savoie, Rhône Alpes

Camping la Colombière

www.alanrogers.com/fr74060
la.colombiere@wanadoo.fr
04 50 35 13 14
www.camping-la-colombiere.com

Open (Touring Pitches):
1 April - 31 October.

Sites et Paysages la Colombière is a family owned site, located on the edge of the small village of Neydens, a few minutes from the A40 autoroute and only a short drive from Geneva. It is an attractive site with 93 pitches (10/16A electricity), all reasonably level and separated by fruit trees, flowering shrubs and hedges. Forty-one new pitches and a toilet block have recently been added in an attractive, landscaped field. Neydens makes a good base for visiting Geneva and the region around the lake. It is a very pleasant, friendly site where you may drop in for a night stop - and stay for several days! The site is open all year for motorcaravans and suitable caravans. English is spoken.

Three sanitary blocks (one heated) include facilities for disabled visitors. Motorcaravan services. Fridge hire. Gas supplies. Good bar/restaurant (all season) and terrace overlooking the pool (1/5-15/9). New heated, indoor pool, spa pool and jacuzzi. Games room. Organised visits and activities (all season). Bicycle hire. Hire car. Archery. Boules. Playground. WiFi throughout (charged). Max. 1 dog.

Ideal For...

 Beach

 Dogs

 Fishing

 Watersports

 Golf

 Play Area

Scan me for more information.

22 accommodations
122 pitches
GPS: 45.94036, 6.42842
Post Code: F-74450

Haute-Savoie, Rhône Alpes

www.alanrogers.com/fr74070
contact@campinglescale.com
04 50 02 20 69
www.campinglescale.com

Open (Touring Pitches):
19 December - 12 April, 27 May - 27 September.

Camping l'Escale

You will receive a good welcome in English from the Baur family at this beautifully maintained and picturesque site, situated at the foot of the Aravis mountain range. There are 149 pitches with 123 for touring. Of average size, part grass, part gravel they are separated by trees and shrubs that give a little shade. All pitches have 2-10A electricity and 86 are fully serviced. Rock pegs are essential. A 200-year-old building houses a bar/restaurant decorated in traditional style and overlooks the indoor pool. It offers regional dishes in a delightful, warm ambience. The village is 200 m. away and has all the facilities of a resort with activities for both summer and winter holidays.

Good toilet blocks (heated in winter) have all the necessary facilities for disabled campers. Drying room for skis, clothing and boots. Superb pool complex with interconnected indoor (all season) and outdoor pools and paddling pools (1/7-30/8), jacuzzi and water jets. Cosy bar/restaurant and takeaway (all season). Play area. Tennis. Activities for adults and children. Video games. Discounts on organised walks and visits to Chamonix/Mont Blanc. Traditional chalets and mobile homes to rent. WiFi in some areas (free).

Ideal For...

 Dogs

 Fishing

 Golf

 Play Area

 Disabled Facilities

 Pets Accepted

Scan me for more information.

18 accommodations
135 pitches
GPS: 45.62248, 6.78475
Post Code: F-73700

Savoie, Rhône Alpes

Camping Bourg St-Maurice

www.alanrogers.com/fr73020
bourgsaintmaurice@huttopia.com
04 79 07 03 45
europe.huttopia.com/en/site/bourg-st-maurice

Open (Touring Pitches):
19 May - 16 October.

Huttopia Bourg-Saint-Maurice is on a small, level plain at an altitude of 830 m. on the River Isère, surrounded by mountains and attracts visitors all year round (except for a short time when they close). The site's 153 unseparated, flat pitches (135 for touring) are marked by numbers on the tarmac roads and all have electrical connections (10A). Most are on grass but some are on tarmac hardstanding making them ideal for use by motorcaravans or in winter. Trees give shade in most parts, although some pitches have almost none. Duckboards are provided for snow and wet weather. Formerly known as Camping le Versoyen, this is a good base for winter skiing, summer walking, climbing, rafting or canoeing, or for car excursions.

Two well maintained toilet blocks can be heated and have British and Turkish style WCs. No facilities for disabled visitors. Laundry. Motorcaravan service facilities. No shop but bread available to order. Heated rest room with TV. Small bar with takeaway in summer. Play area. Free shuttle in high season to funicular railway. Free WiFi in central lodge.

Ideal For...

 Dogs

 Fishing

 Golf

 Play Area

 Pets Accepted

 Bar on Site

Scan me for more information.

48 accommodations
125 pitches
GPS: 44.91679, -0.14148
Post Code: F-33330

Gironde, Aquitaine

www.alanrogers.com/fr33080
info@camping-saint-emilion.com
05 57 24 75 80
www.camping-saint-emilion.com

Open (Touring Pitches):
28 April - 25 September

Camping Saint-Emilion

Yelloh! Village Saint Emilion (formerly La Barbanne) is a pleasant site in the heart of the Bordeaux wine region, only 2.5 km. from the famous town of Saint Emilion. It became part of the Yelloh! group in 2010. With 173 pitches, 125 for touring, the owners have created a carefully maintained, well equipped site. The large, level and grassy pitches have dividing hedges and electricity (long leads necessary). The original parts of the site bordering the lake have mature trees, good shade and pleasant surroundings, whilst in the newer area the trees have yet to provide full shade and it can be hot in summer. Twelve pitches for motorcaravans are on tarmac surrounded by grass.

Two modern, fully equipped toilet blocks include facilities for children and for campers with disabilities. Motorcaravan services. Well stocked shop. Bar, terrace, takeaway, restaurant. Breakfast service. Two swimming pools, one heated with water slide. Enclosed play area with seats for parents. Children's club. Tennis. Boules. Volleyball. Fishing. Minigolf. Bicycle hire. Evening entertainment. WiFi over site (charged). Max. 1 dog.

Ideal For...

 Dogs

 Fishing

 Golf

 Play Area

 Disabled Facilities

 Pets Accepted

Scan me for more information.

282 accommodations
600 pitches
GPS: 45.22297, -1.16465
Post Code: F-33990

Gironde, Aquitaine

www.alanrogers.com/fr33110
info@cca33.com
05 56 09 10 25
www.cca33.com

Open (Touring Pitches):
13 May - 18 September.

Camping de la Côte d'Argent

Airotel Camping de la Côte d'Argent is a large, well equipped site for leisurely family holidays. It makes an ideal base for walkers and cyclists with over 100 km. of cycle lanes in the area. Hourtin-Plage is a pleasant invigorating resort on the Atlantic coast and a popular location for watersports enthusiasts. The site's top attraction is its pool complex, where wooden bridges connect the pools and islands and there are sunbathing and play areas plus an indoor heated pool. The site has 600 touring pitches (all with 10A electricity), not always clearly defined, arranged under trees with some on sand. High quality entertainment takes place at the impressive bar/ restaurant near the entrance.

Very clean sanitary blocks include provision for disabled visitors. Washing machines. Motorcaravan services. Large supermarket, restaurant, takeaway, pizzeria and bar. Four outdoor pools with slides and flumes (1/6-18/9). Indoor pool (all season). Fitness room. Massage (Institut de Beauté). Tennis. Play areas. Miniclub, organised entertainment in season. Bicycle hire. WiFi throughout site (charged). ATM. Charcoal barbecues are not permitted. Hotel (12 rooms).

Ideal For...

 Kids

 Beach

 Dogs

 Fishing

 Watersports

 Walking

Scan me for more information.

HOURTIN
PLAGE
Airotel

Carcans plage Nr Hourtin - By Michel VENOT - CC BY-SA 3.0

400 accommodations
820 pitches
GPS: 44.73439, -1.19598
Post Code: F-33950

Gironde, Aquitaine

Camping les Viviers

www.alanrogers.com/fr33460
reception@lesviviers.com
05 56 60 70 04
www.lesviviers.com

Open (Touring Pitches):
1 April - 17 September.

Les Viviers is a large family site on the Lège-Cap-Ferret peninsula. The pitches are dispersed around a 33-hectare wood, 400 of which are occupied by mobile homes and chalets. The site borders the Bassin d'Arcachon and is 5 km. from the nearest Atlantic beach. Pitches are well shaded and of a good size. Most have electrical connections. A large range of amenities are on offer, including a well stocked supermarket, restaurant, pizzeria and a twice weekly street market. A lively activity and entertainment programme is on offer in peak season.

Toilet blocks have free preset showers and facilities for children and disabled visitors. Supermarket. Bar/snack bar, restaurant/ pizzeria and takeaway. Swimming pool complex with covered pool. Minigolf. Gym. Games room. Play area. Entertainment and activity programme. Mobile homes and chalets to rent. WiFi (charged). Gas and charcoal barbecues are not permitted.

Ideal For...

 Kids

 Beach

 Dogs

 Fishing

 Watersports

 Play Area

Scan me for more information.

Bassin d'Arcachon and Dune du Pyla

62 accommodations
200 pitches
GPS: 45.00207, 1.0711
Post Code: F-24290

Dordogne, Aquitaine

www.alanrogers.com/fr24060
le-paradis@perigord.com
05 53 50 72 64
www.le-paradis-campsite.com

Open (Touring Pitches):
1st April - 20th October

Camping le Paradis

Le Paradis is an excellent, very well maintained riverside site, halfway between Les Eyzies and Montignac. The site is landscaped with a variety of mature shrubs and trees. The gardens are beautiful, which gives a wonderful sense of tranquillity. It is very easy to relax on this ecologically friendly site. Systems of reed filters enhance the efficient natural drainage. This is a family run site and you are guaranteed a warm and friendly welcome. There are 200 good sized pitches with 62 mobile homes to rent. The 134 touring pitches are level and with easy access, all with 10A Europlug, water and drainage. The new covered pool complements the good open-air pools.

---

2 sanitary blocks equipped with showers, private washing cubicles and facilities for babies. Laundrette : Washing machines, dryers and iron. Shop. Bar. Restaurant and Takeaway. Heated outdoor pools. Indoor pool with Spa, Sauna and Hammam. Playground area. Football field. Tennis court. Sport field. River access. Kids club, sports activities and entertainment programmes in July and August. Bicycle hire. Canoe trips. Fishing. WiFi : lowspeed free, high speed charged.

Ideal For...

 Kids

 Dogs

 Fishing

 Watersports

 Play Area

 Disabled Facilities

Scan me for more information.

119 accommodations
118 pitches
GPS: 44.825, 1.25388
Post Code: F-24200

Dordogne, Aquitaine

Domaine de Soleil Plage

www.alanrogers.com/fr24090
info@soleilplage.fr
05 53 28 33 33
www.soleilplage.fr

Open (Touring Pitches):
9 April - 30 September

This site is in one of the most attractive sections of the Dordogne valley, with a riverside location. There are 238 pitches, in three sections, with 118 for touring units. Additionally, there are a number of mobile homes, fully renovated chalets and new cottages for rent. The site offers river swimming from a sizeable sandy bank or there is a very impressive heated pool complex. All pitches are bound by hedges and are of adequate size, with electricity (16A, Europlug), 44 also have water and a drain. Most pitches have some shade. If you like a holiday with lots going on, you will enjoy this site.

Three modern unisex toilet blocks (designated male and female facilities in one). One has been completely renovated to a high standard with heating and family shower rooms. Washing machines and dryer. Motorcaravan services. Well stocked shop, bar with TV and attractive restaurant with local menus and a terrace with views towards the cliffs (all 4/5-16/9). Picnics available to order. Very impressive heated main pool, new covered pool, paddling pool, spa pool and two slides. Tennis. Minigolf. Three play areas. Fishing. Canoe and kayak hire. Bicycle hire. Currency exchange. Small library. WiFi throughout (charged). Activities and social events (high season). Max. 2 dogs.

Ideal For...

 Beach

 Dogs

Fishing

 Watersports

 Golf

 Play Area

Scan me for more information.

72 accommodations
114 pitches
GPS: 44.95776, 1.2729
Post Code: F-24590

Dordogne, Aquitaine

Camping les Péneyrals

www.alanrogers.com/fr24320
infos@peneyrals.com
05 53 28 85 71
www.peneyrals.com

Open (Touring Pitches):
4 May - 11 September.

Within easy reach of all the attractions of the Périgord region, M. and Mme. Havel have created an attractive and friendly family campsite at les Péneyrals. There are 250 pitches, 114 of which are for touring. The pitches at the bottom of the hill tend to be quieter as they are further from the main facilities, but are all level and grassy (some on terraces), with electricity (5/10A), and most have some shade. An attractive bar and restaurant with terrace overlook the excellent pool complex and at the bottom of the site is a small fishing lake.

Three modern, unisex toilet blocks provide good quality facilities, including provision for babies and disabled visitors. Motorcaravan services. Good value shop, excellent restaurant and takeaway. Pool complex with two large pools (one heated), paddling pool with games and four slides with splash pool. Indoor heated pool. Bicycle hire. Minigolf. Tennis (charged). Badminton. Play area. Games room, WiFi over site (charged), TV room and small library. Fishing.

Ideal For...

 Dogs

 Fishing

 Golf

 Play Area

 Disabled Facilities

 Pets Accepted

Scan me for more information.

35 accommodations
99 pitches
GPS: 44.95161, 0.85042
Post Code: F-24260

Dordogne, Aquitaine

Saint-Avit Loisirs

www.alanrogers.com/fr24180
contact@saint-avit-loisirs.com
05 53 02 64 00
www.saint-avit-loisirs.com

Open (Touring Pitches):
26 March - 24 September.

Although Castel Camping Caravaning Saint-Avit Loisirs is set amidst rolling countryside, far from the hustle and bustle of the main tourist areas of the Dordogne, the facilities are first class, providing virtually everything you could possibly want without the need to leave the site. This makes it ideal for families with children of all ages. The site is in two sections. One part is dedicated to chalets and mobile homes which are available to rent, whilst the main section of the site contains 199 flat and mainly grassy, good sized pitches, 99 for touring, with electricity (6/10A). With a choice of sun or shade, they are arranged in cul-de-sacs off a main access road and are easily accessible.

Three modern unisex toilet blocks provide high quality facilities, but could become overstretched (particularly laundry and dishwashing) in high season. Motorcaravan services. Shop, bar, good quality restaurant, cafeteria. Outdoor swimming pool, children's pool, water slide, crazy river, heated indoor pool with jacuzzi. Fitness room. Soundproofed disco. Minigolf. Boules. Tennis. Quad bikes. Play area. Bicycle hire. Canoe trips on the Dordogne and other sporting activities organised. Good walks and cycle routes from site. Additional charge for some activities. WiFi over site (charged).

Ideal For...

 Kids

 Beach

 Dogs

 Fishing

 Golf

 Play Area

Scan me for more information.

30 accommodations
135 pitches
GPS: 45.55035, 0.7947
Post Code: F-24470

Dordogne, Aquitaine

Château le Verdoyer

www.alanrogers.com/fr24010
chateau@verdoyer.fr
05 53 56 94 64
www.verdoyer.fr

Open (Touring Pitches):
25 April - 30 September.

Camping Château le Verdoyer has been developed in the park of a restored château and is owned by a Dutch family. This 22-hectare estate has three lakes, two for fishing and one with a sandy beach and safe swimming area. There are 135 good sized touring pitches, level, terraced and hedged. With a choice of wooded area or open field, all have electricity (5/10A) and most share a water supply between four pitches. There is a swimming pool complex and high season activities are organised for children (5-13 yrs) but there is no disco. This site caters well for those with disabilities, with two fully adapted chalets, wheelchair access to all facilities and even a hoist into the pool.

Well appointed sanitary blocks include baby baths and facilities for disabled visitors. Serviced launderette. Motorcaravan services. Fridge rental. Shop and takeaway (15/5-15/9). Bar (15/5-30/9). Restaurant (25/4-30/9). Bistro (July/Aug). Two swimming pools, slide and paddling pool. Play areas. Tennis. Minigolf. Bicycle hire. Fishing. Small library. Kids' club (July/Aug). WiFi (free in courtyard). Computer in reception for Internet access.

Ideal For...

Kids

Beach

 Dogs

 Fishing

 Golf

 Play Area

Scan me for more information.

141 accommodations
354 pitches
GPS: 44.20447, -1.29099
Post Code: F-40200

Landes, Aquitaine

Club Marina Landes

www.alanrogers.com/fr40080
contact@clubmarina.com
05 58 09 12 66
www.marinalandes.com

Open (Touring Pitches):
15 May - 24 September

Well maintained and clean, with helpful staff, Airotel Club Marina-Landes would be a very good choice for a family holiday. Activities include discos, play groups for children, specially trained staff to entertain teenagers and concerts for more mature campers. There are numerous sports opportunities and a superb sandy beach nearby. The site has 355 touring pitches (312 with 10A electricity) and 141 mobile homes and chalets to rent. The pitches are on firm grass, most with hedges and they are large (mostly 100 sq.m. or larger). A nightly curfew ensures that all have a good night's sleep. A new 1900m^2 leisure pool features flumes a covered heated pool with spa.

Five toilet blocks (opened as required) are well maintained with showers and many washbasins in cabins. Facilities for babies, children and disabled visitors. Laundry facilities. Motorcaravan services. Fridge hire. Shop (freshly baked bread) and bar, restaurant, snack bar, pizzas and takeaway, heated covered pool and outdoor pools (all open all season). Minigolf. Tennis. Bicycle hire. Play area. Entertainment and activities (high season). Gas or electric barbecues only. WiFi throughout (charged).

Ideal For...

 Kids

 Beach

 Dogs

 Fishing

 Watersports

 Golf

Scan me for more information.

260 accommodations
190 pitches
GPS: 44.46052, -1.13065
Post Code: F-40600

Landes, Aquitaine

www.alanrogers.com/fr40100
info@larive.fr
05 58 78 12 33
www.larive.fr

Open (Touring Pitches):
7 April - 2 September

Camping Resort & Spa La Rive

Surrounded by pine woods, La Rive has a superb beach-side location on Lac de Sanguinet. With approximately 500 pitches (including mobile home accommodation), it provides 190 mostly level, numbered and clearly defined touring pitches of 80-100 sq.m. all with electricity connections (10A), 100 also with water and waste water. The swimming pool complex is wonderful with pools linked by water channels and bridges. There is also a jacuzzi, paddling pool and two large swimming pools all surrounded by sunbathing areas and decorated with palm trees. An indoor pool is heated and open all season. This is a friendly site with a good mix of nationalities.

Three good clean toilet blocks have washbasins in cabins and mainly British style toilets. Facilities for disabled visitors. Baby baths. Motorcaravan services. Shop with gas. New bar/restaurant complex with entertainment. Swimming pool complex (supervised July/Aug) with aquapark for children. Games room. Play area. Tennis. Bicycle hire. Boules. Fishing. Water-skiing. Watersports equipment hire. Tournaments (June-Aug). Skateboard park. Trampolines. Miniclub. No charcoal barbecues on pitches. Communal barbecue areas. WiFi throughout (charged).

Ideal For...

 Kids

 Beach

 Dogs

 Fishing

 Watersports

 Golf

Scan me for more information.

1172 accommodations
1536 pitches
GPS: 43.79778, -1.40111
Post Code: F-40660

Landes, Aquitaine

Camping Le Vieux Port

www.alanrogers.com/fr40180
contact@resasol.com
05 58 48 22 00
www.levieuxport.com

Open (Touring Pitches):
1 April - 24 September.

Camping Village Resort & Spa le Vieux Port is a well established destination appealing particularly to families; this lively site has approximately 1500 pitches (87 for touring) of mixed sizes, most with electricity (6A). They also offer a variety of accommodation for rental. The camping area is well shaded by pines and pitches are generally of a good size, attractively grouped around the toilet blocks. There are many tour operators here and well over a third of the site is taken up with mobile homes and chalets. An enormous 7,000 sq.m. aquatic park is now open and is the largest on any French campsite. This heated complex is exceptional, boasting five outdoor pools (all 25°C), three large water slides plus waves and a heated spa. There is also a heated indoor pool.

Twelve well appointed toilet/shower blocks with facilities for disabled visitors. Three Laundry rooms. Motorcaravan services. Supermarket and various smaller shops in high season. Several restaurants, takeaway and three bars (all open all season). Large pool complex (all season) including covered pool and themed bar. Tennis. Multisports pitch. Minigolf. Mini club for kids (Jul/Aug). Outdoor fitness area. Bicycle hire. Riding centre. Organised activities including discos and karaoke evenings (seasonal). Spa, massages &beauty area. Communal barbecues only. WiFi over site (charged).

Ideal For...

 Kids

 Beach

 Dogs

 Fishing

 Watersports

 Walking

Scan me for more information.

170 pitches
GPS: 43.46203, -1.56708
Post Code: F-64200

Pyrénées-Atlantiques, Aquitaine

Camping Biarritz

www.alanrogers.com/fr64330
biarritz.camping@gmail.com
05 59 23 00 12
www.biarritz-camping.fr

Open (Touring Pitches):
30 March - 7 October

Nestled at the foot of the Pyrenees, this campsite in the heart of the Basque country, is ideally placed for you to visit Biarritz and experience all this culture-rich region has to offer. Biarritz Camping is just over 2km from the centre of town, only 700m from the sandy beach, and offers 170 pitches to campers. Pitches are large and partially in shade with electricity (10A) available. There are also mobile homes and bungalow tents available to rent. A bar serving snacks and takeaway food is on site and you'll find restaurants and cafés in easy walking distance. A shop on site sells essentials and fresh bread daily. Activities on site include petanque, table tennis and a children's playground as well as evening entertainment during July and August. Nearby, there is a surf school on the beach, an equestrian centre, golf and a number of thalassotherapy spas which have been popular in Biarritz for nearly 200 years.

Bright and comfortable shower and toilet blocks with facilities for families and disabled guests. Washing machine and dryer. Safety deposit boxes available to rent. Bar serving snacks and takeaway food. Shop selling essentials plus fresh bread daily and beach essentials. Petanque, Table tennis. Children's playground. Evening entertainment some evenings during July and August.

Ideal For...

 Beach

 Walking

 Golf

 Play Area

 Disabled Facilities

 Bar on Site

Scan me for more information.

131 accommodations
356 pitches
GPS: 43.95166, -1.35212
Post Code: F-40560

Landes, Aquitaine

Camping Club Eurosol

www.alanrogers.com/fr40060
contact@camping-eurosol.com
05 58 47 90 14
www.camping-eurosol.com

Open (Touring Pitches):
10 May - 18 September.

Privately owned, Camping Club International Eurosol is an attractive, friendly and well maintained site extending over 15 hectares of undulating ground, amongst mature pine trees giving good shade. Of the 356 touring pitches, 231 have electricity (10A) with 120 fully serviced. A wide range of mobile homes and chalets, which are being updated, are available for rent. This is very much a family site with multi-lingual entertainers. Many games and tournaments are organised and a beach volleyball competition is held regularly in front of the bar. The adjacent boules terrain is floodlit. An excellent sandy beach 700 metres from the site has supervised bathing in high season and is ideal for surfing.

Four main toilet blocks and two smaller blocks are comfortable and clean with facilities for babies and disabled visitors. Motorcaravan services. Fridge rental. Well stocked shop and bar (all season). Restaurant, takeaway (1/6-7/9). Stage for live shows arranged in July/Aug. Outdoor swimming pool, paddling pool (all season) and heated, covered pool (May-July). Tennis. Multisports court. Bicycle hire. WiFi (charged). Charcoal barbecues are not permitted.

Ideal For...

 Kids

 Beach

 Dogs

 Fishing

 Golf

 Play Area

Scan me for more information.

166 accommodations
294 pitches
GPS: 44.94542, 1.44137
Post Code: F-46200

Lot, Midi-Pyrénées

www.alanrogers.com/fr46010
info@lapaillebasse.com
05 65 37 85 48
www.lapaillebasse.com

Open (Touring Pitches):
1 April - 16 September.

Domaine de la Paille Basse

Castel Domaine de la Paille Basse was originally a medieval hamlet made up of three abandoned farmsteads which were restored at the end of the 70's. Emphasis was laid on keeping the former aspects of the buidings, along with treasuring the unspoilt nature around. Today, the 3rd generation looks after this jewel, making sure the guests have the most enjoyable stay. Domaine de la Paille Basse is set in a rural location 9 km from Souillac and stretches over a crest, 250m above sea level, offering wonderful views over the surrounding landscape. It is easily accessible from the A20 and well placed for excursions into the Dordogne and it is part of a large domaine of 80 hectares, all available to campers for walks and recreation.

Three main toilet blocks have modern equipment and are kept very clean. There is also a cabin for disabled visitors & a baby area. Laundry. Small shop with a large selection of wine (seasonal). Restaurant, bar (open late in high season), terrace, pizza takeaway. Crêperie. Two swimming pools, paddling pool (unheated), water slides. Sun terrace. Soundproofed disco (seasonal). TV (with satellite). Cinema below the pool area. Tennis. Football pitch. Basketball pitch. Petanque pitch. Beach-volley pitch. Play areas. Table tennis. Library. WiFi in bar area (charged). Mini farm. Entertainment for all (seasonal). Electric barbecues are not permitted.

Ideal For...

 Kids

 Beach

 Dogs

 Fishing

 Watersports

 Walking

Scan me for more information.

35 accommodations
100 pitches
GPS: 43.98299, 0.50183
Post Code: F-32480

Gers, Midi-Pyrénées

Le Camp de Florence

www.alanrogers.com/fr32010
info@lecampdeflorence.com
05 62 28 15 58
www.lecampdeflorence.com

Open (Touring Pitches):
1 April - 10 October.

Castel Camp de Florence is an attractive and very well equipped site on the edge of an historic village in pleasantly undulating Gers countryside. The 197 large, part terraced pitches (110 for touring units) all have 10A electricity, 20 with hardstanding and 16 fully serviced. They are arranged around a large field with rural views, giving a feeling of spaciousness. The 13th-century village of La Romieu is on the Santiago de Compostela pilgrims' route. The Pyrenees are a two hour drive, the Atlantic coast a similar distance. The site has been developed by the friendly Mijnsbergen family.

Three toilet blocks (one heated) provide all the necessary facilities. Washing machines and dryers. Motorcaravan services. Restaurant (1/5-25/9, also open to the public). Takeaway. Bread. Swimming pool area with water slide (1/5-30/9). Jacuzzi. Protected children's pool (open to public in afternoons). New playgrounds, games and animal park. Bouncy castle. Trampoline. Outdoor fitness machines. Games room. Tennis. Pétanque. Bicycle hire. Discos, picnics, musical evenings. WiFi over site (charged, free in bar). Max. 2 dogs.

Ideal For...

 Kids

 Beach

 Dogs

 Fishing

 Walking

 Golf

Scan me for more information.

41 accommodations
119 pitches
GPS: 44.10240, 3.09100
Post Code: F-12100

Aveyron, Midi-Pyrénées

www.alanrogers.com/fr12350
millau@huttopia.com
05 65 61 18 83
europe.huttopia.com/en/site/millau

Open (Touring Pitches):
27 April - 2 October.

Huttopia Millau

Huttopia Millau is just 500 m. from the lively market town of Millau which lies in the valley below the imposing Millau suspension bridge. There are 160 good sized, slightly sloping grassy pitches with varying degrees of shade, good views over the wooded hills and some enjoy a riverside location. There are 119 pitches for touring with 6/10A electricity for which long leads are needed. The site has a heated swimming pool and snack bar/bar, pleasant for unwinding after a busy day touring making it ideal for long or short stays. The site is situated at the confluence of the Dourbie and Tarn rivers making this a good spot for all the family to have fun in the clear shallow waters.

Modern, well equipped and clean toilet block with all necessary facilities including those for disabled visitors. Laundry facilities. Breakfast service. Snack bar/bar (June/July). Swimming pool (May-Sept). Small TV room. Family recreation room. Play area. Kids' club (5-7 yrs and 8-11 yrs). Activity and entertainment programme, mainly off site. River fishing and bathing. Free WiFi on part of site. Glamping tents for hire.

Ideal For...

 Kids

 Beach

 Dogs

 Fishing

 Watersports

 Play Area

Scan me for more information.

45 accommodations
75 pitches
GPS: 43.765786, 4.097426
Post Code: F-30250

Gard, Languedoc-Roussillon

Domaine de Massereau

www.alanrogers.com/fr30290
camping@massereau.com
04 66 53 11 20
www.massereau.com

Open (Touring Pitches):
2 April - 29 October.

Two brothers, one a wine producer and one an hotelier, opened Domaine de Massereau in August 2006. It is set within a 50-hectare vineyard dating back to 1804, and the idea was to promote their wine, so tours are arranged and they now produce their own olive oil as well. There are 149 pitches, with 75 available for touring units, all with electricity (45 with 16A electricity, water and drainage). Pitch sizes range from 150-250 sq.m. but the positioning of trees on some of the pitches could limit the usable space. The area is lightly wooded and most pitches are now hedged with flowering shrubs. The other pitches are used for chalets and mobile homes to rent. The site is a member of the Castels Group and good English is spoken.

The modern toilet block incorporates excellent facilities for children and disabled visitors. Laundry area. Motorcaravan services. Well stocked shop and newspapers. Restaurant, bar, pizzeria and outdoor grill, takeaway, (all season). Heated swimming pool with slide (all season). Paddling pool. Sauna, steam bath, jacuzzi and massage. Play area. Trampoline. Minigolf. Bicycle hire. Multisports area. Fitness trail. Pétanque. Short tennis. TV room. Barbecue hire. Fridge hire. Tent hire (2 person). Gas. WiFi (charged). Charcoal barbecues are not allowed.

Ideal For...

 Beach

 Dogs

 Fishing

 Play Area

 Disabled Facilities

 Pets Accepted

Scan me for more information.

162 accommodations
217 pitches
GPS: 43.29, 3.39817
Post Code: F-34450

Hérault, Languedoc-Roussillon

www.alanrogers.com/fr34200
info@californie-plage.fr
04 67 21 64 69
www.californie-plage.fr

Open (Touring Pitches):
1 April - 30 September

Camping Club Californie Plage

Though some 4 km. from Vias-Plage with its long sandy beach, Californie Plage does have direct access to three sandy coves, and a few much sought-after pitches overlooking the sea. The site is traditionally laid out, with around 100 mobile homes available to rent on one side of the central road and over 200 touring pitches on the other. Pitches are on level sandy ground, separated by hedging, with electricity (10A, Europlug) and mostly of 100 sq.m. with shade from tall trees; those close to the beach are slightly smaller with less shade. There is a covered pool on the site and situated across the road in the grounds of its sister site is a superb tropical swimming pool complex with the inevitable toboggans etc. and even a naturist swimming pool (open in high season).

Good standard sanitary facilities with washbasins in cabins, baby rooms and facilities for disabled visitors. Washing machines, dryer. Motorcaravan services. Shop, bars, restaurant, takeaway. Beach café, tapas, fish dishes. Covered pool. Range of pools on sister site across road (July/Aug). Bicycle hire. Games room. Play area. Sports nets. Extensive entertainment and activity programme. Children's activities in July/Aug. No electric barbecues. WiFi over site (charged).

Ideal For...

 Beach

 Dogs

 Fishing

 Golf

 Play Area

 Disabled Facilities

Scan me for more information.

225 accommodations
128 pitches
GPS: 43.28202, 3.37105
Post Code: F-34450

Hérault, Languedoc-Roussillon

www.alanrogers.com/fr34410
contact@mediterranee-plage.com
04 67 90 99 07
www.mediterranee-plage.com

Open (Touring Pitches):
28 March - 27 September.

Le Méditerranée Plage

Camping le Méditerranée Plage is a somewhat unusual but comfortable beach site set in a quiet part of the coast, with not only an impressive entertainment complex, but two good sized pools (one heated) and a children's farm with cute small animals and a circus to boot! A supermarket and snack bar provide for daytime needs, with evening entertainment beside the main bar and restaurant. Méditerranée Plage is very well cared for, with 410 pitches (some 128 for touring units, all with 6A electricity) situated in tree-lined avenues on level grass. Nearer the beach, they become sandier and have smaller trees. The sand is built up high, so the sea is not visible from the site.

Two large, heated toilet blocks are modern, one with a special smart nursery unit, plus two smaller ones. There is a mixture of British and Turkish style WCs Facilities for disabled visitors. Laundry. Motorcaravan services. Supermarket. Restaurant (facing stage for entertainment) and bar. Snack bar. Hairdressers. TV room. Play area. Games room. Multisports court. Tennis. Archery. Windsurfing possible from beach. Bicycle hire. Activity programme, children's entertainment. Evening entertainment. Minifarm. WiFi (charged).

Ideal For...

 Beach

 Dogs

 Fishing

 Watersports

 Play Area

 Disabled Facilities

Scan me for more information.

140 accommodations
311 pitches
GPS: 43.29254, 3.39975
Post Code: F-34450

Hérault, Languedoc-Roussillon

Camping & Spa Club Cap Soleil

www.alanrogers.com/fr34825
reception@capsoleil.fr
04 67 21 64 77
www.capsoleil.fr

Open (Touring Pitches):
31 March - 23 September

Camping Club Cap Soleil is sat beside the Mediterranean on Vias beach, a long sandy cove surrounded by wild lagoons and nestled in a green haven. The campsite is situated in the south of France, in the beautiful Languedoc-Roussillon region, where you will certainly be enchanted by the area, the quality of life and the friendly welcome. Ideally located, the Cap Soleil campsite allows you to take advantage of this rich area, less than one kilometre away from the canal du midi.

---

700 metres from the beach. Shops. Hairdresser. Barber. Massages. Restaurant, bar and take away on site. Aquapark with 5 slides. Indoor heated swimming pool. Wellness/Spa area with heated pools, jacuzzi, sauna and hammam.Tennis. Multisports field. Archery. Pétanque. Children's playground. Children's club. Evening shows (seasonal).

Ideal For...

 Kids

 Beach

 Dogs

 Fishing

 Watersports

 Golf

Scan me for more information.

300 accommodations
590 pitches
GPS: 43.23708, 3.26234
Post Code: F-34350

Hérault, Languedoc-Roussillon

www.alanrogers.com/fr34090
infocamping@layolewineresort.com
04 67 37 33 87
www.campinglayole.com

Open (Touring Pitches):
30 April - 24 September.

Domaine de la Yole

Camping Caravaning Domaine de la Yole is an impressive, busy, holiday village with over 1,200 pitches with a wide range of facilities. There are 590 pitches for touring with the remainder occupied by a range of mobile homes plus some tents to rent. Pitches are of a good size, all are level, hedged and have electricity (5A), water and waste water points and, importantly for this area, all have shade. Some fully serviced pitches are available. The pool area is impressive, more like an aqua park with six pools and water slides (heated in low season) and plenty of sunbathing areas. The central shopping and entertainment area form the heart of the site providing everything you need. The beach is a long stretch of beautiful sand with trampolining, paragliding and jet-skis available.

Well maintained toilet blocks include baby rooms. Facilities for families and/or disabled visitors. Washing machines, dryers. Motorcaravan services. Fridge hire. Shops. Good restaurant, terrace, amphitheatre for daily entertainment. Large pool complex with six pools and water slides. Full and half size tennis courts. Multisports court. Play areas. High wire adventure park. Bicycle hire. Minigolf. Miniclub. Youth club. Boules. WiFi over site (charged). Site-owned farm, vineyard and winery. No electric barbecues. Max. 2 dogs.

Ideal For...

 Kids

 Beach

 Dogs

 Fishing

 Watersports

 Golf

Scan me for more information.

250 accommodations
260 pitches
GPS: 43.26308, 3.31976
Post Code: F-34410

Hérault, Languedoc-Roussillon

www.alanrogers.com/fr34070
info@leserignanplage.com
04 67 32 35 33
www.leserignanplage.com

Open (Touring Pitches):
26 April - 01 October.

Camping le Sérignan-Plage

Yelloh! Village le Sérignan-Plage is a lively and vibrant site with direct access onto a superb 600 m. sandy beach (including a naturist section), plus two swimming pool complexes and an indoor pool, this is a must for a Mediterranean holiday. It is a busy, friendly, family orientated site with a very comprehensive range of amenities and activities for children. There are now over 1,200 pitches with 260 for touring units. They are fairly level, on sandy soil and all have 10A electricity. The collection of spa pools (balnéo) built in Romanesque style with colourful terracing and columns is overlooked by a very smart restaurant, Le Villa, available to use in the afternoons (used by the adjacent naturist site in the mornings).

Seven modern blocks of individual design with good facilities including showers with washbasin and WC. Facilities for disabled visitors. Baby bathroom. Launderette. Motorcaravan services. Supermarket, bakery and newsagent. Other shops (2/6-14/9). ATM. Restaurants, bars and takeaway. Hairdresser. Balnéo spa (afternoons). Gym. Heated indoor pool. Outdoor pools (all season). Tennis courts. Multisports courts. Play areas. Trampolines. Children's clubs. Evening entertainment. Sporting activities. Bicycle hire. Bus to Sérignan village (July/Aug). Beach (lifeguards 15/6-15/9). WiFi over site (charged). Gas barbecues only.

Ideal For...

 Beach

 Dogs

 Fishing

 Watersports

 Play Area

 Disabled Facilities

Scan me for more information.

124 accommodations
236 pitches
GPS: 43.1327, 3.1389
Post Code: F-11430

Aude, Languedoc-Roussillon

Camping Les Ayguades

www.alanrogers.com/fr11240
infos@loisirs-vacances-languedoc.com
04 68 49 81 59
www.camping-soleil-mer.com

Open (Touring Pitches):
15 March - 12 November

Sites with direct access to the sea are popular, particularly those with a long season. Camping LVL Les Ayguades is situated between Gruissan Plage and Narbonne Plage and is overlooked by the Montagne de la Clape. The site is owned by an association which has recently updated the facilities and is committed to preserving the environment running the site with this in mind. There are 236 sandy pitches of various sizes, all with 10A electricity. The pitches are hedged and there is some shade. The site also has 70 chalets and mobile homes to rent, plus 15 privately owned. An upstairs restaurant has panoramic views of the sea.

Two fully equipped toilet blocks have been renovated and include facilities for disabled visitors. Launderette. Motorcaravan services. Shop, bar and takeaway (28/6-31/8). Restaurant (15/4-10/11). Play area and skate park. Children's club. Evening entertainment in high season. Direct access to the Beach. Heated swimming pool with jaccuzi . Free WiFi.

Ideal For...

 Naturist

 Kids

 Beach

 Dogs

 Play Area

 Disabled Facilities

Scan me for more information.

90 accommodations
270 pitches
GPS: 43.14696, 3.00439
Post Code: F-11100

Aude, Languedoc-Roussillon

www.alanrogers.com/fr11080
info@campinglanautique.com
04 68 90 48 19
www.campinglanautique.com

Open (Touring Pitches):
1 March - 31 October.

Camping la Nautique

This well established site is owned and run by a friendly Dutch family. It is an extremely spacious site situated on the Etang de Bages, where flat water combined with strong winds make it one of the best windsurfing areas in France. La Nautique has 390 huge, level pitches, 270 for touring, all with 10A electricity and fully equipped individual sanitary units. Six or seven overnight pitches with electricity are in a separate area. A range of mobile homes are available to rent. The flowering shrubs and trees give a pleasant feel while providing some shade. Hedges separate the pitches making some quite private and providing shade. The ground is quite hard and stony.

Each pitch has its own fully equipped sanitary unit. Extra facilities for disabled visitors. Laundry. Motorcaravan services. Shop. Bar/ restaurant with terrace, TV, and takeaway (all 1/5-30/9). Snack bar (July/Aug). Outdoor heated swimming pool, water slide and paddling pool (1/5-30/9). Play areas. Tennis. Minigolf. Pétanque. Miniclub (high season). Games room. Bicycle hire. WiFi (charged). Only electric barbecues are permitted. Torch useful.

Ideal For...

 Beach

 Dogs

 Fishing

 Watersports

 Golf

 Play Area

Scan me for more information.

124 accommodations
130 pitches
GPS: 43.13662, 3.02562
Post Code: F-11100

Aude, Languedoc-Roussillon

www.alanrogers.com/fr11070
info@lesmimosas.com
04 68 49 03 72
www.camping-les-mimosas.fr

Open (Touring Pitches):
26 March - 15 October

Camping les Mimosas

Six kilometres inland from the beaches of Narbonne and Gruissan, Yelloh! Village les Mimosas is a family owned site which benefits from a less hectic situation than others by the sea. Set amongst the vineyards, it is welcoming, peaceful in low season, but lively in July and August with plenty to amuse and entertain the younger generation, including a separate paddling pool for toddlers, but still offering facilities for the whole family. A free club card is available in July/August for use at the children's club, gym, sauna, tennis, minigolf, billiards etc. There are 266 pitches, 130 for touring, hedged and on level grass, and of a very good size, most with 6/10A electricity. There are a few 'grand confort' pitches with reasonable shade, mostly from two metre high hedges.

Sanitary buildings refurbished to a high standard include a baby room. Washing machines. Shop and restaurant (all season, incl. breakfast). Takeaway. Bar (low season only at w/ends). Small lounge, amusements (July/Aug). Landscaped heated pool with slides and islands (12/4-mid Oct), plus the original large pool and excellent new paddling pool and play room. Play area. Minigolf. Mountain bike hire. Tennis. Wellness area with massage, beauty treatments and sauna. Gym. Children's activities, sports, entertainment (high season). Bicycle hire. Multisports court. WiFi throughout (charged).

Ideal For...

 Kids

 Beach

 Dogs

 Fishing

 Watersports

 Play Area

Scan me for more information.

57 accommodations
123 pitches
GPS: 42.50593, 2.04564
Post Code: F-66120

Pyrénées-Orientales,
Languedoc-Roussillon

Camping Font-Romeu

www.alanrogers.com/fr66250
font-romeu@huttopia.com
04 68 30 09 32
europe.huttopia.com/en/site/font-romeu

Open (Touring Pitches):
15 June - 11 September.

This is a large, open site of some seven hectares, with 123 touring pitches (72 with 10A electricity), nestling on the side of the mountain at the entrance to Huttopia Font-Romeu. This part of the Pyrenees offers some staggering views and the famous Mont Louis is close by. An ideal base for climbing, hiking and cycling, it would also provide a good stopover for a night or so whilst travelling between Spain and France, or to and from Andorra. The terraced pitches are easily accessed, with those dedicated to caravans and motorcaravans at the top of the site, whilst tents go on the lower slopes. Trees provide shade to many of the pitches from the sun which can be quite hot at this altitude.

Three bright and clean toilet blocks, one of which is in the centre of the tent pitches. Toilet for children and excellent facilities for disabled visitors. Laundry facilities at each block. Shop (for basics). Bar, restaurant and takeaway service (weekends only outside July/Aug). Outdoor heated swimming pool. Large games hall. No charcoal barbecues (communal area available). Max. 1 dog.

Ideal For...

 Beach

 Dogs

 Watersports

 Walking

 Golf

 Play Area

Scan me for more information.

200 accommodations
150 pitches
GPS: 42.6757, 3.03135
Post Code: F-66140

Pyrénées-Orientales,
Languedoc-Roussillon

Camping Mar Estang

www.alanrogers.com/fr66090
contactme@marestang.com
04 68 80 35 53
www.marestang.com

Open (Touring Pitches):
16 April - 18 September.

Le Mar Estang is a large, impressive, 'all singing, all dancing' site with something for everyone. Situated on the edge of Canet, between the Etang (part of the Réserve Naturelle de Canet/Saint Nazaire) and the sea, there is access to the sandy beach from the site by two tunnels under the road. If you don't fancy the beach, the site has not one but two attractive pool complexes linked by a bridge. They are amazing, providing slides, toboggans, hot tub, paddling pool and a heated pool, all with lifeguards. You can swim seriously, learn to swim or scuba dive or just enjoy the fun pools. Who needs the beach! There are 600 pitches in total, some 150 for touring units, with 6A electricity, and some degree of shade, on sandy ground. The rest are used by tour operators or have site-owned mobile homes to rent.

Nine well equipped sanitary blocks are well placed around the site. Facilities for babies. Laundry. Motorcaravan services. Shops, bars, restaurant and takeaway, swimming pools with lifeguards, jacuzzi and solarium (all open all season). Fitness club. Children's clubs. Artistic workshops (pottery, crafts etc). Daily sports and entertainment programme. Day trips. Evening entertainment with cabaret. Disco. Communal barbecue only. Sailing club. Beach club. Tennis. Bicycle hire. Play areas. WiFi throughout (charged). Direct access to beach.

Ideal For...

 Kids

 Beach

 Dogs

 Fishing

 Watersports

 Golf

Scan me for more information.

179 accommodations
704 pitches
GPS: 42.7083, 3.03552
Post Code: F-66141

Pyrénées-Orientales,
Languedoc-Roussillon

Camping le Brasilia

www.alanrogers.com/fr66070
info@lebrasilia.fr
04 68 80 23 82
www.brasilia.fr

Open (Touring Pitches):
23 April - 8 October.

Situated across the yacht harbour from the resort of Canet-Plage, le Brasilia is an impressive, well managed family site directly beside the beach. The state-of-the-art reception incorporates an information centre. Although large, it is pretty, neat and well kept with an amazingly wide range of facilities - indeed, it is camping at its best. The touring pitches are neatly hedged, all with electricity (6-10A) and 304 with water and drainage. They vary in size from 80 to 120 sq.m. and some of the longer pitches are suitable for two families together. There is a variety of shade from pines and flowering shrubs, with less on pitches near the beach. A member of Yelloh! Village and Leading Campings group.

Nine modern sanitary blocks are very well equipped and maintained, with British style WCs and washbasins in cabins. Good facilities for children and for disabled campers. Laundry room. Motorcaravan services. Range of shops. Gas supplies. Bars and restaurant. Renovated pool complex (heated). New wellness centre including jacuzzi, massage and beauty rooms. Play areas. Sports field. Tennis. Sporting activities. Library, games and video room. Hairdresser. Internet café and WiFi. Daily entertainment programme. Bicycle hire. Fishing. Post office. Weather forecasts. No charcoal barbecues. Free WiFi in bar.

Ideal For...

 Kids

 Beach

 Dogs

 Fishing

 Watersports

 Walking

Scan me for more information.

250 accommodations
80 pitches
GPS: 42.7675, 3.02972
Post Code: F-66440

Pyrénées-Orientales,
Languedoc-Roussillon

www.alanrogers.com/fr66190
contact@campinglestropiques.com
04 68 28 05 09
www.campinglestropiques.com

Open (Touring Pitches):
4 April - 4 October.

Camping Club les Tropiques

Camping Sunêlia les Tropiques is a very attractive site with a large pool complex, only 400 metres from a sandy beach. It will provide families with children of all ages with an ideal seaside holiday. There are 450 pitches with 78 for touring units, all with 10A electricity. Pleasant pine and palm trees with other Mediterranean vegetation give shade and provide a pleasant environment. Activities are provided for all including a large range of sports, activities, cabarets and shows.

Modern, fully equipped sanitary facilities, provision for disabled visitors. Launderette. Shop. Bar and restaurant. Takeaway and pizzeria (1/7-31/8). Swimming pool (heated in low season) and water slides. Paddling pool. Wellness centre. Outdoor fitness equipment. Tennis (floodlit). Multisports area (basketball, football, volleyball). Pétanque. Archery (1/7-31/8). TV/billiards room. Play area. Disco (every evening). Miniclub (6-12 yrs and teenagers' club for 13-17 yrs July/Aug). Bicycle hire (all season). WiFi throughout (charged).

Ideal For...

 Beach

 Dogs

 Fishing

 Watersports

 Golf

 Play Area

Scan me for more information.

352 accommodations
140 pitches
GPS: 42.77855, 3.0301
Post Code: F-66420

Pyrénées-Orientales, Languedoc-Roussillon

Le Floride & L'Embouchure

www.alanrogers.com/fr66290
contact@floride.fr
04 68 86 11 75
www.floride.fr/en

Open (Touring Pitches):
29 March - 4 November

A well established and multi-lingual, family run enterprise, Campsite Resort Le Floride & L'Embouchure is really two sites in one – l'Embouchure the smaller one with direct access to the beach and le Floride on the opposite side of the road. Fifty pitches have their own individual sanitary facility and in total the site offers 632 reasonably sized pitches, 140 for touring, all with 10A electricity. A good range of chalets and mobile homes are available for rent, including a recent Polynesian-style village. It is relatively inexpensive, especially outside the July/August peak period and the majority of the comprehensive facilities are open from end of March until the beginning of November.

Four fully equipped toilet blocks on le Floride and two on l'Embouchure where 50 pitches near the beach have individual facilities. Facilities for babies and disabled visitors. Family shower room. Motorcaravan services. Grocery store. Souvenir shop. Bar and restaurant (from 10/4), takeaway (15/6-5/9). Excellent pool complex with indoor heated pool (all season). Beauty Centre. Hammam. Hairdressers. Excellent play area. Day care for kids. Multisports court. Gym. Tennis. Multilingual entertainment and sports programmes (1/5-30/9). Bicycle hire. Charcoal barbecues are not permitted. Max. 1 dog. WiFi over site (free).

Ideal For...

 Kids

 Beach

 Dogs

 Fishing

 Watersports

 Play Area

Scan me for more information.

500 accommodations
10 pitches
GPS: 42.57093, 3.02906
Post Code: F-66702

Pyrénées-Orientales,
Languedoc-Roussillon

Camping Club la Sirène

www.alanrogers.com/fr66560
contact@camping-lasirene.fr
04 68 81 04 61
www.camping-lasirene.fr

Open (Touring Pitches):
20 April - 28 September.

From the moment you step into the hotel-like reception area you realise that this large site offers the holidaymaker everything they could want, including a super pool complex, in a well managed and convenient location close to Argelès-sur-Mer and the beaches. There are 740 pitches over the 17-hectare site, and 520 mobile homes and chalets. They are modern in design, all less than five years old, and laid out in pretty avenues with flowering shrubs and shade from tall trees. There are now just ten touring pitches, with 16A electricity and water, and some 200 taken by tour operators. All the shops and amenities are near reception making the accommodation areas quite peaceful and relaxing.

Two well equipped toilet blocks with facilities for babies and disabled visitors (key access). Laundry. Traditional restaurant and fast food bar, bar and takeaway, large shop and bazaar, large aqua park, paddling pools, slides, jacuzzi (all season). Games room. Two play areas. Multisports field. Four tennis courts. Archery. Minigolf. Football. Theatre, evening entertainment, discos, show time spectacular. Riding. Bicycle hire. Watersports. WiFi throughout (free). Gas and electric barbecues only.

Ideal For...

 Beach

 Dogs

 Fishing

Watersports

 Golf

 Play Area

Scan me for more information.

92 accommodations
143 pitches
GPS: 43.82343, 6.43095
Post Code: F-04120

Alpes-de-Haute-Provence, Provence

Gorges du Verdon

www.alanrogers.com/fr04250
gorgesduverdon@huttopia.com
04 92 83 63 64
europe.huttopia.com/en/site/gorges-du-verdon

Open (Touring Pitches):
21 April - 2 October.

Located at an altitude of 660 metres, between pinewoods and the River Verdon, Huttopia Gorges du Verdon is a family site with large, shaded or semi-shaded pitches and a range of chalets and mobile homes. The site has been entirely renovated. It has an inviting swimming pool and offers direct access to the Verdon (with its own river beach). The main sight here is, of course, the stunning canyon of the Gorges du Verdon, a grandiose area of vertiginous cliffs towering above the emerald river below. There are some superb walks and this is also an ideal location for white-water rafting or canoeing.

Two modern sanitary blocks (one in each section of the site). Children's toilets. Facilities for disabled visitors and babies. Well stocked shop, bar/restaurant/takeaway. Swimming pool and new paddling pool (all season). River beach. Good play areas. Volleyball. Boules. Games room. Fishing. Kayaking. Children's club. Activity and entertainment (July/Aug). Mobile homes, 'wood and canvas' tents and chalets for rent. WiFi around reception (free).

Ideal For...

 Kids

 Beach

 Dogs

 Fishing

 Watersports

 Play Area

Scan me for more information.

380 accommodations
200 pitches
GPS: 43.3988, 6.675417
Post Code: F-83520

Var, Côte d'Azur

Domaine de la Bergerie

www.alanrogers.com/fr83170
info@domainelabergerie.com
04 98 11 45 45
www.domainelabergerie.com

Open (Touring Pitches):
23/4 - 30/9 (accommodation 1/3 - 31/10).

Castel Camping Domaine de la Bergerie is an excellent site near the Côte d'Azur which will take you away from all the bustle of the Mediterranean to total relaxation amongst the cork, oak, pine and mimosa in its woodland setting, whilst only ten minutes away from the sea. The 60-hectare site is well spread out with semi-landscaped areas for mobile homes and 200 separated pitches for touring caravans and tents. All pitches average over 80 sq.m. and have electricity, with one area also having water and drainage. Eight premium pitches with cabins equipped with kitchenette and bathroom have been added. The restaurant/bar, a converted farm building, is surrounded by shady patios, inside it oozes character with beams and archways leading to intimate corners.

Four toilet blocks are kept clean and include washbasins in cubicles, facilities for babies & disabled visitors. Supermarket. Bar/restaurant/takeaway (seasonal). Indoor heated pool with Jacuzzi, sauna and steam bath. Outdoor pool complex, aquagym, slides & paddling pools. Fitness centre. Bicycle hire. Tennis. Archery. Roller skating. Minigolf. English-speaking childrens & teenagers clubs. Minifarm. Fishing. Paintball (July/Aug). WiFi throughout (charged). Only gas barbecues permitted.

Ideal For...

- Kids
- Beach
- Dogs
- Fishing
- Watersports
- Golf

Scan me for more information.

363 accommodations
20 pitches
GPS: 43.44583, 6.72727
Post Code: F-83600

Var, Côte d'Azur

Domaine du Colombier

www.alanrogers.com/fr83230
info@domaine-du-colombier.com
04 94 51 56 01
www.domaine-du-colombier.com

Open (Touring Pitches):
26 March - 10 October.

Domaine du Colombier is located between Cannes and Saint Tropez, alongside a main road 2 km. from the centre of Fréjus and 4.5 km. from the fine sandy beaches of Fréjus and Saint Raphaël. There are 20 touring pitches, ranging in size from 80-100 sq.m. and all with 16A electricity and 363 units of rental accommodation. Over recent years there has been much ongoing investment in high quality facilities. An attractive heated pool complex (3,600 sq.m) includes a long river, paddling pool, waterslides, lagoon and whirlpool, all surrounded by sun loungers. Plenty of activities and excursions are arranged all season and the site caters principally for families.

Two high quality, fully equipped and heated sanitary blocks with baby rooms. Laundry. Well stocked shop. Bar/restaurant and takeaway. Soundproofed nightclub. Large heated swimming pool complex. Spa. Balnéotherapy. Hairdresser. Fitness facilities. Three play areas and four sports areas. Charcoal barbecues are not permitted. Picnic area with communal barbecue. Bicycle, fridge, safe and barbecue hire. Internet access and WiFi over site (charged).

Ideal For...

 Kids

 Beach

Dogs

 Fishing

 Watersports

 Golf

Scan me for more information.

331 accommodations
164 pitches
GPS: 43.453775, 6.832817
Post Code: F-83530

Var, Côte d'Azur

Caravaning Esterel

www.alanrogers.com/fr83020
contact@esterel-caravaning.fr
04 94 82 03 28
www.esterel-caravaning.co.uk

Open (Touring Pitches):
19 March - 24 September.

Camping Caravaning Esterel is a quality, award-winning caravan site east of Saint Raphaël, set among the hills beyond Agay. The site is 3.5 km. from the sandy beach at Agay where parking is perhaps a little easier than at most places on this coast, but a shuttle from the site runs to and from the beach several times daily in July and August. It has 164 touring pitches (tents are not accepted) with 10A electricity and a water tap. A number of 'deluxe' pitches are available with heated bathroom, jacuzzi, dishwasher and washing machine. Pitches are on shallow terraces, attractively landscaped with good shade and a variety of flowers, giving a feeling of spaciousness.

Heated toilet blocks (one newly refurbished with facilities for babies and children). New en-suite facilities for disabled visitors. Laundry room. Motorcaravan services. Small supermarket. Gift shop. Takeaway. Bar/restaurant. Swimming pool complex (two heated), separate 'jungle' pool for children (covered and heated). Fitness centre. Spa with sauna. Disco. Archery. Minigolf. Tennis. Pony rides. Pétanque. Squash. Playground. Nursery (4 months to 3 years). Clubs for children and teenagers. Family activities. TV room/library. Bicycle hire. Internet access. Organised events in season. No barbecues. WiFi throughout.

Ideal For...

- Kids
- Beach
- Dogs
-  Fishing
-  Watersports
-  Golf

Scan me for more information.

GERMANY

With its wealth of scenic and cultural interests, Germany is a land of contrasts. From the flat lands of the north to the mountains in the south, with forests in the east and west, regional characteristics are a strong feature of German life, and present a rich variety of folklore and customs.

Each region in Germany has its own unique identity. Home of lederhosen, beer and sausages is Bavaria in the south, with small towns, medieval castles and Baroque churches. In the south west, Baden Württemberg is famous for its ancient Black Forest and its spas, and boasts the most hours of sunshine. Further west is the stunningly beautiful Rhine Valley, where the river winds through steep hills dotted with castles, ruins and vineyards. Eastern Germany is studded with lakes and rivers, and undulating lowlands that give way to mountains. The north has busy cities such as Bremen and Hamburg as well as traditional North Sea family resorts.

The capital city of Berlin, situated in the north east of the country, and once divided by the Berlin Wall, is an increasingly popular tourist destination, with its blend of old and modern architecture, zoos and aquariums, museums, green spaces and lively nightlife.

Language: German
Capital: Berlin
Currency: Euro (€)
Time Zone: Central European Time (GMT/UTC plus one hour)
Telephone Country Code: 00 49
Tourist Office: www.germany-tourism.co.uk

Say Hello
Guten tag (goo-ten tahk)

Say Goodbye
Auf Wiedersehen (owf vee-der-say-en)

Public Holidays
New Year's Day; Good Fri; Easter Mon; Labour Day; Ascension; Whit Mon; Unification Day 3 Oct; Christmas, 25, 26 Dec. In some areas: Epiphany 6 Jan; Corpus Christi 22 Jun; Assumption 15 Aug; Reformation 31 Oct; All Saints 1 Nov (plus other regional days).

Motoring
An excellent network of (toll-free) motorways (autobahns) exists in the West and the traffic moves fast. Remember in the East a lot of road building is going on, amongst other works, so allow plenty of time when travelling and be prepared for poor road surfaces.

100 pitches
GPS: 54.26514, 11.07734
Post Code: D-23749

Grube, Schleswig-Holstein

Rosenfelder Strand

www.alanrogers.com/de25360
info@rosenfeder-strand.de
04365 979722
www.rosenfelder-strand.de

Open (Touring Pitches):
28 March - 19 October.

Rosenfelder Strand is a beautiful campsite high above the East Sea beaches. The site has its own sandy beach in a sheltered area, making it safe for children to bathe. The level pitches (some hardstanding) are marked and numbered, and vary in size from 100-140 sq.m. A significant number are fully serviced. The rural location of this site ensures a quiet holiday, the only sounds being birds and the rushing of the sea. Rosenfelder Strand offers many opportunities for an active holiday as well opportunities for riding, watersports and biking.

Four toilet blocks scattered around the site, two very high quality ones with washbasins (open style and in cabins), controllable hot showers and superb facilities for children in the 'Landhaus' block. Family showers. Baby room. Facilities for disabled visitors. Full laundry. Supermarket. Restaurant with open-air terrace. Beach bar. Bouncy cushion. Playgrounds. Trampoline area. Beach. Fishing. Riding. Boat launching. Bicycle hire. Massage and aerobics. Minigolf. Beach volleyball. Dog shower. No dogs in high season.

Ideal For...

 Dogs

 Fishing

 Watersports

 Golf

 Play Area

 Disabled Facilities

Scan me for more information.

160 accommodations
372 pitches
GPS: 54.40805, 11.17374
Post Code: D-23769

Wulfen auf Fehmarn, Schleswig-Holstein

www.alanrogers.com/de30030
info@wulfenerhals.de
043 718 6280
www.wulfenerhals.de

Open (Touring Pitches):
All year.

Camping Wulfener Hals

This is a top class, all year round site suitable as a stopover or as a base for a longer stay. Attractively situated by the sea, it is large, mature (34 hectares) and well maintained. It has over 800 individual pitches (372 for touring) of up to 160 sq.m. in glades. Some are separated by bushes providing shade in the older parts, less so in the newer areas nearer the sea. There are many hardstandings and all pitches have electricity (16A), water and drainage. Some new rental accommodation has been added, including a 'honeymoon mobile home.' A member of Leading Campings group.

Five heated sanitary buildings have first class facilities including showers and both open washbasins and private cabins. Family bathrooms to rent. Facilities for disabled visitors. Beauty and cosmetic facilities (all year), wellness (all year). Laundry. Motorcaravan services. Shop, bar, restaurants and takeaway (April-Oct). Swimming pool (May-Oct). Sauna. Solarium. Jacuzzi. Sailing, catamaran, windsurfing and diving schools. Boat slipway. Golf courses (18 holes, par 72 and 9 holes, par 3). Riding. Fishing. Archery. Well organised and varied entertainment programmes for all ages. Bicycle hire. Catamaran hire. WiFi over part of site (charged).

Ideal For...

 Kids

 Beach

 Dogs

Year Round Camping

 Fishing

 Watersports

Scan me for more information.

6 accommodations
120 pitches
GPS: 53.96142, 10.33737
Post Code: D-23795

Klein Rönnau, Schleswig-Holstein

Klüthseecamp Seeblick

www.alanrogers.com/de30080
info@kluethseecamp.de
045 518 2368
www.kluethseecamp.de

Open (Touring Pitches):
All year except February.

Klüthseecamp Seeblick is a modern, family run site situated on a small hill between two lakes. It is an ideal location for a family holiday with activities on site for all ages and a useful base to explore the region. The large, open grass, touring part of the site has sunny, shaded and semi-shaded areas on offer. There are 120 touring pitches on fairly level ground, all with electricity (10/16A) and 30 with water and drainage, and pitches for tents in natural surroundings. Klüthseecamp offers wellness, a swimming pool, food and drink, organised entertainment for young and old, and a sandy lakeside beach.

Two modern, heated sanitary blocks, some washbasins in cabins, five bathrooms to rent and free showers. Facilities for children and disabled visitors including electric vehicle. Attractive baby room. Motorcaravan services. Gas supplies. Laundry. Shop with breakfast service. Bar and café in main building, additional beer garden and restaurant by the lake. Outdoor swimming pool (heated May-Sept). Wellness. Sauna, steam bath, massage. Play room/kindergarten. Bouncy castle. Three outside play areas. Large LCD0 projected TV. Bicycle hire. Go-kart hire. Minigolf. Way-marked paths around lake. Kids' and teenagers' clubs including weekly disco. Free WiFi at small restaurant.

Ideal For...

 Beach

 Dogs

 Fishing

 Watersports

 Golf

 Play Area

Scan me for more information.

90 accommodations
330 pitches
GPS: 53.30517, 13.00133
Post Code: D-17237

Gross Quassow, Mecklenburg-West Pomerania

Ferienpark Havelberge

www.alanrogers.com/de38200
info@haveltourist.de
039 812 4790
www.haveltourist.de

Open (Touring Pitches):
All year.

The Müritz National Park is a very large area of lakes and marshes, popular for birdwatching as well as watersports, and Havelberge is a large, well equipped site to use as a base for enjoying the area. It is quite steep in places with many terraces, most with shade, and views over the lake. There are 400 pitches in total with 330 good sized, numbered touring pitches (all with 16A Europlug electrical connections) and 230 pitches on a newly developed area to the rear of the site with water and drainage. Pitches on the new field are level and separated by low hedges and bushes but have no shade. A member of Leading Campings group.

Four sanitary buildings (one new and of a very high standard) provide very good facilities, with private cabins, showers on payment and large section for children. Fully equipped kitchen and laundry. Motorcaravan services. Small shop, modern restaurant, bar, takeaway and wellness (all 1/4-31/10). The lake provides fishing, swimming from a small beach and boats can be launched (over 5 hp requires a German boat licence). Rowing boats, windsurfers and bikes can be hired. Canoe centre with beginners' courses and canoe hire. Accompanied canoe, cycle and walking tours. Play areas and entertainment for all the family in high season. Teepee village. Tree walkway (2.5 m. high with safety wires). WiFi (charged).

Ideal For...

 Kids

 Beach

 Dogs

Year Round Camping

 Fishing

 Watersports

Scan me for more information.

8 accommodations
150 pitches
GPS: 53.923561, 12.10676
Post Code: D-18258

Schwaan, Mecklenburg-West Pomerania

www.alanrogers.com/de37850
info@campingplatz-schwaan.de
03844 813716
www.campingplatz-schwaan.de

Open (Touring Pitches):
1 March – 31 October.

Camping Schwaan

Peacefully located beside a gently flowing river, ideal for swimming and with good shade from mature trees, Camping Schwaan is a large site for those who want to relax in a natural setting. There is ample space for children to play, and being close to the Baltic coast and many interesting towns, it makes a quiet base from which to tour the area. There are 150 touring pitches, eight fully serviced and almost all with 10/16A electricity. They are level, grassy and open, so you can spread yourself out under the tall trees. For those using the Rostock ferry service it is also a useful overnight stop.

Three modern, well maintained sanitary blocks have some individual cabins, controllable showers (payment card), baby bath and facilities for disabled visitors. Washing machines and dryers. Motorcaravan services. Small kitchen. Fresh bread to order. Part of river partitioned off as children's swimming area. Minigolf. Play areas. WiFi over part of site (charged).

Ideal For...

 Beach

 Dogs

 Fishing

 Watersports

 Play Area

 Disabled Facilities

Scan me for more information.

170 pitches
GPS: 52.35857, 13.00633
Post Code: D-14471

Potsdam, Brandenburg

Camping Sanssouci

www.alanrogers.com/de38270
info@camping-potsdam.de
033 195 10988
www.camping-potsdam.de

Open (Touring Pitches):
18 March - 8 January.

Sanssouci is a good, if rather expensive, base for visiting Potsdam and Berlin. It lies about 2 km. from Sanssouci Park on the banks of the Templiner See, in a quiet woodland setting. Looking attractive, reflecting the effort which has been put into its development, it has a modern reception, shop, takeaway, restaurant and bar. There are 240 pitches in total with 170 for touring; all have 6-16A electricity, and many also have their own water tap and drainage. Tall trees mark out these pitches. There is a separate area for tents by the lake.

Top class sanitary facilities are in two excellent, modern, heated blocks containing hot showers, washbasins in cabins and facilities for babies. Useful facility for wheelchair users. Bathrooms to rent. Laundry. Gas supplies. Kitchen. Motorcaravan services. Shop. Restaurant/bar. Swimming and sailing in the lake. Wellness. Rowing boats, motorboats, canoes and pedaloes for hire. Fishing. Play area. Bicycle hire (E-bikes on request). Hairdresser. Internet café and WiFi throughout (charged). Public transport tickets and discounts for Berlin attractions.

Ideal For...

 Beach

 Dogs

 Fishing

 Watersports

 Golf

 Play Area

Scan me for more information.

280 pitches
GPS: 52.37012, 13.684351
Post Code: D-12527

Berlin, Berlin

Campingplatz Krossinsee

www.alanrogers.com/de38300
info@campingplatz-krossinsee.de
03067 58687
www.campingplatz-berlin.de

Open (Touring Pitches):
All year.

Am Krossinsee is an efficiently run site and a good base for visiting the capital of Germany. The Krossinsee itself is one of many clean lakes in the southeast of Berlin and is suitable for swimming, fishing and boating, with access by key through a gate from the woodland site. More than half the 450 pitches here are for tourers and are of varying but reasonable size, mainly with some degree of slope, most with 10A electrical connections and a fair amount of shade. A separate area is set aside for tents. For visits in high season, you should try to arrive as early as possible as reservations are not taken.

The sanitary facilities are of above average quality for a city site, situated in a modern building with plenty of private cabins, smallish showers (token from reception), hand and hair dryers, a baby room and a well equipped unit for disabled visitors. Kitchen. Laundry. Lake swimming, fishing, boating (hire facilities) windsurfing school and woodland walks. Bicycle hire. WiFi.

Ideal For...

Year Round Camping

Play Area

Disabled Facilities

Scan me for more information.

47 accommodations
164 pitches
GPS: 51.36975, 12.31400
Post Code: D-04159

Leipzig, Saxony

Campingplatz & Motel Auensee

www.alanrogers.com/de38470
info@camping-auensee.de
03414 651600
www.camping-auensee.de

Open (Touring Pitches):
All year.

It is unusual to find a good site in a city, but this large, neat and tidy site is one. It is far enough away from roads and the airport to be reasonably peaceful during the day and quiet overnight, and has 164 pitches, all for touring units. It is set in a mainly open area with tall trees and attractive flower beds, with some chalets and 'trekker' cabins to rent in the adjoining woodland, home to shoe-stealing foxes. The individual, numbered, flat grassy pitches are large (at least 100 sq.m), all with 16A electricity and five on hardstanding, arranged in several sections.

Five central sanitary buildings with WCs, washbasins in cabins and showers. Rooms for babies and disabled visitors (key access). Kitchen and laundry rooms. Motorcaravan services. Restaurant and snack bar (April-Oct). Entertainment rooms. Multisports court. Play area. Barbecue area. Good English spoken.

Ideal For...

 Dogs

 Year Round Camping

 Fishing

 Play Area

 Disabled Facilities

 Pets Accepted

Scan me for more information.

2 accommodations
198 pitches
GPS: 51.120401, 13.980103
Post Code: D-01900

Dresden, Saxony

Camping LuxOase

www.alanrogers.com/de38330
info@luxoase.de
03595 256666
www.luxoase.de

Open (Touring Pitches):
All year excl. February.

This is a well organised and quiet site located just north of Dresden, with easy access from the autobahn. The site has very good facilities and is arranged on grassland beside a lake, which is reached from the site through a gate. Although the site is fairly open, trees do provide shade in some areas. There are 198 large touring pitches (plus 40 seasonal in a separate area), marked by bushes or posts on generally flat or slightly sloping grass. All have 10/16A electricity and 132 have water and drainage. At the entrance is an area of hardstanding (with electricity) for late arrivals. A member of Leading Campings group.

Two excellent buildings provide modern, heated facilities with private cabins, a family room, baby room, units for disabled visitors and eight bathrooms for hire. Special facilities for children with novelty showers and washbasins. Kitchen. Gas supplies. Motorcaravan services. Shop and bar (1/3-31/12) plus restaurant (15/3-31/12). Lake swimming. Jacuzzi. Sauna. Fitness room. Fishing. Play area. Sports field. Minigolf. Train, bus and theatre tickets from reception. Regular guided bus trips to Dresden, Prague etc. Bicycle hire. Internet point. WiFi throughout (charged).

Ideal For...

 Kids

 Beach

 Dogs

 Fishing

 Walking

 Golf

Scan me for more information.

8 accommodations
150 pitches
GPS: 50.73367, 10.75667
Post Code: D-99330

Frankenhain, Thuringia

Oberhof Camping

www.alanrogers.com/de38550
info@oberhofcamping.de
03620 576518
www.oberhofcamping.de

Open (Touring Pitches):
All year.

Beside a lake, at an altitude of 700 metres and quietly hidden in the middle of the Thüringer forest, Oberhof Camping has seen many changes since the departure of its former owners, the East German secret police. There are 150 touring pitches, all with electricity (10A Europlug), 20 with water and drainage. From this fairly open site there are views of the surrounding forests and of the lake, which is bordered by wide grass areas ideal for a picnic or for just lazing around and enjoying the view. The site is very quiet and has direct access to marked routes for rambling and cycling in the forest. Eight small bungalows and an apartment are to rent.

Two sanitary blocks with all usual facilities including free hot water, plus 15 bathrooms to rent. Facilities for disabled visitors in one block. Baby room. Laundry. Motorcaravan services. Gas sales. Modern reception building with shop and attractive restaurant and takeaway (1/4-31/10). Shop with fresh bread (all year). Children's club room. Play area. On the lake: fishing (licence required), swimming and boating. WiFi (charged).

Ideal For...

Beach

Dogs

Year Round Camping

Fishing

Watersports

Play Area

Scan me for more information.

50 pitches
GPS: 49.83286, 9.99829
Post Code: D-97230

Estenfeld, Bavaria (N)

Camping Estenfeld

www.alanrogers.com/de37420
cplestenfeld@freenet.de
09305 228
www.camping-estenfeld.de

Open (Touring Pitches):
15 May - 10 November.

In the heart of the Franconian wine region and just five kilometres from the A7/E455, Estenfeld has been family owned and managed since it opened in 1953. It is only seven kilometres to the university city of Würzburg, which has a wealth of attractions. The site's 50 grass pitches are all for tourers and have electricity hook-ups (16A, 40 Europlugs). There are eight special pitches for motorcaravans and groups are accommodated in a separate area. A bike would be a real asset here as there are miles of scenic cycling routes through the vineyards and villages.

Heated sanitary block with hot showers, baby changing and a hairdryer. Washing machine and dryer. Motorcaravan services. Shop. Bar. Breakfast service. Restaurant. Takeaway. Play area. WiFi (free).

Ideal For...

 Dogs

 Fishing

 Golf

 Play Area

 Pets Accepted

 Bar on Site

Scan me for more information.

190 pitches
GPS: 48.435176, 13.109415
Post Code: D-84364

Bad Birnbach, Bavaria (S)

Camping Arterhof

www.alanrogers.com/de36960
info@arterhof.de
08563 96130
www.arterhof.de

Open (Touring Pitches):
All year.

Based around a Bavarian farmstead, Gutshof-Camping Arterhof is an excellent site combining the charm of the old together with the comfort of the new. An attractive courtyard at the front of the site houses reception, a farm shop and a café with a flower decked terrace. To the rear is a tropical indoor pool containing soft water at a comfortable 30°C as well as a sauna, solarium, fitness room and much more. The 190 touring pitches with some hedge separation, on grass or pebble standing, all have TV, electricity, fresh and waste water connections, and 12 have their own pitch-side sanitary facilities. For winter camping, 50 of the pitches have a gas supply.

Modern, attractive, well maintained sanitary blocks with heated floor, free showers, washbasins in cabins, hairdryers and bathrooms to rent. Hairdressing salon, cosmetic studio. Laundry facilities. Motorcaravan services. Swimming pools. Wellness centre. Traditional restaurant serving southern Bavarian dishes with meat from the farm's own Aberdeen Angus cattle. Play area. Live music Fridays. WiFi.

Ideal For...

Beach

Dogs

Year Round Camping

Fishing

Golf

Play Area

Scan me for more information.

20 accommodations
200 pitches
GPS: 48.42001, 13.19261
Post Code: D-94086

Bad Griesbach, Bavaria (S)

www.alanrogers.com/de36970
info@camping-bad-griesbach.de
08532 96130
www.camping-bad-griesbach.de

Open (Touring Pitches):
All year.

Feriencamping Dreiquellenbad

This excellent site is part of a wellness, health and beauty spa complex where camping guests have free use of the indoor and outdoor thermal pools, sauna, Turkish bath and jacuzzi. A large selection of treatments are also available (on payment) and the complex has its own doctor. The site has 200 pitches, all with fresh and waste water, electricity and TV connections. In addition, there is a new camping car area (29 units) with its own service point. This is a site where visitors should take full advantage of the facilities, and plenty of information is available at the helpful English-speaking reception. A member of Leading Campings Group.

Excellent sanitary facilities include private cabins and free showers, facilities for disabled visitors, special child facilities and a dog shower. Two private bathrooms to rent. Laundry facilities. Bar/restaurant. Motorcaravan services. Shop. Gym. Luxury leisure complex (heated outdoor pool 1/3-15/11, indoor pool and wellness all year). Play area. Bicycle hire. Fishing. Internet. WiFi. No charcoal barbecues.

Ideal For...

 Dogs

Year Round Camping

 Fishing

 Golf

 Play Area

 Disabled Facilities

Scan me for more information.

350 pitches
GPS: 48.75397, 11.46416
Post Code: D-85053

Ingolstadt, Bavaria (S)

www.alanrogers.com/de36160
ingolstadt@azur-camping.de
08419 611616
www.azur-camping.de

Open (Touring Pitches):
All year.

Waldcamping Auwaldsee

With easy access from the nearby A9, Azur Waldcamping Auwaldsee lies along the northern banks of a small lake. There are 650 pitches, of which 350 are for touring units. These are level, grassed and have 16A electricity. Access roads (some overgrown when we visited) lead to large, open grass areas with unmarked pitches which are shaded in places by mature trees. Opposite reception is a traditional Bavarian restaurant with a large beer garden – a good place to try the Bavarian speciality wheat beer. With its location in the centre of Bavaria the site is a useful base to tour the region or as stopover point to those travelling further afield.

Two heated sanitary blocks. Washing machines and dryers. Motorcaravan services. Shop and snack bar. Boating, swimming and fishing on Auwaldsee.

Ideal For...

 Beach

 Dogs

Year Round Camping

 Fishing

 Disabled Facilities

 Pets Accepted

Scan me for more information.

50 pitches
GPS: 48.43759, 10.92937
Post Code: D-86444

Affing-Mühlhausen bei Augsburg, Bavaria (S)

www.alanrogers.com/de36420
info@lech-camping.de
08207 2200
www.lech-camping.de

Open (Touring Pitches):
14 April - 17 September.

Lech Camping

Situated just north of Augsburg, this beautifully run site with its own small lake, is a pleasure to stay on. Gabi Ryssel, the owner, spends her long days working very hard to cater for every wish of her guests - from the moment you arrive and are given the key to one of the cleanest toilet blocks we have seen, plus plenty of tourist information, you are in very capable hands. The 50 level, grass and gravel pitches are roomy and have shade from pine trees. Electricity connections are available (10/16A Europlug). This is an immaculate site with a separate area for disabled visitors to park near the special facilities provided. The site is located beside a busy main road. A key (deposit payable) is needed to access washrooms and water points.

The new toilet block (cleaned several times daily) provides British style WCs and good showers with seating area and non-slip flooring. Baby room. Separate family bathroom to rent. Five star facilities for disabled visitors. Separate room with washing machine and laundry sinks. Motorcaravan services. Small shop, lakeside restaurant/bar/takeaway (all season). Small playground (partially fenced). Bicycle hire. Free WiFi. Trampolines. Surf boards and rowing boats (free).

Ideal For...

 Beach

 Dogs

 Fishing

 Watersports

 Golf

 Play Area

Scan me for more information.

4 accommodations
120 pitches
GPS: 48.73807, 8.57710
Post Code: D-75323

Bad Wildbad, Baden-Württemberg

Family - Resort Kleinenzhof

www.alanrogers.com/de34060
info@kleinenzhof.de
07081 3435
www.kleinenzhof.de

Open (Touring Pitches):
All year.

In the northern Black Forest, popular with walkers and cyclists alike, this large and busy site runs along the bank of a small but safe stream in a dramatic wooded valley. Of the 300 or so pitches, 120 are for tourers, all with 16A electricity and water, and most with drainage. The four shower blocks are of the highest quality. In the middle of the site is a hotel, bar and restaurant complex, which incorporates indoor and outdoor pools available free to campers.

Four excellent sanitary blocks, all heated, are clean with many washbasins in cabins and showers. Facilities for disabled visitors. Baby changing. Children's bathroom. 12 family bathrooms to rent (10 renovated in 2015). Dog shower. Laundry facilities and dishwasher. Motorcaravan services. Gas. Shop. Bar and restaurant (at hotel). Indoor pool. Outdoor pool (15/5-11/9) and paddling pool. Impressive indoor sports/games hall with toddler annexe. Playgrounds. TV and games room. Fishing. Go-kart hire. WiFi over site (charged).

Ideal For...

 Beach

 Dogs

Year Round Camping

 Fishing

 Play Area

 Disabled Facilities

Scan me for more information.

20 accommodations
362 pitches
GPS: 47.96042, 7.95083
Post Code: D-79199

Kirchzarten, Baden-Württemberg

www.alanrogers.com/de34400
info@camping-kirchzarten.de
076 619 040910
www.camping-kirchzarten.de

Open (Touring Pitches):
All year.

Camping Kirchzarten

Set in a green valley among the foothills of the Black Forest, this family managed site is well placed for visiting the popular Titisee, Feldberg and Totdnau areas, and is only 8 km. from Freiburg. It is divided into 486 numbered pitches, 362 of which are for touring, all with electricity (16A Europlug). Most pitches, which are side by side on gently sloping ground, are of reasonable size and clearly marked out, though there is nothing to separate them. There are increasing numbers of hardstanding pitches suitable for motorcaravans. From about late June to mid August, this site becomes very busy, and booking is advised.

The superb main sanitary building includes a large, central section for children, private cabins (some for hire) and a laundry room. The sanitary block near reception has been rebuilt to exemplary standards. Cooking stoves. Washing machines, dryers and irons (all on payment by meter) are available among the other buildings. Motorcaravan services. New bar/restaurant and takeaway (all year). Shop (15/4-31/10). Swimming pool complex (15/5-15/9). Wellness. TV room, play room and youth room. Large playground. Bicycle hire (electric). WiFi over site (charged). Children's activities in season.

Ideal For...

 Dogs

Year Round Camping

 Golf

 Play Area

 Disabled Facilities

 Pets Accepted

Scan me for more information.

305 pitches
GPS: 47.85973, 7.76375
Post Code: D-79244

Münstertal, Baden-Württemberg

Campingplatz Münstertal

www.alanrogers.com/de34500
info@camping-muenstertal.de
07636 7080
www.camping-muenstertal.de

Open (Touring Pitches):
All year.

Münstertal is an impressive site pleasantly situated in a valley on the western edge of the Black Forest. It has been one of the top graded sites in Germany for 25 years and first time visitors will soon realise why when they see the standard of the facilities here. There are 305 individual pitches in two areas, either side of the entrance road on flat gravel, their size varying from 70-100 sq.m. All have electricity (16A), water, drainage, TV and radio connections. The large indoor pool and the outdoor pool are both heated and free. The adjacent Health and Fitness Centre offers a range of treatments.

Three toilet blocks are of truly first class quality, with washbasins, all in cabins, showers with full glass dividers, baby bath, a unit for disabled visitors and individual bathrooms, some for hire. Dishwashers in two blocks. Laundry. Drying room. Motorcaravan services. Well stocked shop (all year). Restaurant, particularly good (closed Nov). Heated swimming pools, indoor all year, outdoor (with children's area). New health and fitness centre. Sauna and solarium. Games room. Extensive playing fields. Fishing. Bicycle hire. Tennis courses in summer. Riding. WiFi over site (charged). Konus Card for free bus and train travel.

Ideal For...

 Kids

 Dogs

 Year Round Camping

 Fishing

 Golf

 Play Area

Scan me for more information.

5 accommodations
70 pitches
GPS: 47.98064, 7.88153
Post Code: D-79117

Freiburg, Baden-Württemberg

www.alanrogers.com/de34380
information@camping-freiburg.com
07617 679333
www.camping-freiburg.com

Open (Touring Pitches):
1 April - 28 October.

Camping Am Möslepark

This is a small, quiet, family run site in the suburbs of Freiburg. Its grass pitches, set on small terraces, are shaded by many mature trees. Most of the 70 pitches are for touring units and have electricity (10/16A Europlug). On the upper part of the site is a long established and very attractive restaurant. Open in the evenings, the restaurant specialises in dishes freshly prepared from organic ingredients; vegetarian and local specialities are also part of the menu. Additionally a small bar and bistro is part of a wellness centre which adjoins the site.

Well maintained sanitary facilities provide some washbasins in cabins and showers with free hot water (a new block with facilities for disabled visitors and a kitchen for tent campers is scheduled). Space for baby changing. Small dining room with metered hotplate and kettle. Motorcaravan service area. Small shop. Play area. Bicycle hire. Free WiFi over site. The adjoining wellness centre has sauna, steam bath, massage and jacuzzi plus a small swimming pool (reduced rate entrance for campers). Accommodation to rent.

Ideal For...

 Dogs

 Fishing

 Golf

 Play Area

 Disabled Facilities

 Pets Accepted

Scan me for more information.

10 accommodations
100 pitches
GPS: 49.56066, 7.06118
Post Code: D-66625

Nohfelden/Bosen, Saarland

Campingplatz Bostalsee

www.alanrogers.com/de35320
campingplatz@bostalsee.de
06852 92333
www.bostalsee.de

Open (Touring Pitches):
All year.

Located in the beautiful Saar-Hunsrück National Park, this impressive and busy site has 438 pitches of which 100 are for touring (100 sq.m). Touring visitors are accommodated in areas between the seasonal pitches, most accessed by hard pathways. All pitches have electricity. There are ten generous hardstanding pitches for motorcaravans and 24 serviced pitches with electricity, water and drain. There are five areas for tents and rental units. Two large toilet blocks offer exemplary facilities for all visitors. A sports field, play areas and a multisports court will keep active children busy. This site offers exceptional value for one of this quality.

Heated sanitary facilities in two large blocks. Family bathrooms (charged). Facilities for disabled visitors. Sauna and solarium (charged). Motorcaravan services. Washing machines and dryers. Microwave and fridge. Small supermarket (15/3-15/11). Bread (1/4-1/10). Restaurant, snack bar, takeaway (all year). Multisports field. Play areas. Recreation room. TV/video room. Library. Boules. Entertainment for children to 12 years old in school holidays. Bicycles, mountain bikes, pedal boats, canoes, rowing boats, sailing boats, surf boards for hire. Communal barbecue pits. Internet access. WiFi near reception (charged).

Ideal For...

 Beach

 Dogs

Year Round Camping

 Fishing

 Watersports

 Golf

Scan me for more information.

187 pitches
GPS: 50.57428, 7.25189
Post Code: D-53424

Remagen, Rhineland Palatinate

www.alanrogers.com/de32150
info@camping-goldene-meile.de
02642 22222
www.camping-goldene-meile.de

Open (Touring Pitches):
All year.

Camping Goldene Meile

This site is on the banks of the Rhine between Bonn and Koblenz. Although there is an emphasis on permanent caravans, there are about 200 pitches for touring units (out of 500), most with 6A electricity and 100 with water and drainage. They are either in the central, more mature area or in a newer area where the numbered pitches of 80-100 sq.m. are arranged around an attractively landscaped, small lake. Just five are by the busy river and there may be some noise from the trains that run on the other side.

The main toilet block is heated and well maintained, with some washbasins in cabins, showers (token) and facilities for wheelchair users. A smaller block (renovated in 2012) serves the newer pitches (no showers). Laundry and cooking facilities. Motorcaravan services. Gas. Shop, bar, restaurant and takeaway (all 1/4-30/10 and some weekends). Play areas. Entertainment for children (July/Aug). Bicycle hire. WiFi over site (charged). Main gate is closed 22.00-07.00 (also 13.00-15.00).

Ideal For...

 Beach

 Dogs

Year Round Camping

 Watersports

 Walking

 Play Area

Scan me for more information.

6 accommodations
154 pitches
GPS: 49.35174, 7.78066
Post Code: D-67705

Trippstadt, Rhineland Palatinate

Camping Sägmühle

www.alanrogers.com/de32580
info@saegmuehle.de
06306 92190
www.saegmuehle.de

Open (Touring Pitches):
All year excl. 1 November - 11 December.

Freizeitzentrum Sägmühle is peacefully situated beside a lake, in a wooded valley in the heart of the Palatinate Nature Park, and there are many kilometres of walks to enjoy, as well as castles to explore. There are 303 pitches in total, of which 154 are available for touring, at least 80 sq.m. or more on flat grass, each with electricity (4/16A). Fifty of these are fully serviced and some have hardstanding. One area is close to the lake and it is a pleasant change to find a site that keeps the lakeside pitches for touring units.

Each area has its own sanitary facilities, which feature private cabins, baby bathroom, facilities for disabled visitors, launderette. Motorcaravan services. Restaurant serving local specialities and takeaway (lunchtime and evening). Bread available in high season. Solarium. Tennis. Play areas. Boules. Minigolf. Lake fishing. Beach volleyball. Entertainment daily in high season. Guided tours for ramblers and mountain bikers. Electric barbecues are not permitted. WiFi on part of site (charged).

Ideal For...

 Beach

 Dogs

 Walking

 Golf

 Play Area

 Disabled Facilities

Scan me for more information.

100 pitches
GPS: 49.97871, 7.9554
Post Code: D-65366

Geisenheim, Hessen

Campingplatz Geisenheim

www.alanrogers.com/de32930
info@rheingaucamping.de
06722 75600
www.rheingaucamping.de

Open (Touring Pitches):
3 March - 31 October.

Geisenheim is in a lovely position on the north bank of the Rhine and within walking distance of the picturesque small town of Rüdesheim. There are 100 slightly sloping touring pitches each with 16A electricity, plus some attractive seasonal pitches. The touring pitches are on the part of the site nearest the river and are on well maintained grass. Some have shade and some are marked out by hedges. There are four special hardstandings for long, heavy motorcaravans, but these must be booked in advance. A level pedestrian/cycle path runs alongside the river in both directions and there are many small picturesque villages in the area to visit.

Toilet block with showers and washbasins in cubicles. Laundry. Motorcaravan services. Small shop. Separately run restaurant (1/3-31/10). Fishing adjacent. WiFi throughout (charged).

Ideal For...

 Beach

 Dogs

 Pets Accepted

Scan me for more information.

200 pitches
GPS: 49.97966, 7.93647
Post Code: D-65385

Rüdesheim am Rhein, Hessen

Campingplatz am Rhein

www.alanrogers.com/de32240
info@campingplatz-ruedesheim.de
06722 2582
www.campingplatz-ruedesheim.de

Open (Touring Pitches):
1 May - 3 October.

This site, with direct access to The Rhine, is only 600 metres from Rüdesheim's attractive town centre. It has been run by the Richter family since 1984 and is ideally placed to explore this most important wine producing region with its thousands of acres of vineyards. The colourful seven acre touring site offers 200 level pitches on grass with shade from trees and arrangement is open plan. All pitches have 10A electricity and 40, normally allocated to motorcaravans, also have hardstanding, water and drainage. This is understandably a major tourist area and the site, although usually quiet and peaceful, may become busy at times.

Two sanitary blocks with washbasins in cabins, one with controllable hot showers. Washing machines and dryer. Motorcaravan services. Shop. Bar and snacks. Play area. Gates closed to vehicles and riverside 22.00-08.00.

Ideal For...

 Dogs

 Fishing

 Play Area

 Disabled Facilities

 Pets Accepted

 Bar on Site

Scan me for more information.

5 accommodations
50 pitches
GPS: 52.00412, 8.06467
Post Code: D-48336

Sassenberg, North Rhine-Westphalia

Eichenhof Münsterland

www.alanrogers.com/de31720
info@campmuensterland.de
02583 1585
www.campmuensterland.de

Open (Touring Pitches):
All year.

Campingpark Münsterland Eichenhof is a spacious 13 ha. family run site of 350 pitches, of which 50 close to reception are for touring, all with electricity (16A), water and waste water, TV and WiFi connections. Some of the touring pitches have shade whilst others are more open. There is a large football field with an open area for tents adjacent, and a small animal enclosure. A well stocked shop and excellent restaurant with bar area can provide a relaxing end to a busy day swimming or paddle boating at the Feldmarksee lake which is connected to the campsite by a traffic free pathway. Mobile homes and caravans are available to rent.

Modern heated shower facilities. Shop (1/4-19/10). Restaurant (all year). Bar. Direct lake access. Football field. Play areas. Accommodation to rent. Bicycle hire, Small animal petting corner. WiFi throughout (free).

Ideal For...

 Beach

 Dogs

 Year Round Camping

 Fishing

 Golf

 Play Area

Scan me for more information.

140 pitches
GPS: 50.90438, 6.99188
Post Code: D-51105

Köln-Poll, North Rhine-Westphalia

Campingplatz Stadt Köln

www.alanrogers.com/de32050
info@camping-koeln.de
02218 31966
www.camping-koeln.de

Open (Touring Pitches):
1 April - 18 October.

The ancient city of Cologne offers much for the visitor. This wooded park is pleasantly situated along the river bank, with wide grass areas on either side of narrow tarmac access roads with low wire mesh fencing separating it from the public park and riverside walks. There are 140 unmarked, level or slightly undulating touring pitches, all with 16A electricity and there is shade for some from various mature trees. Tents have their own large area. Because of its position close to the autobahn bridge over the Rhine, there is road and river noise.

The toilet block, which has been totally renovated, is heated with free hot water in washbasins and by a 50 cent coin in the showers. New facilities for disabled visitors. Large open-fronted room for cooking and eating with microwave oven. Washing machine and dryer. Small shop for bread and basic supplies (mid May-Sept). Evening snacks (March-Oct). Fishing. Bicycle hire. Drinks machine. WiFi (charged).

Ideal For...

 Beach

 Dogs

 Fishing

 Golf

 Disabled Facilities

 Pets Accepted

Scan me for more information.

10 accommodations
200 pitches
GPS: 53.424383, 10.294977
Post Code: D-21423

Drage, Lower Saxony

Stover Strand International

www.alanrogers.com/de28990
info@stover-strand.de
04177 430
www.camping-stover-strand.de

Open (Touring Pitches):
All year.

This is a large site, part of which directly borders the River Elbe, with 500 pitches, of which 200 are for touring (all with electricity, water and drainage). The main part of the site is located behind a dyke and contains reception and the principal sanitary facilities. Pitches bordering and overlooking The Elbe are serviced by excellent, modern mobile sanitary units containing WCs and washbasins. Along the Elbe's banks there are sandy areas useful for playing and sunbathing in summer with some showers. Next to the site's main building there is a further area set aside for touring units and this has easy access to the main sanitary facilities, the bar and restaurant and children's playground.

Modern sanitary facilities with washing machines and dryer, facilities for disabled visitors, and a baby room. Kitchen with cooking facilities. Motorcaravan services. Supermarket. Bar. Restaurant. Play areas. Family entertainment (July/Aug). Bicycle hire. Fishing. Sport boat harbour with 100 moorings. Boat slipway. Car rental. WiFi (charged).

Ideal For...

 Beach

 Dogs

Year Round Camping

 Fishing

 Watersports

 Golf

Scan me for more information.

69 accommodations
726 pitches
GPS: 52.931639, 9.965254
Post Code: D-29649

Wietzendorf, Lower Saxony

Südsee-Camp

www.alanrogers.com/de30700
info@suedsee-camp.de
051 969 80116
www.suedsee-camp.de

Open (Touring Pitches):
All year.

Südsee-Camp in the Lüneburger Heide is a large, well organised holiday centre where children are especially well catered for. There are 726 touring pitches of varying types and sizes, 580 with electricity (4-10A), fresh water and drainage; 440 of these have a TV connection. Modern sanitary blocks are well maintained and contain all necessary facilities, including some areas specially built for children. Although centred around a large sandy shored lake, complete with shipwreck, the main swimming attraction is the South Sea Tropical swimming pool. A member of Leading Campings group.

Twelve modern, well maintained sanitary blocks with all the expected facilities, including those for disabled visitors and private bathrooms to rent. Special areas for children (Kinderland), facilities for babies. Laundry rooms. Kitchens. Bar (1/4-1/11). Shop, restaurants and takeaway (all year). Pool complex (on payment in high season). Fitness room. Bicycle and pedal car hire. High ropes adventure course. Jungle golf. Overnight parking outside site. WiFi over part of site (charged).

Ideal For...

- Kids
- Beach
- Dogs
- Year Round Camping
- Fishing
- Watersports

Scan me for more information.

16 accommodations
375 pitches
GPS: 52.48597, 7.99215
Post Code: D-49597

Rieste, Lower Saxony

Alfsee Ferien & Erholungspark

www.alanrogers.com/de30250
info@alfsee.de
054 649 2120
www.alfsee.de

Open (Touring Pitches):
All year.

Alfsee has plenty to offer for the active family and children of all ages. It is a really good base for enjoying the many recreational activities available here on the lake. The smaller lake has a 780 m. water ski cableway (on payment) and there is also a separate swimming area with a sandy beach. The Alfsee itself is now a nature reserve. Many birdwatching excursions are organised by the site. Improvements to this already well equipped site continue. There are now over 800 pitches (many long stay but with 375 for touring units) on flat grass, all with 16A electricity, with some shade for those in the original area. A new camping area provides 290 large pitches. A member of Leading Campings group.

Five excellent heated sanitary blocks with family bathrooms (to rent), baby rooms and laundry facilities. Cooking facilities. Dishwashers. Motorcaravan services. Gas supplies. Shop, restaurants and takeaway (high season). Watersports. Playground, new indoor play centre (on payment) and entertainment for children. Entertainment hall. Grass tennis courts. Trampoline. Minigolf. Go-kart track. Games room. Fishing. Bicycle and E-bike hire. Free WiFi throughout.

Ideal For...

Kids

Beach

Dogs

Year Round Camping

Fishing

Golf

Scan me for more information.

168 pitches
GPS: 53.114833, 8.832467
Post Code: D-28359

Bremen, Bremen

Hanse Camping

www.alanrogers.com/de30210
info@hansecamping.de
0421 3074 6825
www.hansecamping.de

Open (Touring Pitches):
All year.

Formerly known as Camping am Stadtwaldsee, this well designed and purpose built campsite overlooking a lake is ideally placed for those travelling to northern Europe and for people wishing to visit Bremen and places within the region. There is a bus stop outside the site. Of the 220 level pitches 168 are for touring units, standing on grass with openwork reinforcements at the entrances. All have electricity (16A), water and drainage. The pitches are positioned around the spacious grass-roofed sanitary block and are laid out in areas separated by trees and hedges. A restaurant/cafeteria with open-air terrace overlooks the lake.

Modern sanitary block with free hot showers, facilities for disabled visitors, five private bathrooms for rental. Washing machines and dryers. Motorcaravan services. Large, modern kitchen. Sitting/ dining room with LCD projector facilities. Small supermarket (1/3-31/12). Lakeside café/restaurant with terrace. Play room. Play area. Lake swimming, windsurfing, fishing and scuba diving (air tank refill facility on site). Tents for hire. WiFi (charged). Bicycle and go-kart hire.

Ideal For...

 Beach

 Dogs

 Year Round Camping

 Watersports

 Golf

 Play Area

Scan me for more information.

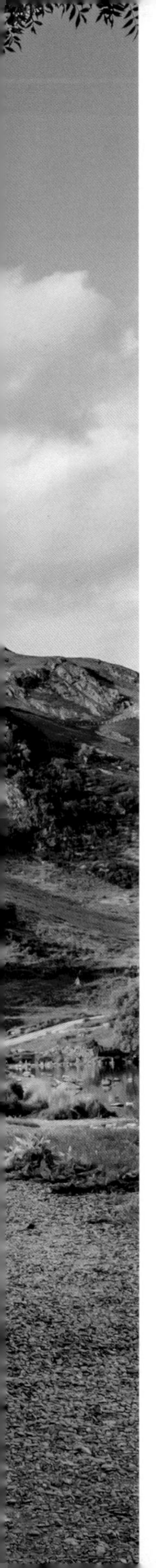

GREAT BRITAIN

The United Kingdom offers a wealth of extraordinary landscapes set against the backdrop of a rich and vibrant history. In terms of character and stunning scenery it offers an unsurpassed choice of holiday activities from coast to country.

Northern England
A beautiful and varied region of rolling hills and undulating moors, along with a wealth of industrial heritage and undiscovered countryside. The Yorkshire moors, the Cumbrian lakes, the Northumbrian ancient forts and fairytale castles, these are all highlights not to be missed.

Southern England
Rich in maritime heritage and historical attractions, the southern region comprises tranquil English countryside replete with picture postcard villages, ancient towns, formidable castles and grand stately homes, coupled with a beautiful coastline and lively seaside resorts.

Eastern England
A perfect mix of gentle countryside and sleepy storybook villages, it's an unspoilt region with endless skies, inland waterways and traditional beach resorts.

Western England
A region of contrasts, with windswept moorlands and dramatic cliffs towering above beautiful sandy beaches.

Wales
Land of ancient myths and Celtic legends, Wales boasts a diverse landscape, from lakes and mountains, rivers and valleys to beautiful coastlines and rolling wooded countryside.

Scotland
From gentle rolling hills and rugged coastlines, to dramatic peaks punctuated with beautiful lochs, Scotland is an untamed land steeped in history.

Northern Ireland
With a diversity of unspoilt landscapes, ranging from wild coastlines to green valleys, rugged mountains and shimmering lakes, to the natural phenomenon of the Giant's Causeway, Northern Ireland is crammed full of sights.

200 pitches
GPS: 50.44537, -4.94355
Post Code: TR9 6DB

Cornwall, South West

Trewan Hall Campsite

www.alanrogers.com/uk0305
enquiries@trewan-hall.co.uk
01637 880 261
www.trewan-hall.co.uk

Open (Touring Pitches):
11 May – 12 September.

Not so much camping as living in the gardens of a beautiful 350-year-old house. Trewan Hall's 36 acres have been slowly and carefully developed over 50 years by its owners and visitors cannot fail to be impressed by the idyllic setting. The modern facilities are housed mainly within the hall's former outbuildings, and the colourful, well maintained floral gardens are dispersed between the camping areas. The grassy, open plan pitches are set out in level fields with a minimum of six metres between each pitch, most of which are equipped with 10A electricity. Although the site never appears overcrowded, campers seeking an especially tranquil holiday might consider a visit in spring when the rhododendrons are in bloom, or in late summer.

Three modern, well maintained sanitary blocks with free controllable showers and provision for disabled visitors. Family shower rooms with baby changing area. Rooms with baths. Laundry with washing machines and dryers. Drying room. Well stocked shop in reception serves takeaway snacks. Large covered swimming pool (high season). Play area. Theatre with local entertainment for children (July/Aug). Games Rooms with table tennis tables and a Barn with a pool table for teenagers and adults. Library in part of the main house with free WiFi.

Ideal For...

 Kids

 Beach

 Dogs

 Fishing

 Watersports

 Walking

Scan me for more information.

110 pitches
GPS: 51.20484, -4.06417
Post Code: EX34 9SH

Devon, South West

Mill Park

www.alanrogers.com/uk0681
enquiries@millparklimited.com
01271 882647
www.millparklimited.com

Open (Touring Pitches):
31 March - 31 October.

Mill Park is a sheltered touring caravan and camping site set in an attractive wooded valley on the North Devon Coast. It has a shop, a takeaway, games room, laundry, and has many other useful facilities such as gas-changing and ice pack freezing. There is also an on-site pub. It's surrounded by attractive woodland and is an ideal family site as it's just a short walk to quiet beaches, both sand and pebble. Equally close by is the unspoilt and breathtaking beauty of Exmoor and the nearest village, Berrynarbor is just a five minute walk from the site. This village dates back from the sixteenth century and earlier. There is a quaint old country pub, village stores and post office. Buses also pass by the site regularly. They cater very well for families and couples and they do all possible to create a friendly relaxed atmosphere.

---

2 Separate shower blocks - both recently refurbished and kept impecably clean, onsite bar, well stocked shop, fishing lake, small river flowing through the park, childrens play area, games room, book swap, games library, free Internet in bar and games room. Close to beaches, secluded and quiet, very peaceful.

Ideal For...

 Kids

 Beach

 Dogs

 Fishing

 Watersports

 Golf

Scan me for more information.

5 accommodations
11 pitches
GPS: 51.16265, -1.89658
Post Code: SP3 4TQ

Wiltshire, South West

Stonehenge Campsite

www.alanrogers.com/uk1610
stay@stonehengecampsite.co.uk
07786 734732
www.stonehengecampsite.co.uk

Open (Touring Pitches):
10 February - 31 October.

Stonehenge Campsite & Glamping Pods is a small, very attractive family run park tucked away in the beautiful Wiltshire countryside, yet with easy access to the A303 and Stonehenge. There are 15 pitches (11 for touring) laid out in three separate areas. The 13 nearest reception, in a garden setting, are for caravans and motorcaravans, all with 16A electricity and ten on hardstandings. The 20 pitches for tents and small motorcaravans are around the edge of two large open meadows, 12 have 16A electricity. There is plenty of room in the meadows for children and adults to play games. Those with caravans and motorcaravans should phone ahead for availability.

Small, modern, heated toilet blocks near reception with some en-suite shower units. Family room. Washing machine/dryer. Very well appointed campers' kitchen. No facilities for disabled campers. Small shops with local produce. Takeaways deliver. WiFi over site (charged). Campfire pits for hire.

Ideal For...

 Beach

 Dogs

 Fishing

 Watersports

 Golf

 Pets Accepted

Scan me for more information.

Pure freedom at Lobb Fields

Natural beauty | Relaxation | Togetherness

Lobb Fields is a stunning south-facing caravan and camping park, just outside Braunton in North Devon. Perfect for all the best beaches; Saunton, Croyde, Putsborough and Woolacombe.

Friendly, always helpful staff and every facility you'd expect from a four star park... and more!

- Unlimited hot water showers
- Dog friendly
- Glamping tents available
- On-site surf hire
- Wi-Fi
- Children's play area
- Snack Shack delicious hot food
- Spectacular coastal views

www.lobbfields.com | T: 01271 812090 | E: info@lobbfields.com

10 accommodations
160 pitches
GPS: 51.632383, -0.038383
Post Code: N9 0AR

Edmonton, London

www.alanrogers.com/uk3230
edmontoncampsite@leevalleypark.org.uk
02088 036900
www.visitleevalley.org.uk

Open (Touring Pitches):
All year.

Lee Valley Camping Park

Certainly one of the only sites in this guide with a multiplex cinema just outside the gate, you are greeted here by a very attractive entrance with flower displays. The site offers 160 spacious level pitches, 44 with hardstanding and 100 with 10A electricity hook-ups. The pitches are well laid out around a large field and there is a tent area just behind two grassy mounds. The grass and gardens are well trimmed and kept very tidy. The site also offers hook-up points for tents. The adjacent sports complex has been rebuilt and was used for the 2012 Olympics.

Two modern, heated toilet blocks include spacious showers and two large en-suite units for disabled visitors. Baby changing area. All facilities are accessed by combination locks. Laundry. Motorcaravan services. Shop. Play area. Accommodation available to rent. WiFi throughout (charged).

Ideal For...

 Kids

 Dogs

 Year Round Camping

 Fishing

 Watersports

Golf

Scan me for more information.

300 pitches
GPS: 51.200725, 0.39333
Post Code: TN12 6PY

Kent, South East

The Hop Farm Campsite

www.alanrogers.com/uk3055
touring@thehopfarm.co.uk
01622 870838
www.thehopfarm.co.uk

Open (Touring Pitches):
1 March - 30 September.

Set in 400 acres of the Garden of England, The Hop Farm Touring & Camping Park is a popular family visitor attraction. There are plenty of activities to entertain children including adventure play areas (indoor and outdoor), a driving school, funfair rides, the Magic Factory and the Great Goblin Hunt. This is also the venue for many special events throughout the summer including music festivals, shows and other gatherings. To one side, and overlooking all this activity and the attractive cluster of oasts, is the touring park which provides over 300 grass and hardstanding pitches on flat, open fields. Electricity (16A) and water are available. There is also plenty more space for tents.

Brick built toilet block with open washbasins, preset showers (with curtain) and toilets. Further prefabricated units when the park is full for events. Small shop (in reception) for essentials. Free entry for campers and caravanners to the Family Park with restaurant and café. Nature walks. Boat launching. Fishing. Dogs accepted but not permitted inside the visitor attraction. Activities and entertainment at the visitor attraction.

Ideal For...

 Kids

 Beach

 Dogs

 Fishing

 Golf

 Play Area

Scan me for more information.

6 accommodations
160 pitches
GPS: 52.44636, 1.02514
Post Code: NR16 2HE

Norfolk, East of England

Applewood Country Park

www.alanrogers.com/uk3385
info@applewoodholidays.co.uk
01953 715319
www.applewoodholidays.co.uk

Open (Touring Pitches):
01 February - 31 October

Whether you're looking to explore Norfolk's many historic sights and lively market towns, set out for an adventure to take in the beautiful countryside and stunning coastline or simply want to relax, Applewood Countryside Park is your perfect choice of campsite. A tranquil, family-friendly caravan park and campsite set within 13-acres of grassy parkland, it caters for touring caravans, motorhomes, tents, glampers, rally groups and clubs. Spacious pitches with electric hook up are separated by mature laurel hedges allowing plenty of privacy. The park then has a large central area with unmarked pitches for those who do not need electricity. There is a further area with pitches which can be booked exclusively and a large field too, perfect for rallies and larger groups. Six glamping pods are also available for hire.

Two toilet blocks, one new and one refurbished, provide clean and adequate facilities. Exclusive hook-up points and shower and toilet facilities for disabled visitors. Washing machine and dryer. Gas supplies. Rally field. Children's play area. Free WiFi. Dogs welcome at no extra charge. Secure storage facility. Function room.

Ideal For...

 Kids

 Beach

 Dogs

 Fishing

 Walking

 Golf

Scan me for more information.

87 pitches
GPS: 53.5888, -3.044
Post Code: PR8 3ST

Mersey, North West

Willowbank Touring Park

www.alanrogers.com/uk5360
info@willowbankcp.co.uk
01704 571566
www.willowbankcp.co.uk

Open (Touring Pitches):
14 February - 31 January.

Well situated for the Sefton coast and Southport, Willowbank Holiday Home & Touring Park is set on the edge of sand dunes amongst mature, wind swept trees. Entrance to the park is controlled by a barrier, with a pass-key issued at the excellent reception building which doubles as a sales office for the substantial, high quality caravan holiday home development. There are 79 touring pitches, 30 on gravel hardstandings, 16 on grass and a further 33 pitches, all with 10A electricity; these are on grass hardstanding using an environmentally friendly reinforcement system. Large units are accepted by prior arrangement.

The purpose built, heated toilet block is of a high standard including an excellent bathroom for disabled visitors, although the showers are rather compact. Baby room. Laundry. Motorcaravan services. Play area. Field for ball games. Beauty treatments. WiFi throughout (charged).

Ideal For...

 Beach

 Dogs

 Fishing

 Watersports

 Walking

Golf

Scan me for more information.

55 accommodations
245 pitches
GPS: 53.09725, -0.20219
Post Code: LN4 4LR

Lincolnshire, Heart of England

Tattershall Lakes

www.alanrogers.com/uk3685
tattershall.holidays@away-resorts.com
01526 348800
www.tattershall-lakes.com

Open (Touring Pitches):
1 March - 31 October.

Tattershall Lakes Country Park is an extensive park with seven lakes of varying sizes offering opportunities for enthusiasts of watersports and fishing. The pleasant village of Tattershall is within walking distance. The touring fields are flat with views across the main lake. There are 245 pitches, numbered but with no markings to separate them; all have 16A electrical connections and 25 also have individual taps, drainage & hardstanding. Ten tent pitches are on a small peninsula in the lake. Fifty-five lodges and static caravans for rent with a further 437 in private ownership.

Toilet block with preset showers and open-style washbasins can be busy. En-suite unit for disabled visitors. Washing machines and dryers. Two additional prefabricated units provide very basic en-suite units (shower, toilet, washbasin). Small, well stocked shop. Coffee shop serving meals, snacks and takeaways. Comfortable bar with discos and entertainment. Upstairs bar overlooking the lake has a TV, electronic games and darts. Water-skiing and jet-ski lakes. Four fishing lakes. Golf course. Archery. Bicycle and pedalo hire. Full programme of activities and entertainment for all ages. Brand new indoor swimming pool and spa complex, complete with lake view hot tubs. Artificial beach. Outdoor entertainment area with floating stage and amphitheatre style seating. All facilities available all season. WiFi (free).

Ideal For...

 Beach

 Dogs

 Fishing

 Watersports

 Golf

 Play Area

Scan me for more information.

35 pitches
GPS: 54.0797, -1.0166
Post Code: YO60 6QP

North Yorkshire, Yorkshire

York Meadows Caravan Park

www.alanrogers.com/uk4605
reception@
yorkmeadowscaravanpark.com
01347 878508
www.yorkmeadowscaravanpark.com

Open (Touring Pitches):
1 March - 31 October.

Set in a grassy meadow, this newly created park is surrounded by farmland, half a mile from Sherriff Hutton with its two pubs and village shops. A total of 70 pitches are available, 35 of which are for touring, 30 with hardstanding and electricity (16A) and five super pitches with hardstanding and all services. A further area has room for 38 tents, some with electricity. These are separated from the touring section by trees and a children's play area. The park is a haven for wildlife with trees and meadows all around. It is very peaceful here yet within easy reach to visit the historic city of York, just eight miles away.

The heated toilet facilities are in a single block along with reception and provide a mix of washbasins in cubicles and open vanity units. Separate shower room for disabled visitors. Laundry facilities. Small shop in reception selling essentials. Slides, swings and a zip wire frame for children (safety surface). WiFi (free but limited reception). Max. 2 dogs.

Ideal For...

 Dogs

 Fishing

 Golf

 Play Area

 Disabled Facilities

 Pets Accepted

Scan me for more information.

90 pitches
GPS: 54.209333, -1.073783
Post Code: YO62 5YQ

North Yorkshire, Yorkshire

www.alanrogers.com/uk4560
reception@
goldensquarecaravanpark.com
01439 788269
www.goldensquarecaravanpark.com

Open (Touring Pitches):
1 March - 31 October.

Golden Square Camping Park

Golden Square Caravan & Camping Park is a popular, high quality, family-owned park. An exceptionally attractive caravan park has been created from an old quarry with a number of separate, level bays that have superb views over the North Yorkshire Moors. The pitches are individually marked with car parking alongside. In very dry weather the ground can be hard so rock pegs would be needed (even in wet weather the park is well drained). All pitches have 10A electricity, 24 have drainage and six are deluxe pitches (with waste water, sewerage, electricity, water and TV aerial connections). There are some seasonal pitches and holiday caravan homes for sale.

Two stone-built toilet blocks are first rate, modern and well equipped with underfloor heating, with some washbasins in private cubicles. Showers are free. Bathroom (£1) also houses baby facilities. Both ladies and men have full facilities for disabled visitors. Laundry facilities. Motorcaravan services. Tourist information room also houses a microwave. Well stocked shop. Two excellent play areas. Games field and a barn with games. Bicycle hire. All year caravan storage. CCTV. WiFi throughout (charged).

Ideal For...

 Dogs

 Fishing

 Golf

 Play Area

 Disabled Facilities

 Pets Accepted

Scan me for more information.

15 accommodations
65 pitches
GPS: 54.5931, -3.112583
Post Code: CA12 4TE

Keswick, Cumbria

Castlerigg Hall Camping Park

www.alanrogers.com/uk5660
info@castlerigg.co.uk
01768 774499
www.castlerigg.co.uk

Open (Touring Pitches):
12 March - 7 November.

Castlerigg Hall Caravan & Camping Park is a well laid out park that was started in the late 1950s by the Jackson family, who over the years have developed and improved the site whilst maintaining its character. Good use has been made of the traditional stone buildings to house the reception and shop, whilst another building houses a modern amenity block along with a really excellent campers' kitchen. Gently sloping with some shelter, the 120 pitches have fine views across Keswick, Derwentwater and the western Fells. Each terrace has a maximum of eight pitches with 10/16A electricity and almost all with water and drainage. The 65 hardstanding pitches, 52 of which are fully serviced, overlook the lake.

The main toilet block is beautifully fitted out, fully tiled and heated, with showers, vanity style washbasins (2 in cabins) and hair care areas. Unit for disabled visitors (key). Baby area. Two other toilet blocks are older in style but newly decorated and clean. Fully equipped laundry and dishwashing area. Sitting room and campers' kitchen with microwave, toasters, kettle and hot plates. Restaurant with locally sourced food. Reception houses tourist information and a well stocked shop (with gas). WiFi (free). Arts and crafts gallery.

Ideal For...

 Beach

 Dogs

 Fishing

 Watersports

 Walking

 Golf

Scan me for more information.

9 accommodations
151 pitches
GPS: 53.09513, -4.18802
Post Code: LL54 7YY

Gwynedd, North Wales

Bryn Gloch Camping Park

www.alanrogers.com/uk6600
eurig@bryngloch.co.uk
01286 650216
www.northwalescamping.co.uk

Open (Touring Pitches):
All year, limited facilities 1 November - 28 February.

Bryn Gloch Caravan & Camping Park is a tranquil, well maintained, family owned touring park in the impressive Snowdonia area. An unusual feature is the mountain railway which runs along one side of the park. Six flat, spacious meadows accommodate 231 units and afford some breathtaking views of the surrounding landscape. Tarmac access roads serve 151 touring pitches with 131 having hardstandings, 10A electricity, water and drainage. In addition, there are four caravan holiday homes and 24 serviced pitches for tents. The park has a barbecue and picnic area, a children's play area, and a large field for ball games, dog walks and fishing borders the river.

Two very clean, modern main toilet blocks include washbasins in cabins, large showers, a heated family bathroom (hot water £1), baby room and complete facilities for visitors with disabilities (coded access). The far field has a prefabricated unit containing all facilities, for use in peak season. Well equipped laundry and separate drying room. Motorcaravan services and car wash. Shop (1/3-31/10). TV and games rooms with computer and pool tables. Minigolf. Entrance barrier (code). WiFi throughout (free). Dog walks.

Ideal For...

 Beach

 Dogs

 Year Round Camping

 Fishing

 Watersports

 Golf

Scan me for more information.

6 accommodations
120 pitches
GPS: 52.17121, -3.31621
Post Code: LD1 5RT

Powys, Mid Wales

Fforest Fields Camping Park

www.alanrogers.com/uk6320
office@fforestfields.co.uk
01982 570406
www.fforestfields.co.uk

Open (Touring Pitches):
1 March - 3 January.

Fforest Fields Caravan & Camping Park is a secluded park is set on a family hill farm within seven acres in the heart of Radnorshire. This is simple country camping and caravanning at its best, with no clubhouse, swimming pool or games room. The facilities include 80 large pitches on level grass on a spacious and peaceful, carefully landscaped field by a stream. Electrical connections (6-16A) are available and there are 17 hardstanding pitches, also with electricity. Several additional areas without electricity are provided for tents. There are two new lakes, one for boating and fly fishing, the other for coarse fishing.

The toilet block is spotlessly clean and has underfloor heating, family rooms, drying rooms, laundry, and spacious controllable showers. Reception stocks essentials. Room for campers with fridges and freezers, microwave, table and chairs. Fishing. Torches are useful. Free WiFi over site.

Ideal For...

 Beach

 Dogs

 Fishing

 Watersports

 Golf

 Disabled Facilities

Scan me for more information.

70 pitches
GPS: 51.99325, -3.78023
Post Code: SA20 0RD

Carmarthenshire, West Wales

Erwlon Caravan & Camping Park

www.alanrogers.com/uk5955
enquiries@erwlon.co.uk
01550 721021
www.erwlon.co.uk

Open (Touring Pitches):
All year.

Just outside Llandovery and on the edge of the Brecon Beacons National Park, Erwlon is an attractive and welcoming campsite. Of the 110 pitches, seven are used for privately owned caravan holiday homes, 33 have seasonal caravans and 70 are for touring units. Fifty are on hardstanding with electricity connections and 12 have water and drainage as well. There is a flat field for tents at the bottom of the park with some electrical outlets; an open-sided, covered area for eating, food preparation and bicycle storage is at the planning stage. The site has a relaxed atmosphere where consideration for others minimises the need for formal rules.

New heated toilet block with washbasins in cabins, four family rooms (basin, shower, toilet) and a room for families and disabled visitors which includes a baby unit. Combined, well equipped laundry and dishwashing room. Motorcaravan services. Fridge freezer. Fishing. WiFi over site (charged).

Ideal For...

 Beach

 Dogs

Year Round Camping

 Fishing

 Walking

 Golf

Scan me for more information.

25 accommodations
107 pitches
GPS: 51.872983, -5.2569
Post Code: SA62 6QT

Pembrokeshire, West Wales

www.alanrogers.com/uk5995
info@caerfaibay.co.uk
01437 720274
www.caerfaibay.co.uk

Open (Touring Pitches):
1 March - 11 November.

Caerfai Bay Camping Park

Caerfai Bay Caravan & Tent Park is located near to St Davids, Britain's smallest city, noted for its cathedral and Bishop's Palace. This cliff-top park, just a 15 minute walk from St Davids, has direct access to the Pembrokeshire Coastal Path and a magnificent sandy beach. Family-run with an emphasis on peace, quiet and relaxation, the perfect spot for walkers, rock climbers, water sports enthusiasts, star gazers & wildlife lovers. There are 107 touring pitches (inc.78 for tents) and 59 electric hook-ups (10A), & 33 hardstandings. The site is spread over three open fields with magnificent seaviews, one for caravans and motorhomes with hardstanding and electric as well as accommodation to rent; two for tents with some electric points. Main access roads are tarmac.

Three main buildings house the sanitary facilities (two are heated), one by reception contains facilities for disabled visitors and families, dishwashing, laundry, cooking facilities (hot plate, microwave and fridge). A small block offers 3 unisex cubicles (WC and basin). The third, in the tent field, includes 4 family rooms, dishwashing, microwave, fridge, toaster, wet suit washing and drying area. Motorcaravan services. Bicycle storage. Gas. Dog walking area (dogs not accepted in the tent field in high season). WiFi (charged). Secure charging points for phones/tablets. Lounge with tourist information, maps & book exchange.

Ideal For...

 Beach

 Dogs

 Fishing

 Watersports

 Walking

 Golf

Scan me for more information.

8 accommodations
80 pitches
GPS: 54.840183, -4.26015
Post Code: DG7 2ET

Dumfries and Galloway,
Lowlands

Mossyard Caravan Park

www.alanrogers.com/uk6890
enquiry@mossyard.co.uk
01557 840226
www.mossyard.co.uk

Open (Touring Pitches):
End March - 31 October

Mossyard is a family run park set within a working farm right beside the sea in a sheltered bay. The park and farmhouse appear together suddenly over the horizon as you approach, with some breathtaking views across the Solway where the Galloway Hills and the waters of Fleet Bay meet. There are 37 grass touring pitches, 12 for caravans and motorcaravans on an elevated area that slopes in parts. The remaining 25 pitches for any unit are on a level field which adjoins the beach. There are dishwashing and toilet facilities on the lower field. Electrical connections (16A) are available to all.

Some of the farm buildings around the main farmhouse have been utilised for the sanitary facilities, which are of traditional design. Showers are coin-operated (20p). Roomy facilities for disabled visitors can also be used as a family bathroom. Purpose built building with laundry, dishwashing area and information room with freezer and fridge for visitors' use. No shop, but supermarkets deliver.

Ideal For...

 Beach

 Dogs

 Fishing

 Watersports

 Walking

 Golf

Scan me for more information.

5 accommodations
60 pitches
GPS: 55.91104, -3.43588
Post Code: EH53 0HT

Edinburgh, Heart of Scotland

www.alanrogers.com/uk7045
queries@linwater.co.uk
01313 333326
www.linwater.co.uk

Open (Touring Pitches):
Open all Year from March 2017.

Linwater Caravan Park

Linwater Caravan Park is a peaceful, family run park situated on farmland close to Edinburgh. They offer a variety of accomodation including 60 large pitches for caravans, motorhomes and tents (a mixture of grass and hardstanding including 44 with 16A electricity connections); plus glamping units known as timber tents and a luxury self catering lodge. The site has an immaculately presented amenities block with toilets; privacy cublicles with wash basins; shower facilities; laundry and dish washing facilities as well as a diabled toilet and baby changing area.There is a chemical waste disposal area which is also suitable for drive over disposals of motorhomes. The site has a shop which sells the basics just in case you have forgotten anything, and new for 2017 is a playpark for the kids to enjoy.

Scandiavian style amenities block with showers, private washing cubicles, baby changing, limited access ablution room and laundry. Chemical waste disposal area. Shop in reception with basic food supplies and tourist information. Takeaways from local village will deiver to pitch. Play area with climbing frame and swings suitable for children up to 12 years old. River fishing available (trout and coarse). Dog walk. Free internet and Wifi access.

Ideal For...

 Kids

 Dogs

 Fishing

 Watersports

 Golf

 Play Area

Scan me for more information.

25 accommodations
250 pitches
GPS: 56.767039, -3.845791
Post Code: PH18 5SR

Perth and Kinross, Heart of Scotland

Blair Castle Caravan Park

www.alanrogers.com/uk7300
mail@blaircastlecaravanpark.co.uk
01796 481263
www.blaircastlecaravanpark.co.uk

Open (Touring Pitches):
23 February - 26 November.

This attractive, well kept park is set in the grounds of Blair Castle, the traditional home of the Dukes of Atholl. It has a wonderful feeling of spaciousness with a large central area left free for children's play or for general use. There is space for 250 touring units, all with 10/16A electricity connections, 63 with hardstanding and 44 fully serviced pitches with water and waste water facilities. Caravan holiday homes, 85 privately owned and 18 for hire, are in separate areas along with five woodland lodges also available for hire. A quality park, quiet at night and well managed. The castle is open to the public, its 30 fully furnished rooms showing a picture of Scottish life from the 12th century to the present day, while the beautiful grounds and gardens are free to those staying on site.

The five toilet blocks can be heated and are of excellent quality and very clean. Large hot showers, some incorporating WC and washbasin, and further cubicles with WC and washbasin. Facilities for disabled visitors. Baby changing. Laundry. Motorcaravan services. Shop. Beauty treatments and hair salon. Games room and Internet gallery. WiFi throughout. Gas supplies. American motorhomes are accepted (eight pitches available, length up to 20 m. or 5 tons).Glamping style pods are available to rent.

Ideal For...

 Beach

 Dogs

 Fishing

Watersports

 Golf

 Play Area

Scan me for more information.

3 accommodations
60 pitches
GPS: 57.45205, -2.7916
Post Code: AB54 4UJ

Aberdeenshire, Grampian

Huntly Castle Caravan Park

www.alanrogers.com/uk7550
enquiries@huntlycastle.co.uk
01466 794999
www.huntlycastle.co.uk

Open (Touring Pitches):
31 March - 29 October.

Huntly Caravan Park was opened in '95 and its hardworking owners, the Ballantynes, are justly proud of their neat, well landscaped 15-acre site that is affiliated to the Caravan Club (non-members welcome). The 10 level grass and 50 hardstanding touring pitches are separated and numbered, with everyone shown to their pitch. Arranged in three bays with banks of heathers and flowering shrubs separating them, most pitches have 16A electrical hook-ups and 15 are fully serviced with water and waste water. Two bays have central play areas and all three have easy access to a toilet block, as has the camping area.

The three heated toilet blocks are well designed and maintained, with washbasins (in cubicles for ladies) and large showers. Each block also has a family shower room, dishwashing sinks and a room for disabled visitors. Laundry room. Milk and papers may be ordered at reception. WiFi (charged).

Ideal For...

 Beach

 Dogs

 Fishing

 Golf

 Play Area

 Disabled Facilities

Scan me for more information.

50 pitches
GPS: 57.578569, -4.118101
Post Code: IV10 8RX

Highlands and Islands, Highland

www.alanrogers.com/uk7663
fortrosebaycampsite@gmail.com
01381 621927
www.fortrosebaycampsite.co.uk

Open (Touring Pitches):

Fortrose Bay Campsite

Located on the shores of the Moray Firth, Fortrose Bay campsite is equipped with all the basic amenities. The ownership of the site changed in 2015 and whilst some of the facilities are old, they are kept in perfect condition.The new owners are currently working to improve the site facilities including the addition of a brand new shower unit.

The campsite is licensed as a seasonal touring site with 50 pitches. Electric Hookups are available (16amps.) The two spotless toilet blocks are fitted with electric razor points and hairdryer sockets. The kitchen and laundry area has sinks and a microwave along with clothes washing and drying facilities. Chemical waste and grey water disposal areas can be found througout the site. Well behaved dogs are welcome.

Ideal For...

 Beach

 Dogs

 Fishing

 Watersports

 Walking

 Golf

Scan me for more information.

50 pitches
GPS: 55.194019, -6.518764
Post Code: BT57 8TN

Bushmills, Co. Antrim

www.alanrogers.com/uk8360
info@ballynesscaravanpark.com
028 2073 2393
www.ballynesscaravanpark.com

Open (Touring Pitches):
16 March - 1 November.

Ballyness Caravan Park

Ballyness is immaculately cared for and is designed with conservation in mind. In keeping with the surrounding countryside, it is extensively planted with native trees and shrubs. A pathway encircles several ponds which attract local wildlife and birds. The overall appearance of this eight-hectare park with its black stone pillared entrance gate and broad tarmac drive is attractive. There are 50 hardstanding pitches all with electricity (16A), water and drainage. Privately owned caravan holiday homes are placed away from the touring pitches.

One spotlessly clean and well decorated, cottage-style heated sanitary block (key coded). Facilities for disabled visitors (toilet and shower). Shop for basic food supplies, gas and camping essentials. Family room with bath. Games and TV room. Laundry room. Play area and play park. Motorhome Service area. Dedicated dog walk. Free WiFi throughout.

Ideal For...

 Beach

 Dogs

 Fishing

 Watersports

 Golf

 Play Area

Scan me for more information.

GREECE

Greece is made up of clusters of islands with idyllic sheltered bays and coves, golden stretches of sand and coastal caves with volcanic black sand. Its rugged landscape is a monument to nature with dramatic gorges, lakes, rivers and waterfalls.

Nestling between the waters of the Aegean, Ionian and Mediterranean seas, Greece has over 13,000 km of coastline. A largely mountainous country, its backbone is formed from the Pindus range, which extends as far as Crete, the largest of Greece's 6,000 islands, themselves peaks of the now submerged landmass of Aegeis.

Mount Olympus, known from Greek mythology as the abode of the gods, is the highest mountain (2,917 m).

The Greek islands have something to offer every visitor – the vibrant nightlife of Mykonos, the 'honeymoon' island of Santorini; Rhodes, where the modern city sits alongside the medieval citadel, and Corfu with its Venetian and French influences. The mainland is home to some of the most important archaeological sites, including the Acropolis, the Parthenon and Delphi.

Language: Greek
Capital: Athens
Currency: Euro (€)
Time Zone: Central European Time (GMT/UTC plus one hour)
Telephone Country Code: 00 30
Tourist Office: www.gnto.co.uk

Public Holidays
New Year's Day 1 Jan; Epiphany 6 Jan; Shrove Monday Orthodox Easter; Independence Day 25 Mar; Easter: Good Friday, Easter Sunday and Easter Monday (Orthodox); Whit Sunday and Monday (Orthodox); Assumption Day 15 Aug; Ochi Day (National Fest) 28 Oct; Christmas 25-26Dec.

Motoring
Speed limits are 100-120 km/h on highways unless otherwise stated; 50 km/h in residential areas unless otherwise marked. An international driver's licence is required. Road signs are written in Greek and repeated phonetically in English. Road tolls exist on two highways in Greece, one leading to Northern Greece and the other to the Peloponnese.

2 accommodations
100 pitches
GPS: 38.478533, 22.474733
Post Code: GR-33054

Central Greece, Centre

Camping Delphi

www.alanrogers.com/gr8520
info@delphicamping.com
226 508 2209
www.delphicamping.com

Open (Touring Pitches):
1 April - 15 October.

Camping Delphi enjoys a stunning location on the slopes of Mount Parnassus, just four kilometres from ancient Delphi. There are some truly outstanding views over valleys of olive groves across to the Gulf of Corinth. The site's 100 fairly level pitches all offer electricity connections (10A) and some benefit from the great views. This is a well managed and well equipped site with an attractive pool and a friendly bar featuring an exhibition of paintings by Avyeris Kanatas, a former owner of the site. The prevailing ambience here is geared towards a peaceful, relaxing stay.

Two toilet blocks, one modern and one refurbished. Facilities for disabled visitors. Washing machine. Motorcaravan services. Shop, bar and restaurant (1/5-30/9). Internet café. Swimming pool. Tennis. Play area. Max. 1 dog. WiFi throughout (free).

Ideal For...

 Beach

 Dogs

 Play Area

 Disabled Facilities

 Pets Accepted

 Bar on Site

Scan me for more information.

35 accommodations
120 pitches
GPS: 39.310267, 23.109783
Post Code: GR-38500

Thessaly, Centre

Camping Sikia

www.alanrogers.com/gr8280
info@camping-sikia.gr
242 302 2279
www.camping-sikia.gr

Open (Touring Pitches):
1 April - 31 October.

Camping Sikia is an attractive, well maintained site enthusiastically run by the Pandelfi family. The site offers 120 pitches of varying sizes all with 16A electricity. They are arranged on terraces and may become quite dusty during the dry season, but most are well shaded by olive trees. There are superb views from many pitches – the sea to the south and the mountains to the north. Rental accommodation is also available. The calm sea and golden beaches of the Pagasitikos Gulf make this a perfect spot for family holidays. The site is just 100 m. from a sand and shingle beach on the edge of a rocky bay.

Two modern and one refurbished sanitary blocks with British style WCs, open washbasins and preset showers. Separate facilities for disabled visitors. Laundry area with sinks, washing machines and ironing facilities. Shop. Bar. TV room. Restaurant. Communal barbecue areas. Fishing. Dogs are not allowed on the beach. Internet corner. WiFi throughout (free).

Ideal For...

 Beach

 Dogs

 Fishing

 Watersports

 Play Area

 Disabled Facilities

Scan me for more information.

10 accommodations
120 pitches
GPS: 39.310833, 23.1091
Post Code: GR-38500

Thessaly, Centre

Camping Hellas International

www.alanrogers.com/gr8285
info@campinghellas.gr
242 302 2267
www.campinghellas.gr

Open (Touring Pitches):
All year.

There is a warm welcome from the English-speaking brother and sister team who own and run Camping Hellas. The campsite has been in the family since the sixties, when tourists first asked if they could camp overnight and use the facilities of the taverna. It is in a beautiful setting in a 500-year-old olive grove, right next to the beach and the calm blue waters of the Pagasitikos gulf. There are around 120 pitches all with 16A electricity. Pitch sizes vary and some parts are more level than others, but shade is plentiful thanks to the olive trees.

One modern and one old sanitary block, both very clean with British style toilets and open washbasins. Very good facilities for disabled visitors. Laundry room with sinks and washing machines, ironing facilities. Motorcaravan services. Shop, bar, restaurant and takeaway from 1 May. TV room. Dogs are not allowed on the beach. WiFi over site (free).

Ideal For...

 Beach

 Dogs

Year Round Camping

 Watersports

 Disabled Facilities

 Pets Accepted

Scan me for more information.

10 accommodations
66 pitches
GPS: 38.00861, 23.67194
Post Code: GR-12136

Attica, South

Camping Athens

www.alanrogers.com/gr8590
info@campingathens.com.gr
210 581 4114
www.campingathens.com.gr

Open (Touring Pitches):
All year.

Camping Athens is an all-year site, located to the west of the city and convenient for visiting Athens. The site prides itself on friendly Greek hospitality and offers 66 touring pitches, all with 16A electricity connections. The pitches are of a reasonable size and are generally well shaded. Smaller pitches are available for tents. The two toilet blocks are of modern design and well maintained. To visit the city, there is a bus stop opposite the site entrance. The site's restaurant is most welcoming after a day's sightseeing, and a selection of Greek starters, helped along by cool wine, can be thoroughly recommended.

Two modern toilet blocks. Washing machines. Shop. Bar. Takeaway food and restaurant (all May-Oct). Excursions can be arranged. Barbecues and open fires are forbidden. Free WiFi over site.

Ideal For...

 Beach

 Dogs

Year Round Camping

 Golf

 Pets Accepted

Scan me for more information.

5 accommodations
GPS: 38.09943, 23.79175
Post Code: GR-14564

Attica, South

www.alanrogers.com/gr8595
camping@hol.gr
210 807 5579
www.camping-neakifissia.gr/

Open (Touring Pitches):
All year.

Camping Nea Kifissia

Many visitors to Greece will want to spend some time in Athens, the capital. Camping Nea Kifissia offers one of the best opportunities to do that, being in a quiet location with easy access. A small site, run personally by the Komianidou family, there are 66 level pitches, some with shade, in well kept grounds. A regular bus service runs to the Kifissia metro station for fast and regular transport to all the sights. The Acropolis, Parthenon and the Porch of Caryatids are essential viewing, as are the many museums. Athens' shops and the flea market near Monastiraki also have much to offer.

A centrally positioned toilet block includes showers, WCs and washbasins. Washing machine. Bar and coffee shop (1/6-15/9). Swimming pool (1/6-15/9). WiFi over site (free). Communal barbecue area. English spoken in reception.

Ideal For...

 Dogs

Year Round Camping

 Pets Accepted

 Bar on Site

Scan me for more information.

30 accommodations
210 pitches
GPS: 37.836617, 21.1338
Post Code: GR-27050

Peloponnese, South

www.alanrogers.com/gr8330
ionionfl@otenet.gr
262 309 6828
camping.ionion-beach.gr

Open (Touring Pitches):
All year.

Camping Ionion Beach

This is a very attractive and well kept site in a beautiful location by the Ionian Sea, created from former farmland by the Fligos family. Much has changed since they welcomed their first guests in 1982, when they still left plenty of space for growing potatoes. Now it is a modern site with a large pool and a paddling pool and two blocks of apartments to rent. Separated by a variety of trees and oleander bushes, there are 210 pitches of 80-100 sq.m, all with 16A electricity. Those at the front of the site enjoy views over the sea and the island of Zakinthos.

Three excellent sanitary blocks with British style WCs, and showers with washbasins in cabins. Facilities for disabled campers. Motorcaravan services. Turkish style chemical disposal point. Laundry room. Shop, bar, restaurant (1/4-30/10). Swimming pool (no depth markings) and paddling pool (1/5-31/10). Excellent play area. WiFi over site (charged).

Ideal For...

 Beach

 Dogs

Year Round Camping

 Watersports

 Play Area

 Disabled Facilities

Scan me for more information.

5 accommodations
71 pitches
GPS: 36.72817, 22.54614
Post Code: GR-23200

Peloponnese, South

www.alanrogers.com/gr8685
info@gythiocamping.gr
273 302 2522
www.gythiocamping.gr

Open (Touring Pitches):
1 January - 31 October.

Camping Gythion Bay

Camping Gythion Bay is in the Peloponnese, three kilometres west of Gythion town on the road to Areopolis. It has 71 unmarked pitches set amongst orange, fig, olive and pine trees, all with 16A electricity. Some trees limit access but the owner is dealing with this to improve the site. Indeed he has also been busy refurbishing the toilets, showers and other facilities. With a good beach alongside the site, there are good opportunities for windsurfing and storage for boards is available. This is a good starting point for excursions to the Caves of Diros and for wider exploration of Lakonia and especially Inner and Outer Mani and Sparta.

Four toilet blocks (totally renovated) include British and Turkish style WCs plus facilities for disabled visitors. Laundry with washing machines. Motorcaravan services. Small shop (1/6-15/9) including gas. Bar, restaurant and takeaway (1/6-30/9). Outdoor swimming pool. Play area. Fishing, windsurfing and limited boat launching. Small beach. Free WiFi over part of site.

Ideal For...

 Beach

 Dogs

 Fishing

 Watersports

 Play Area

 Disabled Facilities

Scan me for more information.

39 accommodations
200 pitches
GPS: 37.53202, 22.89165
Post Code: GR-21060

Peloponnese, South

Camping Triton II

www.alanrogers.com/gr8635
info@tritonii.gr
27 52 09 21 28
www.tritonii.gr

Open (Touring Pitches):
All year.

What do we look for in a good campsite in Greece? Given the excellent Greek weather, the answer is probably a good, flat pitch with some shade, excellent toilets and showers that are spotlessly clean, a small shop and proximity to a beach and local tavernas. Well, here you have it all! This is an exceptional and well managed site with 200 touring pitches (50-120 sq.m, 16A electricity) under high screens, just across the road from Drepano beach. Local tavernas are within strolling distance and the town's shops are about a mile away.

Excellent refurbished toilet blocks include showers, WCs and washbasins. Baby bath. Facilities for disabled visitors. Laundry with washing machines and ironing board. Electric hobs for cooking. Fridge and freezer. Small shop (1/5-30/9). Play area. WiFi over site (free). Tropical Village bungalows to rent.

Ideal For...

 Dogs

Year Round Camping

 Fishing

 Play Area

 Pets Accepted

Scan me for more information.

5 accommodations
40 pitches
GPS: 37.64317, 21.61975
Post Code: GR-27065

Peloponnese, South

Camping Alphios

www.alanrogers.com/gr8340
alphios@otenet.gr
262 402 2951

Open (Touring Pitches):
1 April - 15 October.

High above ancient and modern Olympia, Camping Alphios enjoys spectacular views, both across the adjoining countryside and to the coast at Pyrgos. It provides 97 pitches, 40 for tourers, all with 16A electricity and many with high reed screens that provide shade. Olympia is a popular tourist destination with dozens of coaches each day bringing tourists from around the world to this small town and the adjacent archaeological sites. However, the area also offers opportunities for walking and cycling in some wonderful scenery and this site provides a good base for excursions to the surrounding northern Peloponnese countryside.

Two toilet blocks include showers, WCs and washbasins. Two kitchens with sinks, electric hobs and fridges. Laundry with washing machines. Small shop. Bar and restaurant (1/5-15/10). Small swimming pool. WiFi over site (free).

Ideal For...

 Dogs

 Pets Accepted

 Bar on Site

Scan me for more information.

6 accommodations
95 pitches
GPS: 39.686272, 19.838511
Post Code: GR-49100

Ionian Islands, Islands

www.alanrogers.com/gr8375
campco@otenet.gr
266 109 3595
www.kardacamp.gr

Open (Touring Pitches):
15 April - 6 October.

Camping Karda Beach

The popular holiday island of Corfu offers many sporting and leisure activities and access to it is easy, and comparatively cheap, via one of the many ferries from either Igoumenitsa or one of the Italian ports serving the Greek mainland. Camping Karda Beach offers a quiet low season site with excellent facilities, close to the beach and the island's main town, Kerkyra. It also offers a popular high season site for families and those looking for good weather, good beaches and lots of activities close at hand. It has 101 good grassy pitches of which 95 are for touring units, all with electricity (16A Europlug), under tall trees.

Three excellent toilet blocks include showers, WCs and washbasins. Facilities for disabled visitors. Fridges. Laundry. Bar, small shop and restaurant (open all day, 1/5-30/9). Swimming pool with sunbeds (1/5-5/10). Play area and pool. Bungalows to rent. WiFi on part of site (free).

Ideal For...

 Beach

 Dogs

 Fishing

 Watersports

 Golf

 Play Area

Scan me for more information.

IRELAND

Ireland is made up of four provinces: Connaught, Leinster, Munster and Ulster, comprising 32 counties, 26 of which lie in the Republic of Ireland.

Famed for its folklore, traditional music and friendly hospitality, the Republic of Ireland offers spectacular scenery contained within a relatively compact area. With plenty of beautiful areas to discover, and a relaxed pace of life, it is an ideal place to unwind.

Ireland is the perfect place to indulge in a variety of outdoor pursuits while taking in the glorious scenery. There are plenty of waymarked footpaths which lead through woodlands, across cliffs, past historical monuments and over rolling hills. The dramatic coastline, with its headlands, secluded coves and sandy beaches, is fantastic for watersports.

The Cliffs of Moher, in particular, is a prime location for birdwatching and Goat Island, just offshore, is where puffins make their nesting burrows. Fishing is also popular with plenty of opportunity in the numerous streams, rivers, canals and hidden lakes.

In the south the beautiful Ring of Kerry is one of the most visited regions. This 110 mile route encircles the Inveragh Peninsula and is surrounded by mountains and lakes. Other sights include the Aran islands, home to some of the most ancient Christian and pre-Christian remains in Ireland, the Rock of Cashel and the bustling cities of Dublin, Galway and Cork.

Capital: Dublin
Currency: Euro (€)
Time Zone: Greenwich Mean Time (no GMT/UTC offset)
Telephone Country Code: 00 353
Tourist Office: www.ireland.com

Public Holidays
New Year's Day 1 Jan; St Patrick's Day 17 Mar; Good Friday; Easter Monday; 1 May; 5 June; 7 Aug; 30 Oct; Christmas Day/Boxing Day.

Motoring
Driving is on the left hand side and roads are generally well maintained. Tolls exist in the Republic, generally paid at the barrier. Speed limits are 50 kph in built up areas, 120 kph on motorways. Signposts are in both Gaelic and English in most areas (where Irish is the primary language signage is in Gaelic).

15 pitches
GPS: 53.71575, -6.57334

Co. Meath, North

www.alanrogers.com/ir8900
info@slanefarmhostel.ie
041 988 4985
www.slanefarmhostel.ie

Open (Touring Pitches):
1 March - 31 October.

Slane Farm Camping

Slane Farm Camping is a friendly, family run campsite situated on a large working farm, in a rural setting in the heart of the historic Boyne valley, 16 km. west of Drogheda. This small campsite has a sunny field for tents and a separate stony area for motorcaravans and caravans. Electricity (6A Europlug) is available, but long leads may be needed. It is an ideal base for pop concerts in the grounds of Slane Castle, only 5 minutes walk away, so can be quite busy. A well equipped kitchen is available for use by campers and the reception area is well stocked with local information. The owners are always on hand to offer help and advice about the area.

Well maintained, but very basic toilet facilities in nearby farm building. Kitchen. Laundry room. Barbecue. Bicycle hire (delivered to site). WiFi (free). 6 cottages to rent. Hostel accommodating 42 people in private rooms. Twin-axle caravans are not accepted.

Ideal For...

 Beach

 Dogs

 Fishing

 Watersports

 Golf

 Pets Accepted

Scan me for more information.

3 accommodations
44 pitches
GPS: 53.466111, -7.375278

Co. Westmeath, Heart

Lough Ennell Camping Park

www.alanrogers.com/ir8965
eamon@caravanparksireland.com
044 934 8101
www.caravanparksireland.com

Open (Touring Pitches):
Easter/1 April - 30 September.

Natural, rustic charm is the visitor's first impression on arrival at Lough Ennell Camping & Caravan Park. Set in 18 acres of mature woodland beside a Blue Flag lake, Eamon and Geraldine O'Malley run this sheltered and tranquil park with their family, who live on the site. They receive a blend of visitors - seasonal residents in camping holiday homes (private and to rent), caravanners and motorcaravanners and there are ample areas for tents. Pitches are varied, sheltered with trees and natural shrubbery, and with gravel or gravel and grass combinations. There are 44 touring pitches with electricity (7A Europlug) available on 25 hardstanding and grass pitches, with water points on or nearby all pitches; there are also 80 tent pitches. The site is a paradise for fishermen, with brown trout, rainbow trout, pike, tench, roach, perch, rudd and bream available. There is also one lake stocked with carp.

The toilet block provides toilets, washbasins and hot showers (€ 1 coin). Additional dishwashing areas are around the park. Laundry. Small shop (all season). Café and coffee shop with takeaway. TV and games room. Play areas and area for ball games. Small lakeside beach. Fishing. Late arrivals area outside. Security including CCTV. Some breeds of dog are not accepted.

Ideal For...

 Beach

 Dogs

 Fishing

 Watersports

 Golf

 Play Area

Scan me for more information.

17 accommodations
160 pitches
GPS: 52.8884, -6.14528

Co. Wicklow, Heart

River Valley Holiday Park

www.alanrogers.com/ir9150
info@rivervalleypark.ie
040 441 647
www.rivervalleypark.ie

Open (Touring Pitches):
11 March - 4 November.

In the small country village of Redcross, in the heart of County Wicklow, you will find River Valley Caravan & Camping Park, a first rate, family run park. It is within easy reach of beauty spots such as the Vale of Avoca (Ballykissangel), Glendalough and Powerscourt, plus the safe beach of Brittas Bay. The 160 touring pitches are divided into separate, well landscaped areas with an adults-only section. All have 6/10A electricity connections and offer a choice of hardstanding or grass – you select your pitch. A late arrivals area has electricity hook-ups, water and night lighting.

All sanitary blocks are of the highest quality, modern and well designed. Excellent facilities for disabled visitors. Showers are on payment (€ 1 token). Laundry area. Campers' kitchen. Motorcaravan services. Gas supplies. Full bar and restaurant entertainment twice a week. TV and games room. Three tennis courts. Beer garden with entertainment for children (July/Aug). Sports complex. New foot-golf course. Go-kart track. Remote control boats and cars. Movie nights. Adventure and toddlers' playgrounds. Caravan storage. WiFi (free). Archery range. Mini wildlife walk.

Ideal For...

 Beach

 Dogs

 Fishing

 Golf

 Play Area

 Disabled Facilities

Scan me for more information.

54 pitches
GPS: 52.159266, -6.992342

Co. Waterford, South East

Dunmore East Holiday Park

www.alanrogers.com/ir9345
info@dunmoreholiday.ie
087 702 2566
www.dunmoreholiday.ie

Open (Touring Pitches):
1 March - 31 October.

Dunmore Holiday Park is a new purpose built touring park catering for caravans and motorcaravans. It is set in over five acres of meadow surrounded by woodland, overlooking the village and coves of Dunmore East. There are 68 pitches (54 for touring). Twenty-seven are equipped with electricity (16A) and waste water with a shared tap on each pair of pitches. South of the park there are views across the estuary to Hook Head lighthouse, where the River Suir meets the Atlantic Ocean. There are many trails along this spectacular coastline and next to the site is an 18-hole championship golf course.

Sanitary block with hot showers (€ 1), family room and facilities for disabled visitors. Launderette. Motorcaravan services. Campers' kitchen. Playground.

Ideal For...

 Beach

 Dogs

 Fishing

 Watersports

 Golf

 Play Area

Scan me for more information.

1 accommodations
42 pitches
GPS: 52.419981, -8.187867

Co. Tipperary, Shannon

The Glen of Aherlow

www.alanrogers.com/ir9400
rdrew@tipperarycamping.com
062 565 55
www.tipperarycamping.com

Open (Touring Pitches):
All year.

The owners of one of Ireland's newest parks, George and Rosaline Drew, are campers themselves and have set about creating an idyllic park in an idyllic location. This three-hectare park is set in one of Ireland's most picturesque valleys and is open all year. There are beautiful views of the wooded and hilly areas of Slievenamuck and the Galtee Mountains. There are 42 large and level touring pitches, on both hardstanding and grass, each pair sharing a double 10A Europlug post and water point. The Drew family is happy to welcome large groups and rallies, and large units can be accommodated. The new stone-built reception and shop beside the gate is a super addition to the site and includes a coffee shop. The excellent facilities are located in a purpose-built toilet block.

The modern toilet block includes free showers and facilities for disabled visitors. Motorcaravan services. Laundry room with ironing. Campers' kitchen. Recreation and TV rooms. Shop. Coffee shop. Bicycle hire (delivered to site). WiFi (free).

Ideal For...

 Dogs

 Year Round Camping

 Fishing

 Golf

 Disabled Facilities

 Pets Accepted

Scan me for more information.

3 accommodations
99 pitches
GPS: 53.01677, -9.402

Co. Clare, Shannon

www.alanrogers.com/ir9465
ken@doolincamping.com
065 707 4458
www.doolincamping.com

Open (Touring Pitches):
Mid March - mid October.

Nagle's Doolin Camping Park

This neat and tidy seaside site is located just one kilometre from the cliffs of Moher, and a short ferry ride from the sparsely populated Aran Islands. The nearby village of Doolin, famed for its traditional music, has a good range of shops, restaurants and pubs. The four-hectare site, which enjoys spectacular views over the bay to Conemara, has 99 pitches, including 76 level hardstandings (all with 10A electricity, and 21 also with water and drainage) and grass pitches for tents. They are not separated by hedges, but the site is divided into bays by limestone walls. Three new camping pods are available for hire. There is excellent WiFi coverage over the whole site.

One modern, well equipped toilet block is unheated but has good facilities including hot showers (€ 1) and en-suite unit for disabled visitors. Laundry facilities (charged). Kitchen with cooking rings (charged), fridge/freezer and sinks with hot water. Motorcaravan services. Shop (June-Aug). Gas. Games room. Play area. WiFi throughout.

Ideal For...

 Beach

 Dogs

 Fishing

Watersports

 Golf

 Play Area

Scan me for more information.

40 pitches
GPS: 51.94787, -8.54622

Co. Cork, South West

Blarney Camping Park

www.alanrogers.com/ir9480
info@blarneycaravanpark.com
021 451 6519
www.blarneycaravanpark.com

Open (Touring Pitches):
24 March - 31 October.

There is a heart of the country feel about this 'on the farm' site, yet the city of Cork is only an 8 km. drive. What makes this friendly, family run park so appealing is the welcome you receive on arrival and the friendliness throughout your stay. Its secluded location and neat spacious pitches add to its appeal. The terrain on the three-acre park is elevated and gently sloping, commanding views towards Blarney Castle and the surrounding mountainous countryside. The 80 pitches, 40 of which have hardstanding and 10A Europlug, are with caravans near the entrance with tents pitched slightly further away. There are gravel roads, well tended young shrubs and a screen of mature trees. Tidy hedging marks the park's perimeter.

Excellent toilet facilities are housed in converted farm buildings. Reception and small shop are now at entrance. Good facilities for disabled visitors. Laundry room. Campers' kitchen. Motorcaravan services. Shop (1/6-31/8). TV lounge. Playground. WiFi throughout (free). Delightful 18-hole golf and pitch and putt course.

Ideal For...

 Dogs

 Golf

 Play Area

 Disabled Facilities

 Pets Accepted

Scan me for more information.

6 accommodations
30 pitches
GPS: 52.05887, -9.93198

Co. Kerry, South West

Glenross Camping Park

www.alanrogers.com/ir9600
glenross@eircom.net
087 137 6865
www.campingkerry.com

Open (Touring Pitches):
3 April - 30 September.

Glenross Caravan, Camping & Motor Home Park is situated on the spectacular Ring of Kerry and the Kerry Way footpath giving it an immediate advantage. Scenic grandeur around every bend of the road is guaranteed as Glenbeigh is approached. Quietly located before entering the village, the park commands stunning views of Rossbeigh Strand, (within walking distance) and the Dingle Peninsula. On arrival, a good impression is created with the park being well screened from the road, with a new stone entrance and gates. With 30 touring pitches, 27 with hardstanding and all with 10A electricity (Europlug), and six caravan holiday homes, the park is attractively laid out. Dedicated small tent area.

Well maintained and modern sanitary block with refurbished showers (€ 1) includes laundry facilities. Motorcaravan services. Shelter for campers and dining area. Bar, restaurant and takeaway (all year). Games room. Free WiFi throughout.

Ideal For...

 Beach

 Dogs

 Fishing

 Golf

 Pets Accepted

 Bar on Site

Scan me for more information.

20 pitches
GPS: 51.75562, -9.76193

Co. Kerry, South West

Creveen Lodge Camping Park

www.alanrogers.com/ir9570
info@creveenlodge.com
064 668 3131
www.creveenlodge.com

Open (Touring Pitches):
Easter - 31 October.

The Healy Pass is the well known scenic summit of the R574 road that crosses the Beara Peninsula, shortening the original journey from Kenmare Bay in the north to Bantry Bay in the south by nearly 70 km. As this narrow coast road starts to climb steeply, on the mountain foothills you will arrive at Creveen Lodge, a working hill farm with a quiet, homely atmosphere. The park provides 20 attractive pitches, 10 with 10A electricity and an area of hardstanding for motorcaravans. To allow easy access, the steep farm track is divided into a simple one-way system. Creveen Lodge, commanding views across Kenmare Bay, is divided among three gently sloping fields separated by trees.

Well appointed and maintained, the small toilet block provides token operated showers (€ 1). Communal room with cooking facilities, a fridge, freezer, TV, ironing board, fireplace, tables and chairs. Reception is in the farmhouse. Play area. Accommodation (3 cottages, 2 caravans) to rent.

Ideal For...

 Beach

 Dogs

 Fishing

 Watersports

 Play Area

 Pets Accepted

Scan me for more information.

12 accommodations
70 pitches
GPS: 53.79391, -8.91387

Co. Mayo, West

Knock Caravan & Camping Park

www.alanrogers.com/ir8780
caravanpark@knock-shrine.ie
094 938 8100
www.knock-shrine.ie

Open (Touring Pitches):
1 April - 31 October.

This park is in a sheltered, landscaped area immediately south of the world famous Shrine that receives many visitors. Comfortable and clean, the park has neatly trimmed lawns with tarmac roads and is surrounded by clipped trees. The 70 touring pitches are of average size on hardstanding and 52 have 15A electricity connections. There is also an overflow field. Because of the religious connections of the area, the site is very busy in August and indeed there are unlikely to be any vacancies at all for 14-16 August.

Two heated toilet blocks, one dated, have good facilities for disabled visitors and a nice sized rest room attached, hot showers and adequate washing and toilet facilities. Laundry room. Gas supplies. TV rooms. Playground. Free WiFi over site.

Ideal For...

 Dogs

 Fishing

 Golf

 Play Area

 Disabled Facilities

 Pets Accepted

Scan me for more information.

ITALY

Italy, once the capital of the Roman Empire, was unified as recently as 1861, thus regional customs and traditions have not been lost. Its enviable collections of art, literature and culture have had worldwide influence and continue to be a magnet for visitors who flock to cities such as Venice, Florence and Rome.

In the north, the vibrant city of Milan is the fashion capital of the world and home to the famous opera house as well as Da Vinci's 'The Last Supper.' It is also a good starting-off point for the Alps; the Italian Lake District, incorporating Lake Garda, Lake Como and Lake Maggiore; the canals of Venice and the lovely town of Verona.

The hilly towns of central Italy are especially popular, with Siena, San Gimignano and Assisi among the most visited. The historic capital of Rome with its Colosseum and Vatican City is not to be missed.

Naples is an ideal base for visiting Pompeii and the breathtaking scenery of the Amalfi coast but the city also has a charm of its own – winding narrow streets and crumbling façades inset with shrines sit alongside boutiques, bars and lively street markets, amid chaotic traffic.

Language: Italian. There are several dialect forms and some German is spoken near the Austrian border.
Capital: Rome
Currency: Euro (€)
Time Zone: Central European Time (GMT/UTC plus one hour)
Telephone Country Code: 00 39
Tourist Office: www.enit.it

Say Hello in Italian
Ciao (chow)

Say Goodbye in Italian
Arrivederci (ahr-ree-veh-DEHR-chee)

Public Holidays
New Year; Easter Mon; Liberation Day 25 Apr; Labour Day; Republic Day 2 June; Assumption 15 Aug; All Saints 1 Nov; Unity Day 4 Nov; Immaculate Conception 8 Dec; Christmas 25, 26 Dec; plus some special local feast days.

Motoring
Tolls are payable on the autostrada network. If travelling distances, save time by purchasing a 'Viacard' from pay booths or service areas. An overhanging load, e.g. a bicycle rack, must be indicated by a large red/white hatched warning square. Failure to do so will result in a fine.

2 accommodations
95 pitches
GPS: 45.81840, 7.22891
Post Code: I-11014

Etroubles, Valle d'Aosta

Camping Tunnel

www.alanrogers.com/it62160
info@campingtunnel.it
016 578 292
www.campingtunnel.it

Open (Touring Pitches):
Year round with seasonal closures

This is a small, friendly site located near the southern exit of the Gran San Bernardo tunnel. The views from the site are really very pleasant with green hills and towering peaks all around. There is a distinct Italian feel about it and the young English-speaking owners, Silvia and Roberto, are most welcoming and helpful. The site sits on two sides of a quiet road and steady improvements are being made. There are 95 pitches, with 45 of mixed size for touring units, plus a special overnight area for motorcaravans, opposite the main gate. All have electricity (6A Europlug) with drainage and water taps nearby. Gas connections are also available. Some have shade and most are on terraces or gentle slopes. Two fully equipped, air-conditioned mobile homes are available to rent.

The main toilet block is beneath the restaurant building and has recently been refurbished, while the smaller block is central to the upper part of the site. WCs are mixed British and Turkish styles. Showers are modern in one block, outdoor in the other. Good facilities for disabled visitors. Laundry room with washer/dryer and baby changing. Motorcaravan services. Bar and restaurant (1/6-15/9 and 26/12-6/1). New lounge with TV, games and library. Torches and long leads useful. Playground. Pétanque. Communal barbecue. WiFi (free). Nightstop area for motorcaravans with electricity and access to toilets. A small outdoor swimming pool with a hydro-massage bench.

Ideal For...

 Dogs

 Fishing

 Walking

 Golf

 Play Area

 Disabled Facilities

Scan me for more information.

20 pitches
GPS: 45.82331, 8.41398
Post Code: I-28028

Pettenasco, Piedmont

www.alanrogers.com/it62419
info@campingroyal.com
0323 888 945
www.campingroyal.com

Open (Touring Pitches):
1 March - 30 November.

Camping Royal

It would be difficult to find a more beautiful lake than Orta, surrounded by wooded hills and mountains and fringed with ancient towns and villages. Camping Royal, family owned and run, sits on a hillside overlooking the lake. There are 60 pitches, 20 for touring, set on level terraces, each with 5A Europlug and a water point nearby. Although professionally managed, this site has maintained the typical relaxed informality for which Italy is famous. Popular with campers from all over Europe, many return year after year. Nothing seems to be too much trouble to ensure a memorable stay.

Refurbished toilet block has hot showers (20c tokens) and a mixture of British and Turkish style toilets. New wet room for disabled campers by reception. Washing machine and dryer. Laundry and dishwashing sinks. Fridges. Shop with takeaway pizzas. Bar. New swimming pool. Playground. Football field. Room with games, library, cooking hobs and TV. Children's activities (daily in July/August) and some entertainment for adults. Shuttle bus to San Giulio in season (€2 return). Bicycle, scooter and car hire arranged. Internet cabin. WiFi (charged).

Ideal For...

 Beach

 Dogs

 Fishing

 Watersports

 Golf

 Play Area

Scan me for more information.

15 accommodations
234 pitches
GPS: 45.9334, 8.4812
Post Code: I-28831

Feriolo di Baveno, Piedmont

Camping Orchidea

www.alanrogers.com/it62465
info@campingorchidea.it
032 328 257
www.campingorchidea.it

Open (Touring Pitches):
19 March - 9 October.

Camping Orchidea is an immaculate family owned site on the western bank of Lake Maggiore, 35 km. south of the Swiss border and 8 km. from Stresa. This site has direct access to the lake and the banks of the River Stronetta and has a sandy beach. Orchidea has a good range of modern amenities, including a shop, bar and restaurant. Watersports are understandably popular here and pedaloes and kayaks can be rented on site. The 234 touring pitches are grassy and generally well shaded, all with 6A electrical connections. Some pitches are available facing the lake (a supplement is charged in mid and peak season). There are apartments and mobile homes available for rent.

Two toilet blocks are kept clean and have hot and cold water throughout. Special facilities for children and provision for disabled visitors. Laundry facilities. Shop. Restaurant. Bar. Takeaway. Direct lake access. Pedalo and kayak hire. Fishing. Boat launching. Playground. Children's club. Mobile homes for hire. Bicycle hire. WiFi on part of site (charged).

Ideal For...

 Beach

 Dogs

 Fishing

 Watersports

 Golf

 Play Area

Scan me for more information.

287 accommodations
413 pitches
GPS: 45.94960, 8.48058
Post Code: I-28924

Fondotoce di Verbania,
Piedmont

Continental Lido

www.alanrogers.com/it62490
info@campingcontinental.com
0323 496 300
www.campingcontinental.com

Open (Touring Pitches):
23 March - 19 September.

Camping Continental Lido is a large, bustling site situated on the shore of the charming little Lake Mergozzo, about one kilometre from the better known Lake Maggiore. The average size touring pitches are back to back in rows on grass and although a little close together, the rest of the site has a more open feel. All have 6A electricity, TV connections, water, drainage and there is some shade. There are also 287 mobile homes and 14 apartments available to rent. There is an impressive pool complex and a small sandy beach slopes gently into the lake where swimming and watersports can also be enjoyed (no powered craft may be used).

Five high standard toilet blocks have free hot water. Facilities for disabled visitors. Washing machines and dryers. Mini-fridges. Well stocked shop and bar/restaurant with terrace and takeaway. Swimming pool complex (24/4-13/9) with slides, rapids and waves, plus free sun loungers and parasols. Snack bars by pool and lake. Large amphitheatre. TV. Tennis. Golf course (9 holes). Playground. Fishing. Windsurfing, pedaloes, canoes, kayaks. Games room. Bicycle hire. Entertainment and activities (24/3-3/4 & 23/4-11/9). Bus on request to Verbania. Internet access and WiFi.

Ideal For...

 Beach

 Dogs

 Fishing

 Watersports

 Golf

 Play Area

Scan me for more information.

100 accommodations
100 pitches
GPS: 44.07556, 9.96972
Post Code: I-19031

Ameglia, Ligúria

www.alanrogers.com/it64190
info@campingriver.com
0187 659 20
www.campingriver.com

Open (Touring Pitches):
1 April - 30 September.

Camping River

Camping River is a large oblong site on the banks of the Magna river but only the swimming pool/entertainment area has river views. It provides 100 level, 75-100 sq.m. touring pitches (all 3A electricity) mostly under a canopy of tall trees with much welcome shade on hot days. They are mostly separated from the equal number of permanent pitches. It is possible to launch your boat into the Magra river from the campsite and there are good fishing opportunities further up river. A busy entertainment programme is provided from mid June until September.

Two unisex sanitary blocks provide toilets (some Turkish style), washbasins and showers. Facilities for disabled visitors. Motorcaravan services. Shop, restaurant and bar, pizzeria (1/5-30/9). Swimming pool (1/5-15/9) and sun deck. Play area. Football. Hydro massage. Boat launching. Fishing. Mobile homes and bungalows to rent. Entertainment area. Beach shuttle bus. Lessons organised (scuba diving, swimming, dancing). Kayak, windsurf board, bicycle hire. WiFi (free).

Ideal For...

 Beach

 Dogs

 Fishing

 Watersports

 Golf

 Play Area

Scan me for more information.

92 accommodations
107 pitches
GPS: 43.80117, 7.74867
Post Code: I-18038

San Remo, Ligúria

Villaggio dei Fiori

www.alanrogers.com/it64010
info@villaggiodeifiori.it
0184 660 635
www.villaggiodeifiori.it

Open (Touring Pitches):
All year.

Camping Villaggio dei Fiori is open all year round. This open and spacious site is a member of the Sunêlia group and maintains very high standards. It is excellent for exploring the Italian and French Rivieras, a guided tour to Monte Carlo in particular, or for just relaxing by the enjoyable, filtered seawater pools or on the private beach. Unusually, all of the pitch areas at the site are totally paved, with huge pitches for large units. Electricity (3/6A) is available to all 107 pitches. Water, drainage and an outside sink with cold water is available for every four pitches in one area. There is ample shade on some pitches from mature trees and shrubs, which are constantly watered and cared for in summer. The pitches along the seafront are superb and enjoy great views. This is an excellent site and we loved it here!

Four clean and modern toilet blocks have British and Turkish style WCs and hot water throughout. Controllable showers. Baby rooms. Facilities for disabled campers. Private cabins. Laundry facilities. Motorcaravan services. Gas. Bar sells limited essential supplies. Large restaurant. Pizzeria and takeaway. Sea water swimming pools and heated whirlpool spa. Tennis. Excellent play area. Fishing. Satellite TV. Bicycle hire. Free WiFi. Dogs are not accepted.

Ideal For...

 Kids

 Beach

 Year Round Camping

 Fishing

 Watersports

 Golf

Scan me for more information.

133 accommodations
153 pitches
GPS: 45.65708, 10.03740
Post Code: I-25049

Iseo, Lombardy

Camping del Sole

www.alanrogers.com/it62610
info@campingdelsole.it
0309 802 88
www.campingdelsole.it

Open (Touring Pitches):
16 April - 25 September.

Camping del Sole is, in our opinion, one of Italy's best family sites. It lies on the southern edge of Lake Iseo, just outside the pretty lakeside town of Iseo. The site has 306 pitches, of which 180 are for touring, all with 3A electricity and some fine views of the surrounding mountains and lake. Pitches are generally flat and of a reasonable size, but cars must park in the car park. The site has a wide range of excellent leisure amenities, including a large swimming pool. There is a bar and restaurant with a pizzeria near the pool and an entertainment area.

Sanitary facilities are modern and well maintained, including special facilities for children and disabled visitors. Washing machines and dryers (€ 4). Bar, restaurant, pizzeria, snack bar and excellent shop. Motorcaravan services. Bicycle hire. Swimming pool with children's pool (21/5-10/9). Tennis. Football pitch. Fitness area. Canoe and pedal boat hire. WiFi. Dog exercise area. Entertainment in high season.

Ideal For...

 Beach

 Dogs

 Fishing

 Watersports

 Golf

 Play Area

Scan me for more information.

75 pitches
GPS: 46.17067, 9.39268
Post Code: I-22010

Sorico, Lombardy

www.alanrogers.com/it62510
info@campinglariva.com
0344 945 71
www.campinglariva.com

Open (Touring Pitches):
1 April - 3 November.

Camping La Riva

La Riva lies on a waterway at the northern end of Lake Como. It is surrounded by mountains, close to the nature reserve of Pian di Spagna and within walking distance of Sorico, a pretty town with bars, restaurants and shops. The site is beautifully laid out, with 70 level touring pitches on well tended grass, and an average size of 80 sq.m. Many have attractive views across the river to the mountains and most have 6A electrical connections. Reception houses a small bar, with limited snack bar and takeaway. Bread and milk to order. The excellent outdoor pool has a sunbathing terrace. Camping La Riva has a happy, friendly atmosphere.

The centrally located sanitary building contains modern showers (token), British style toilets and washbasins and is kept very clean. Excellent suite for disabled visitors. Washing machine. Swimming pool. Small playground. Bicycle hire. Fishing. Water-skiing. Canoe and pedalo hire. Free WiFi in reception area.

Ideal For...

 Beach

 Dogs

 Fishing

 Watersports

 Golf

 Play Area

Scan me for more information.

6 accommodations
190 pitches
GPS: 45.75418, 10.49821
Post Code: I-25074

Idro, Lombardy

Sportcamping Rio Vantone

www.alanrogers.com/it62580
info@idrosee.eu
0365 831 25
www.idrosee.eu

Open (Touring Pitches):
1 April - 31 October.

Lake Idro, one of the smaller of the northern Italian lakes, is tucked away in the mountains to the west of Lake Garda. Rio Vantone is on the southeast shore of the lake with marvellous views across the water to the villages on the opposite bank and surrounding mountains. The ground slopes gently down to the water's edge with many of the 190 touring pitches in level rows divided by hedges, with others between tall trees. All have 6A electricity and there are 46 with water and drainage. The ones nearest the lake attract a higher charge. The lake is ideal for windsurfing and the surrounding countryside for walking and climbing.

The main, heated sanitary block occupies the ground floor of a large building and is of excellent quality including cabins (WC, washbasin and shower). A smaller block is also open in high season. Facilities for disabled visitors. No hot water 22.00-06.00. Washing machines and dryer. Motorcaravan services. Gas supplies. Cooking rings. Shop. Bar. Excellent restaurant (15/5-15/9). Swimming pools. Lake swimming. Windsurf school. Boat and mountain bike hire. Play area. Torches useful in some areas. WiFi throughout (charged).

Ideal For...

 Beach

 Dogs

 Fishing

 Watersports

 Play Area

 Disabled Facilities

Scan me for more information.

3 accommodations
150 pitches
GPS: 46.53344, 11.53335
Post Code: I-39050

Völs am Schlern, Trentino - Alto Adige

www.alanrogers.com/it62040
info@camping-seiseralm.com
0471 706 459
www.camping-seiseralm.com

Open (Touring Pitches):
20 December - 2 November.

Camping Seiser Alm

What an amazing experience awaits you at Seiser Alm! Elisabeth and Erhard Mahlknecht have created a superb site in the magnificent Südtirol region of the Dolomite mountains. Towering peaks provide a wonderful backdrop when you dine in the charming, traditionally styled restaurant on the upper terrace. Here you will also find the bar, shop and reception. The 150 touring pitches have 16A electricity, gas, water, drainage, satellite connection and WiFi. Guests were delighted with the site when we visited, many coming to walk or cycle, some just to enjoy the surroundings. There are countless things to see and do here, including a full entertainment programme and a brilliant new pool.

One spotless, luxury underground block is in the centre of the site. 16 private units are available. Excellent facilities for disabled visitors. Fairy tale facilities for children. Infrared sensors, underfloor heating and gently curved floors to prevent slippery surfaces. Washing machines and large drying room. Sauna. Supermarket. Quality restaurant and bar with terrace. Swimming pool (heated in cool weather). Entertainment programme six days a week. Miniclub. Children's adventure park and play room. Rooms for ski equipment. Animal enclosure. WiFi (charged). Apartments, mobile homes and maxi-caravans for rent.

Ideal For...

 Kids

 Beach

 Dogs

 Fishing

 Watersports

 Walking

Scan me for more information.

55 accommodations
385 pitches
GPS: 46.00799, 11.28454
Post Code: I-38056

Levico Terme, Trentino - Alto Adige

Camping Lago di Levico

www.alanrogers.com/it62290
info@campinglevico.com
046 170 6491
www.campinglevico.com

Open (Touring Pitches):
20 March - 16 October.

Camping Lago di Levico, by a pretty lakeside in the mountains, is the result of the merging of two popular sites. An impressive new reception has efficient systems and you are soon on one of 430 mostly grassy and shaded pitches. All pitches have 6A electricity, 150 also have water and drainage and 12 have private facilities. The lakeside pitches are really quite special. Staff are welcoming and fluent in English. The swimming pool complex is popular, as is the summer family entertainment. A small shop and a mini-market are on site and it is a short distance to the local village. The restaurant, bar, pizzeria and takeaway are open all season. A steady stream of improvements continues at this site which is great for families.

Four modern sanitary blocks provide hot water for showers, washbasins and washing. Mostly British style toilets. Single locked unit for disabled visitors. Laundry facilities. Freezer. Motorcaravan services and stop-over pitches. Good shop. Bar/restaurant and takeaway. Outdoor swimming pool. Play area. Miniclub and entertainment (high season). Small zoo. Satellite TV and cartoon cinema. Watersports. Kayak hire. Fishing. Tennis. Bicycle hire. Communal barbecues. Torches useful. Max. 1 dog in high season. WiFi throughout (free).

Ideal For...

 Kids

 Beach

 Dogs

 Fishing

 Watersports

 Walking

Scan me for more information.

11 accommodations
268 pitches
GPS: 46.66727, 12.40221
Post Code: I-39030

Sexten, Trentino - Alto Adige

Caravan Park Sexten

www.alanrogers.com/it62030
info@caravanparksexten.it
0474 710 444
www.caravanparksexten.it

Open (Touring Pitches):
All year.

Caravan Park Sexten is 1,520 metres above sea level and has 268 pitches, some very large and all with electricity (16A), TV connections and water and drainage in summer and winter (underground heating stops pipes freezing). Some pitches are in the open to catch the sun, others are tucked in forest clearings by the river. They are mostly gravelled to provide an ideal all year surface. It is the facilities that make this a truly remarkable site; no expense or effort has been spared to create a luxurious environment that matches that of any top class hotel.

The three main toilet blocks are remarkable in design, fixtures and fittings. Heated floors. Controllable showers. Hairdryers. Luxurious private facilities to rent. Children and baby rooms. En-suite facilities for disabled visitors. Laundry and drying room. Motorcaravan services. Shop. Bars and restaurants with entertainment 2-3 nights a week. Indoor pool. Heated outdoor pool (1/6-30/9). Superb wellness facility. Play areas. Good range of activities for all. Tennis. Bicycle hire. Climbing wall. Fishing. Adventure activity packages. Internet access and WiFi (whole site).

Ideal For...

 Dogs

Year Round Camping

 Fishing

 Golf

 Play Area

 Disabled Facilities

Scan me for more information.

165 accommodations
242 pitches
GPS: 45.49833, 10.7375
Post Code: I-37017

Lazise sul Garda, Lake Garda

Camping du Parc

www.alanrogers.com/it62535
duparc@campingduparc.com
045 758 0127
www.campingduparc.com

Open (Touring Pitches):
4 March - 6 November.

Camping du Parc is a very pleasant, family owned site which resembles a Tardis, in that it extends and extends as you progress further through the site. Olive groves are interspersed with the pitch areas which gives an open and green feel. The site is set on a slope that goes down to the lakeside beach of soft sand. The 242 touring pitches are terraced and all have 5A electricity. Units above 10 m. long will be challenged by some of the corners here. Pitches are separated by trimmed hedges and some have shade, others have fine views of the lake.

Four modern sanitary blocks are heated, well placed and have free hot water throughout. Three blocks have facilities for disabled visitors, one for children and babies. Washing machines and dryers. Motorcaravan services. Well stocked mini-market, restaurant with lake views, pizzeria with terrace and views, takeaway (19/3-31/10). Beach bar. Pool bar. Outdoor heated swimming pool (26/3-20/10). Large paddling pool with slides. Children's entertainment programme. Baby club. Play area. Tennis. Fitness suite. Multisports court. Fishing. Free WiFi throughout.

Ideal For...

 Beach

 Dogs

 Fishing

 Watersports

 Golf

 Play Area

Scan me for more information.

200 accommodations
765 pitches
GPS: 45.49716, 10.73806
Post Code: I-37017

Lazise, Lake Garda

Camping Spiaggia d'Oro

www.alanrogers.com/it62545
info@campingspiaggiadoro.com
0457 580 007
www.campingspiaggiadoro.com

Open (Touring Pitches):
20 March - 18 October.

Spiaggia d'Oro is a well equipped family site near Lazise on Lake Garda's eastern bank. This is a large site with 765 grassy touring pitches and a selection of chalets and mobile homes to rent. The site has its own sandy beach with a beach volleyball court. A fitness centre is a recent addition and has been developed with a good range of high specification equipment. The swimming pool complex is impressive with three pools, one for children with a slide and water games. This is a lively site in high season with a varied activity programme and a club for children.

Five modern, suitably positioned toilet blocks provide open style washbasins and showers. Good facilities for disabled visitors. Laundry. Motorcaravan services. Supermarket. Bar. Snack bar. Swimming pools with waterslide. Separate children's pool. Fitness centre. Tennis. Playground. Children's club and entertainment programme. Direct access to beach. Mobile homes and chalets to rent. WiFi on part of site (charged).

Ideal For...

 Beach

 Dogs

 Fishing

 Watersports

 Golf

 Play Area

Scan me for more information.

492 accommodations
400 pitches
GPS: 45.44165, 10.67920
Post Code: I-37019

Peschiera del Garda, Lake Garda

Camping Bella Italia

www.alanrogers.com/it62630
info@camping-bellaitalia.it
045 640 0688
www.camping-bellaitalia.it

Open (Touring Pitches):
12 March - 23 October.

Peschiera is a picturesque village on the southern shore of Lake Garda, and Camping Bella Italia is a very attractive, large, well organised and very busy site in the grounds of a former farm, just west of the centre of the village. Half of the 1,200 pitches are occupied by the site's own mobile homes and chalets and by tour operators; there are some 400 touring pitches, most towards the lakeside and reasonably level on grass under trees. All have 16A electricity, water and waste water and are separated by shrubs. There are some fine views across the lake to the mountains beyond. A superb promenade allows direct access to the town.

Six modern toilet blocks have British style toilets, washbasins and showers. Baby rooms and facilities for disabled visitors. Washing machines. Motorcaravan services. Infirmary. Shops. Gelateria. Bars. Waiter service restaurant and terrace and two other restaurants (one in the old farm building). Swimming pools. Tennis. Archery. Playgrounds (small). Games room. Watersports. Fishing. Bicycle hire. Organised activities and entertainment. Mini club. WiFi over part of site (charged). ATMs. Dogs are not accepted.

Ideal For...

 Beach

 Fishing

 Watersports

 Golf

 Play Area

 Disabled Facilities

Scan me for more information.

50 accommodations
166 pitches
GPS: 45.5253, 10.5434
Post Code: I-25080

Moniga del Garda, Lake Garda

Camping Fontanelle

www.alanrogers.com/it62770
info@campingfontanelle.it
0365 502 079
www.campingfontanelle.it

Open (Touring Pitches):
18 April - 4 October.

Camping Fontanelle, a new member of the HG Hotels group, is situated near the historic village of Moniga and enjoys excellent views across the lake. The site sits on the southwest slopes of Lake Garda and has 166 touring pitches on slightly sloping and terraced ground. A further 50 pitches are used by tour operators but there is little impingement. All are marked and have 6A electricity connections (36 are fully serviced) and there are some very pleasant lakeside pitches (at extra cost). Some for tents and touring units are very secluded, being distant from the campsite facilities, although small blocks with toilets are close by. This is a peaceful, friendly site.

The two main toilet blocks and two smaller blocks are modern and clean, with hot water throughout. Facilities for disabled campers. Washing machines and dryers. Motorcaravan services. Large shop with prices to compete with local supermarkets. Pleasant restaurant/bar. Takeaway. Swimming pools (15/5-15/9, supervised). Tennis. Electronic games. Play area. Live entertainment in high season. Fishing. Boat launching. Only charcoal barbecues permitted. WiFi throughout (free).

Ideal For...

 Beach

 Dogs

 Fishing

 Watersports

 Golf

 Play Area

Scan me for more information.

178 accommodations
266 pitches
GPS: 45.58497, 10.56582
Post Code: I-25010

San Felice del Benaco, Lake Garda

www.alanrogers.com/it62750
fornella@fornella.it
036 562 294
www.fornella.it

Open (Touring Pitches):
23 April - 25 September.

Fornella Camping

Fornella Camping is one of the few campsites on Lake Garda still surrounded by farmed olive trees and retaining a true country atmosphere. Parts of the crisp, clean site have great lake views, others a backdrop of mountains and attractive countryside. The 266 touring pitches are on flat grass, terraced where necessary and most have good shade, all with 6/10A electricity; 101 have water and a drain as well. The remaining pitches are used for mobile homes to rent. The staff speak excellent English and Dutch. A superb lagoon pool complex is here, along with a more traditional pool. These are supplemented by a pleasant bar, and a restaurant with terrace overlooking the lakeside.

Three very clean, modern toilet blocks, well dispersed around the site, have mainly British type WCs and hot water in washbasins (some in cabins), showers and sinks. Facilities for disabled visitors. Washing machines, dryer and irons. Motorcaravan services. Bar/restaurant. Pizzeria and takeaway. Shop. Supervised heated swimming pools and paddling pool (all season). Tennis. Two playgrounds and entertainment for children in season. Bicycle hire (high season). Beach. Fishing. Small marina, boat launching and repairs. WiFi throughout (charged).

Ideal For...

 Beach

 Dogs

 Fishing

 Watersports

 Golf

 Play Area

Scan me for more information.

285 accommodations
2200 pitches
GPS: 45.467883, 12.530367
Post Code: I-30013

Cavallino-Treporti, Veneto

Camping Union Lido Vacanze

www.alanrogers.com/it60200
info@unionlido.com
041 257 5111
www.unionlido.com

Open (Touring Pitches):
21 April - 3 October.

This amazing site is very large, offering absolutely everything a camper could wish for. It is extremely professionally run and we were impressed with the whole organisation. It lies along a 1.2 km. long, broad sandy beach which shelves very gradually and offers a huge number of sporting activities. The site itself is regularly laid out with parallel access roads under a covering of poplars, pine and other trees. There are 2,200 pitches for touring units, all with 6/10/16A electricity and 1,969 also have water and drainage. Because of the size of the site, there is an internal road train and amenities are repeated across the site (cycling is permitted on specific roads). A member of Leading Campings group.

Fourteen superb, fully equipped toilet blocks; 11 have facilities for disabled visitors. Launderette. Motorcaravan services. Gas supplies. Comprehensive shopping areas set around a pleasant piazza (all open till late). Eight restaurants each with a different style plus 11 pleasant and lively bars (all services open all season). Impressive aqua parks (all season). Tennis. Riding. Minigolf. Skating. Bicycle hire. Archery. Two fitness tracks in 4 ha. natural park with play area and supervised play. Diving centre and school. Windsurf school in season. Exhibitions. Boat excursions. Recreational events. Hairdressers. Internet cafés. ATM. Dogs are accepted in designated areas. Free WiFi throughout.

Ideal For...

 Kids

 Beach

 Dogs

 Fishing

 Watersports

 Golf

Scan me for more information.

353 accommodations
2274 pitches
GPS: 45.43750, 12.43805
Post Code: I-30013

Punta Sabbioni, Veneto

Marina di Venezia

www.alanrogers.com/it60450
camping@marinadivenezia.it
041 530 2511
www.marinadivenezia.it

Open (Touring Pitches):
23 April - 2 October.

Camping Village Marina di Venezia is an amazingly large site (2,881 pitches) with every conceivable facility. It has a pleasant feel with cheerful staff and no notion of being overcrowded, even when full. Marina di Venezia has the advantage of being within walking distance of the ferry to Venice. It will appeal in particular to those who enjoy an extensive range of entertainment and activities and a lively atmosphere. Individual pitches are spacious and set on sandy or grassy ground; most are separated by trees or hedges. All are equipped with 10A electricity and water. The site's excellent sandy beach is one of the widest along this stretch of coast and has five pleasant beach bars.

Nine modern toilet blocks are maintained to a very high standard with hot showers and a high proportion of British style toilets. Pleasant facilities for disabled visitors. Laundry. Range of shops. Several bars, restaurants and takeaways. Five beach bars/snack bars. Enormous swimming pool complex with slides and flumes. Several play areas. Tennis. Surfboard and catamaran hire. Wide range of organised entertainment. WiFi throughout (free). Special area and facilities for dog owners (also beach area).

Ideal For...

 Kids

 Beach

 Dogs

 Fishing

 Watersports

 Golf

Scan me for more information.

302 accommodations
422 pitches
GPS: 45.55357, 12.76752
Post Code: I-30020

Eraclea Mare, Veneto

Camping Village Portofelice

www.alanrogers.com/it60220
info@portofelice.it
0421 664 11
www.portofelice.it

Open (Touring Pitches):
7 May - 18 September.

Portofelice is an efficient and attractive coastal site, with a sandy beach which is a short walk through a protected pine wood. The excellent beach is very safe and has lifeguards. There are a total of 422 pitches, half of which are available for touring. These flat and shady pitches have 6/8A electricity (70 also have water, drainage and TV sockets), are well kept and cars are parked separately. Some 302 pitches are dedicated to rental accommodation. The social life of the site is centred around the stunning pool complex where the shops, pizzeria, bar, café and restaurant are also located. This is a tremendous family site.

Three modern sanitary blocks have the usual facilities with slightly more Turkish style toilets than British. Baby room and excellent children's block (0-12 yrs). Facilities for disabled campers. Very large supermarket and bazaar. Pizzeria and takeaway. Bar/restaurant with terraces and waiter service. American diner. Gelateria. Crêperie. Three superb pools with waterfalls, slides and an area specifically equipped for disabled guests, hydro-massage and sunbathing. Playgrounds. Go-kart track. Pedalos. Water dodgems. Tennis. 5-a-side football. Basketball. Volleyball. Sandy beach. Bicycle hire. ATM. Organised activity and entertainment programmes. Miniclub. WiFi throughout (charged). Internet room. Dogs are not accepted.

Ideal For...

 Beach

 Fishing

 Watersports

 Golf

 Play Area

 Disabled Facilities

Scan me for more information.

131 accommodations
378 pitches
GPS: 45.48395, 12.58763
Post Code: I-30016

Lido di Jesolo, Veneto

Camping Jesolo International

www.alanrogers.com/it60370
info@jesolointernational.it
0421 971 826
www.jesolointernational.it

Open (Touring Pitches):
24 April - 27 September.

An absolutely brilliant, family orientated, resort-style site that we love, especially for its positive value for money approach. The array of top quality on-site activities is included in the price, as are some off-site attractions (Aqualandia, etc) others are discounted. Jesolo International is located on a beautiful promontory with 700 m. of white sandy beach and slowly shelving waters. The 368 pitches are flat, mostly shaded and with 10/20A electricity, water and drainage, WiFi and satellite TV connection. Some have private bathrooms. The superb pool complex, has an excellent entertainment programme, presented nightly, which rounds off this outstanding site.

Sanitary facilities include 72 modern, clean bathroom units (shower, WC and basin). Rooms for babies, seniors & disabled campers. Washing machines & dryers. Dishwashers. Motorcaravan services. Supermarket. Family-style restaurant. Pizzeria. Meals and shopping delivery to pitch. Beach bar. Pool bar serving light lunches. Sports centre. Miniclub. Indoor gym. Tennis (free courts & lessons). Golf (free lessons, no green fees). Play area with adventure-style equipment. Sailing (tuition), banana boat, canoes, pedal boats, loungers & sunshades (all free). Offshore pirate ship. Scuba diving (charged). Language course (free). Pony riding (free). Doctor on site. WiFi (free). Dogs not accepted.

Ideal For...

 Beach

 Fishing

 Watersports

 Golf

 Play Area

 Disabled Facilities

Scan me for more information.

663 accommodations
370 pitches
GPS: 45.56709, 12.7943
Post Code: I-30021

Caorle, Veneto

Camping San Francesco

www.alanrogers.com/it60110
info@villaggiosanfrancesco.com
0421 29 82
www.villaggiosfrancesco.com

Open (Touring Pitches):
21 April - 24 September.

Camping San Francesco is a large, beachside site in a quiet location close to the coastal town of Caorle (Little Venice), known for its connection with Ernest Hemingway. Although there are over 600 mobile homes to rent, 370 level, grassy pitches are reserved for tourers. They are close to the beach, shaded, and all have electricity (10A) and fresh and waste water connections. The site has every facility for a comfortable holiday, with swimming pools, an attractive aquapark (extra charge), a good beach for swimming, a large supermarket etc. However, some touring in the area from the site and a trip to Venice are also worthwhile.

Five sanitary blocks with all the usual facilities including free, controllable showers, washbasins in cabins, facilities for disabled visitors, children's area and baby room. Motorcaravan services. Bars, restaurants, pizzeria and ice-cream parlour. Supermarket and shopping centre plus first aid centre and a Murano glass shop. Swimming pools, paddling pools and hydromassage centre. Aquapark with waterslides (charged). Fitness centre. Solarium. Gym. Bowls. Tennis. Playground. Windsurfing school. Diving school. Games room. Entertainment and activity programme. Children's club. Excursions. Mobile homes and chalets for rent. Free WiFi throughout.

Ideal For...

 Kids

 Beach

 Dogs

 Fishing

 Watersports

 Golf

Scan me for more information.

256 accommodations
800 pitches
GPS: 45.44543, 12.46127
Post Code: I-30013

Ca'Savio, Veneto

Camping Ca'Savio

www.alanrogers.com/it60440
info@casavio.it
0419 660 17
www.casavio.it

Open (Touring Pitches):
26 April - 2 October.

Ca'Savio is a very large, family owned site of almost 50 years standing. It is in traditional Italian style and is set on a wide, sandy, Blue Flag beach which is safe for swimming. The beach is separated from the pitches by a pleasant open area and a row of bungalows. There are many activities here, some requiring additional payment. There are 800 touring pitches (all with 10A electricity), 256 mobile homes/bungalows and around 400 tour operator pitches. Rows of pitches lead off a very busy central avenue and they are shaded, mostly flat and varying in size (90-100 sq.m). Many are a long way from water and sanitary facilities. Customers are left to find their own pitches, so leave someone there while you fetch your unit!

Three large toilet blocks include many shower, toilet and washbasin units. The toilets are in cabins with showers and washbasins, so at busy periods there may be a long wait. Supermarket, bazaar and other shops. Restaurants, pizzeria, café and pub. Two very large pool complexes (free). Miniclub. Bicycle hire. Minigolf. Good adventure style playground. Car hire. Internet and WiFi (at the restaurant; charged). Dogs are not accepted.

Ideal For...

 Beach

 Watersports

 Golf

 Play Area

 Disabled Facilities

 Bar on Site

Scan me for more information.

65 accommodations
684 pitches
GPS: 45.7051, 13.4640
Post Code: I-34073

Grado, Friuli - Venézia Giúlia

Camping Tenuta Primero

www.alanrogers.com/it60065
info@tenuta-primero.com
0431 896 900
www.tenuta-primero.com

Open (Touring Pitches):
14 April - 28 September.

Tenuta Primero is a large, attractive, well run, family owned site with direct access to its own private beach, marina and golf course. It offers a wealth of facilities and activities and caters for all members of the family. The 740 pitches are all level, with 6A electricity, some separating hedges and ample tree shade. The site has several restaurants and bars, and the large, elevated, flower decked Terrazza Mare, overlooking the sea, is great for eating and drinking whilst enjoying views over the romantic Adriatic.

Nine traditional sanitary blocks, seven with facilities for disabled visitors. Washing machines and dryers. Motorcaravan services. Swimming pools and paddling pool. Shop, bars and restaurants, pizzeria, takeaway (all May-Sept). Beauty salon. Aerobics. Water gymnastics. Football pitch. Tennis. Boules. Skateboarding. Play areas. Windsurfing. Marina, sailing, boat launching and boat hire. Bicycle hire. Children's and family entertainment. Live music, disco, dancing. Private beach with sunshades, deck chairs and jetty. Internet corner and WiFi (free). Dogs are not accepted. Courses now available for many activities.

Ideal For...

 Beach

 Fishing

 Watersports

 Golf

 Play Area

 Disabled Facilities

Scan me for more information.

293 accommodations
974 pitches
GPS: 45.68198, 13.12577
Post Code: I-33054

Lignano Sabbiadoro, Friuli - Venézia Giúlia

Camping Sabbiadoro

www.alanrogers.com/it60080
campsab@lignano.it
043 171 455
www.campingsabbiadoro.it

Open (Touring Pitches):
28 March - 9 October.

Sabbiadoro is a large, top quality site that caters very well for children. It is divided into two parts with separate entrances and efficient receptions. It has 974 touring pitches and is ideal for families who like all their amenities to be close by. The level, grassy pitches vary in size, are shaded by attractive trees and have electricity (6-10A) and TV connections. The facilities are all in excellent condition and well thought out, especially the pool complex, and everything here is very modern, safe and clean. The site's private beach (with 24-hour guard) is only 250 m. away and has its own showers, toilets and baby rooms.

Well equipped sanitary facilities with free showers includes superb facilities for disabled visitors. Washing machines and dryers. Motorcaravan services. Huge supermarket (all season). Bazaar. Good restaurant, snack bar and takeaway. Heated outdoor pool complex with separate fun pool area, slides and fountains (all season). Heated indoor children's pool. Swimming courses. Play areas. Tennis. Fitness centre. Boat launching. Windsurfing school. Activity centre for children with well organised entertainment (high season) and language school. WiFi throughout (charged). Bicycle hire. Excursions to Venice.

Ideal For...

 Beach

 Dogs

 Fishing

 Watersports

 Golf

 Play Area

Scan me for more information.

The beach at Lignano Sabbiadoro

92 accommodations
120 pitches
GPS: 44.52366, 11.3741
Post Code: I-40127

Bologna, Emília-Romagna

www.alanrogers.com/it66020
info@hotelcamping.com
0513 250 16
www.hotelcamping.com

Open (Touring Pitches):
9 January - 20 December.

Camping Hotel Città di Bologna

This spacious city site was established in 1993 on the edge of the Trade Fair Centre of this ancient and historic city and is very clean and modern. The 120 pitches, with 6A electricity, are numbered and marked out in a very orderly manner and shaded by trees. All pitches are on level 'grasscrete' hardstandings. There are two main areas plus a separate section for very long units. You will always find space here as there is huge over capacity. There is an unassuming restaurant and bar in a central location and the pleasant swimming pool with paddling area is very welcome after a day exploring the city. The site is excellent for an overnight stop or for longer stays to explore the most attractive and unusual city of Bologna.

Modern sanitary blocks include excellent provision for disabled visitors (with British style WCs, free showers and alarms that ring in reception). Washing machines. Motorcaravan services. Restaurant and bar with adjoining terrace where quality meals are offered. Large swimming pool with shallow area for children. Basic play area. Minigolf. Fitness centre. WiFi over site (first 15 mins. free).

Ideal For...

 Dogs

 Fishing

 Golf

 Play Area

 Disabled Facilities

 Pets Accepted

Scan me for more information.

20 accommodations
200 pitches
GPS: 43.95957, 12.46126
Post Code: I-47893

Repubblica di San Marino,
Emília-Romagna

www.alanrogers.com/it66230
info@centrovacanzesanmarino.com
0549 903 964
www.centrovacanzesanmarino.com

Open (Touring Pitches):
All year.

Centro Vacanze San Marino

Centro Vacanze San Marino, at 400 m. above sea level and positioned on an attractive hillside, has lovely views of the Adriatic. This excellent, modern site has a variety of well tended trees offering shade. On level terraces, the main grass pitches are roomy and accessed from tarmac or gravel roads. Separated by hedges, all have electricity (5A). Smaller pitches on lower terraces are for tents. There is a pleasant open feel to this site. Mobile homes and bungalows are available to rent and the site is used by a tour operator (30 pitches). The large swimming pool has a section for children and a broad sunbathing terrace. Make sure you visit the ancient city of San Marino at the top of the mountain (4 km).

Four high quality, heated toilet blocks are kept very clean and have British and Turkish style WCs. Facilities for disabled visitors at the upper level to avoid slopes. Laundry facilities. Motorcaravan services. Gas supplies. Shop (April-Sept). Kitchen. TV room (satellite). Restaurant/pizzeria. Large swimming pool (1/6-1/9) with jacuzzi and solarium. Large enclosed play area. Games room. Free WiFi over part of site. Tennis. Bicycle hire. Mini zoo. Entertainment programme for children (high season).

Ideal For...

 Beach

 Dogs

Year Round Camping

 Golf

 Play Area

 Disabled Facilities

Scan me for more information.

53 accommodations
240 pitches
GPS: 43.72187, 11.22058
Post Code: I-50023

Firenze, Tuscany

Camping Village Firenze

www.alanrogers.com/it66090
internazionale@florencevillage.com
055 237 4704
www.florencevillage.com

Open (Touring Pitches):
19 March - 3 November.

Camping Village Internazionale Firenze is set in the hills about 5 km. south of Florence. This is a well shaded, terraced site with 240 informal touring pitches set around the top of a hill. Although it is a very green site, the camping area is somewhat more open with two electricity pylons at the top of the hill and some noise from the busy motorway which is below and next to the site. It is often lively at night with many young people from tour groups. There is a small restaurant half way up the slope of the site with a reasonable menu. A well located site for visiting Florence rather than for extended stays.

Two traditional toilet blocks include free hot showers. Laundry. Some kitchen facilities. Motorcaravan services. Shop. New bar and restaurant at the lower level. Evening entertainment. Two swimming pools. Swim cap compulsory. Playground. WiFi over part of site (charged). Gas and electric barbecues only.

Ideal For...

 Dogs

 Fishing

 Golf

 Disabled Facilities

 Pets Accepted

 Bar on Site

Scan me for more information.

30 accommodations
362 pitches
GPS: 42.77700, 10.80989
Post Code: I-58043

Castiglione della Pescaia,
Tuscany

www.alanrogers.com/it66605
info@campingsantapomata.it
056 494 1037
www.campingsantapomata.co.uk

Open (Touring Pitches):
24 March - 22 October.

Camping Village Santapomata

Camping Village Santapomata is a traditional type of campsite with direct access to a sandy beach. There are 362 pitches with just 2A electricity, shaded by tall pines. Pitches vary from roomy to rather tight, some are close to the beach and have privacy. The whole site appears a little dated but is popular with some regular visitors and prices are reasonable compared to some in the area. A short walk takes you to the first section of beach where you are required to pay for sun loungers and umbrellas, filling the beach in unbroken rows. The area beyond this is free but you will have a longer walk. Off-pitch parking is compulsory.

Two clean but dated sanitary blocks are equipped with a mixture of Turkish and British style WCs, showers and washbasins. Facilities for disabled visitors. Laundry. Shop. Bar with TV. Restaurant/pizzeria. Takeaway. Play area. Miniclub (July/Aug). Pedalo and canoe hire. WiFi (free). Private beach.

Ideal For...

 Beach

 Dogs

 Fishing

 Watersports

 Golf

 Disabled Facilities

Scan me for more information.

150 accommodations
200 pitches
GPS: 43.18812, 10.53974
Post Code: I-57027

Donoratico, Tuscany

International Camping Etruria

www.alanrogers.com/it66052
info@campingetruria.it
0565 744 254
www.campingetruria.it

Open (Touring Pitches):
24 April - 11 October.

In the heart of the Maremma, on the Etruscan Coast south of Livorno, International Camping Etruria is an ideal place for a peaceful, healthy and enjoyable holiday with family and friends. It is a large, well equipped site with 200 impressive pitches, all with 6A electricity connections and with direct access to a fine sandy beach where there is a popular brasserie, open in the evenings and serving good food. Unlike many pine-dominated sites, there is an attractive open canopy with clever landscaping. The main services are centrally located and are all of a high standard.

Sanitary facilities with hot showers. Motorcaravan services. Supermarket, bar, restaurant, pizzeria and takeaway. Brasserie on beach and lifeguard. Beach chairs, umbrellas and gazebos can be rented at the beach, which has wheelchair access. Cold showers on beach. Water aerobics, beach volleyball, towing boats, pedal boat and canoe rental. Swimming pool complex planned. Playground. Communal barbecue area. Entertainment and activities for children and families. WiFi throughout (charged).

Ideal For...

 Beach

 Dogs

 Play Area

 Disabled Facilities

 Pets Accepted

 Bar on Site

Scan me for more information.

77 accommodations
270 pitches
GPS: 42.77343, 10.84392
Post Code: I-58043

Castiglione della Pescaia,
Tuscany

Maremma Sans Souci

www.alanrogers.com/it66600
info@maremmasanssouci.it
056 493 3765
www.maremmasanssouci.it

Open (Touring Pitches):
26 March - 2 November.

Camping Maremma Sans Souci is a delightful seaside site which has been open since 1965 and sits in natural woodland on the coast road between Follonica and Grosseto. The minimum amount of undergrowth has been cleared to provide 270 individually marked and hedged, flat touring pitches with considerable privacy. All have 6A electrical connections and 40 have a satellite TV point. Cars are parked away from pitches. There is a wide road for motorcaravans but other roads are narrow. Access to some parts is difficult so each pitch is earmarked either for touring units or for tents. An excellent sandy beach is less than 100 m. from one end of the site (400 m. from the other) and is used only by campers. The waters here are among the cleanest in Italy and the beach is very safe for swimming.

Five small, very clean, older style toilet blocks are well situated around the site. Free hot showers. Three blocks have private cabins each with WC, basin and shower. Motorcaravan services. Laundry. Shop. Excellent restaurant (half- and full-board available) and pizzeria. Bar with snacks. ATM. Bicycle hire. Diving school. Excursions organised. WiFi (free). Torches required in some areas. Direct beach access.

Ideal For...

 Beach

 Dogs

 Fishing

 Watersports

 Golf

 Play Area

Scan me for
more information.

110 pitches
GPS: 43.1341, 12.0448
Post Code: I-06061

Castiglione del Lago, Umbria

Camping Listro

www.alanrogers.com/it66530
listro@listro.it
075 951 193
www.listro.it

Open (Touring Pitches):
1 April - 30 September.

This is a simple, pleasant, T-shaped site with the best beach on Lake Trasimeno. Listro provides 100 pitches, all with 3A electricity, many of which are on the lakeside giving stunning views out of your windows and shade is available on most. Facilities are fairly limited with a small shop, bar and snack bar, and there is no organised entertainment. English is spoken and British guests are particularly welcome. The campsite's beach is private and the lake has very gradually sloping beaches making it very safe for children to play and swim. A great site for those who enjoy the peace and quiet of simple camping without the comprehensive facilities and busy activities found on many other lakeside sites. This is reflected in the prices which are very reasonable.

Two sanitary blocks are kept clean. One is rustic in style with outside showers. One includes British style WCs. Facilities for disabled visitors. Washing machine. Motorcaravan services. Bar. Shop. Snack bar. Play area. Fishing. Bicycle hire. Private beach. Guided tours. WiFi over part of site (charged). Dogs are not allowed on the beach.

Ideal For...

 Beach

 Dogs

 Fishing

 Watersports

 Golf

 Play Area

Scan me for more information.

50 accommodations
208 pitches
GPS: 43.0881, 12.1561
Post Code: I-06063

Sant Arcangelo-Magione, Umbria

Villaggio Italgest

www.alanrogers.com/it66520
camping@italgest.com
075 848 238
www.italgest.com

Open (Touring Pitches):
25 March - 30 September.

CampingVillaggio Italgest is a mature, pleasant site with 208 touring pitches (with 6A electricity) on level grass with plenty of shade. Cars are parked away from the pitches. The site offers a wide variety of activities with tours organised daily. The somewhat dated swimming pool complex is next to the bar/restaurant and there is a play area nearby. Directly on the shore on the south side of Lake Trasimeno, Sant Arcangelo is ideally placed for exploring Umbria and Tuscany. The deep lake is a pleasant feature, but may present a hazard to unsupervised children.

The two sanitary blocks have been completely refurbished. They have mainly British style WCs and free hot water in the washbasins and showers. Children's toilets. Baby room. Limited facilities for disabled visitors. Motorcaravan services. Washing machines and dryers. Well equipped campers' kitchen. Shop, bar, restaurant, pizzeria and takeaway (all year). Swimming pool complex with slides and paddling pool (seasonal). Tennis. Play area. TV (satellite) and games rooms. Disco. Films. Watersports, motorboat hire and lake swimming. Fishing. Charcoal barbecues not permitted. Mountain bike and scooter hire. Internet and WiFi (free in some areas). Wide range of activities, entertainment and excursions.

Ideal For...

 Beach

 Dogs

 Fishing

 Watersports

 Golf

 Play Area

Scan me for more information.

111 accommodations
50 pitches
GPS: 42.1558, 12.5732
Post Code: I-00065

Roma, Lazio

I Pini Camping

www.alanrogers.com/it68110
ipini@ecvacanze.it
076 545 3349
www.ecvacanze.it

Open (Touring Pitches):
18 April - 29 September.

I Pini was built a few years ago by a family of experienced campers and is now part of the Elite Club Vacance group. The 117 pitches, with 6-10A electricity, are set on shaded, grassy terraces, some with views of the nearby hills. The beautifully designed restaurant, with a very large terrace, is typical of the thought that has gone into making I Pini a place where you can relax. The pool complex is buzzing with the sound of happy children making use of the novel slides. This tranquil site is 45 minutes from Rome to which buses are available on a daily basis and the site offers plenty of excursions.

The single excellent sanitary block is spotless throughout and hot water is free. Two well equipped units for disabled visitors and separate child's shower. Washing machines and dryers. Motorcaravan services. Bar. Restaurant with large terrace. Snack bar and pizza oven. Pleasant market. Bazaar. Lagoon style swimming pools (with lifeguard). Pool bar. Tennis. Play area. Entertainment (1/6-30/8). Buffet or traditional dinner and pool party (both weekly). Free WiFi. Torches required in some areas. Excursions organised.

Ideal For...

 Dogs

 Fishing

 Play Area

 Disabled Facilities

 Pets Accepted

 Bar on Site

Scan me for more information.

57 accommodations
275 pitches
GPS: 42.130113, 12.173527
Post Code: I-00062

Bracciano, Lazio

Camping Roma Flash

www.alanrogers.com/it68120
info@romaflash.it
0699 805 458
www.romaflash.it

Open (Touring Pitches):
1 April - 30 September.

This pleasant site is in a superb location with magnificent views over Lake Bracciano and Castello Odescalchi. Although it was busy when we visited, it was still peaceful and relaxing. There are 275 flat, shaded pitches with 6A electricity (Europlug). A pleasant, covered restaurant offers pizza and a limited menu. Set alongside the lake with its fabulous views, the restaurant complex has a large terrace, as does a smaller indoor area. Elide speaks excellent English and will happily go out of her way to ensure guests enjoy their holiday. Many of the visitors told us that they return year after year and some stay for 8 to 12 weeks at a time, enjoying all that the Lazio region has to offer.

Two large, but tired sanitary blocks (scheduled for refurbishment) have free hot water throughout and fully adjustable showers. Facilities for disabled visitors in one block. Rooms for children. Laundry facilities. Gas supplies. Bar/restaurant/pizzeria, small shop (all open as site). Swimming pool (1/6-31/8). Play area. Watersports. Games room. Entertainment for children in high season. WiFi (charged). Excursions. Private bus to Roma San Pietro and return. Sports area.

Ideal For...

 Beach

 Dogs

Fishing

 Watersports

 Golf

 Play Area

Scan me for more information.

50 pitches
GPS: 42.15431, 14.71578
Post Code: I-66050

Vasto, Abruzzo

Camping Grotta del Saraceno

www.alanrogers.com/it67985
info@grottadelsaraceno.it
0873 310213
www.grottadelsaraceno.it

Open (Touring Pitches):
4 June - 18 September.

Set on a beautiful stretch of the Adriatic Coast, Camping Village Grotta del Saraceno is on a promontory overlooking an attractive bay with stunning views. The site has rows of pitches with 6A electricity, most with artificial shade, others with shade provided by trees. Unfortunately, the few pitches with sea views are occupied by permanent units. The trio of pools, including fountains, is very pleasant and is floodlit at night. There is a choice of restaurants and a pizzeria and plenty of activities on offer especially for children. The soft sand beach is down 100 steps, and halfway down there is a charming 'ristopub' which sits alongside the famous grotto. If you are at all infirm and looking for a beach holiday, this site is not for you.

A mix of newer and older style sanitary facilities are clean and well maintained and include both British and Turkish style toilets and showers. Laundry. Motorcaravan services. Bazaar. Bar/ snack bar. Ristopub. Central and beach bars. Supermarket. News stand. Greengrocer. Swimming pool complex. Restaurants and pizzeria. Beautician. Hairdresser. Sports fields. Beach volleyball. Auditorium. Games room. Fitness area. Entertainment and activities for children and families. Fishing. Bicycle hire. Torches useful. WiFi on part of site (free). Dogs are not accepted.

Ideal For...

 Beach

 Fishing

 Watersports

 Play Area

 Disabled Facilities

 Bar on Site

Scan me for more information.

84 accommodations
265 pitches
GPS: 42.6577, 14.0353
Post Code: I-64026

Roseto degli Abruzzi, Abruzzo

www.alanrogers.com/it68040
eurcamping@camping.it
085 899 3179
www.eurcamping.it

Open (Touring Pitches):
11 May - 22 October.

Camping Village Eurcamping

Eurcamping is about 2 km. south of the small town of Roseto degli Abruzzi. This is a pleasant and relatively quiet site, situated beside the sea, with 265 well defined pitches. All pitches have 6A electricity, some are very large and many have shade. There are good facilities which are grouped around the reception area including a very pleasant swimming pool and an entertainment area is at the far end of the site. Access to the site's beach of soft sand and rugged stone is just 75 m. from the gate.

Three sanitary blocks with free hot showers. Facilities for disabled visitors. Baby rooms. Motorcaravan services. Laundry. Bar, restaurant, takeaway, pizzeria, shop (all 15/5-15/9). Swimming pools (hats must be worn) with solarium terrace (20/5-10/9). Play area. Outdoor fitness area. Tennis. Bowling. Bicycle hire. Artificial grass football ground. Entertainment in high season. Clubs for children and teenagers. WiFi throughout (charged). Pets restricted to assigned pitches. Bungalows to rent. Free shuttle bus to Roseto beach. Security bracelets are compulsory.

Ideal For...

 Kids

 Beach

 Dogs

 Fishing

 Play Area

 Disabled Facilities

Scan me for more information.

299 accommodations
750 pitches
GPS: 41.20722, 13.79139
Post Code: I-81030

Baia Domizia, Campania

Baia Domizia Villaggio

www.alanrogers.com/it68200
info@baiadomizia.it
082 393 0164
www.baiadomizia.it

Open (Touring Pitches):
28 April - 18 September.

This large, beautifully maintained seaside site is about 70 kilometres northwest of Naples within a pine forest, cleverly left in its natural state. Although it does not feel like it, there are 750 touring pitches in clearings, either of grass and sand or on hardstanding, all with electricity, 80 now also with water and waste water. Finding a pitch may take time as there are so many good ones to choose from, but staff will help in season. Most pitches are well shaded, however there are some in the sun for cooler periods. The central complex is superb with well designed buildings providing for all needs (the site is some distance from the town).

Seven new toilet blocks have hot water in washbasins (many cabins) and showers. Good access and facilities for disabled campers. Washing machines, spin dryers. Motorcaravan services. Gas supplies. Supermarket and general shop. Large bar. Restaurants, pizzeria and takeaway. Ice cream parlour. Swimming pool complex. Playground. Tennis. Windsurfing hire and school. Disco. Cinema. Gym. Excursions. Torches required in some areas. WiFi (charged). Dogs are not accepted.

Ideal For...

 Kids

Beach

 Fishing

 Watersports

 Play Area

 Disabled Facilities

Scan me for more information.

10 accommodations
80 pitches
GPS: 38.908917, 16.80945
Post Code: I-88050

Cropani Marina, Calabria

Casa Vacanze Lungomare

www.alanrogers.com/it68830
info@campinglungomare.com
096 196 1167
www.campinglungomare.com

Open (Touring Pitches):
1 April - 30 September.

Camping Casa Vacanze Lungomare is a small, family run site close to the town of Cropani Marina. There are 100 marked pitches in total and 80 of these are for touring. They are well laid out, all have 3/6A electricity and water points nearby and shade is provided on most by tall pine trees. The site has a private sandy beach which is accessed across a small road, just 20 m. from the pitches. Just outside the site, close to the entrance/reception area there are also a number of mobile homes/chalets available for rent. The friendly and helpful owner is able to arrange excursions to various places of interest.

Two toilet blocks include showers and WCs (Turkish and British style). Facilities for disabled visitors. Washing machine. Motorcaravan services. Bar and restaurant/pizzeria. All weather football pitch. Play area. Entertainment in high season. Accommodation to rent. WiFi on part of site.

Ideal For...

 Beach

 Dogs

 Fishing

 Play Area

 Disabled Facilities

Pets Accepted

Scan me for more information.

5 accommodations
100 pitches
GPS: 36.93639, 15.17472
Post Code: I-96012

Avola, Sicily

Camping Sabbiadoro

www.alanrogers.com/it69215
info@campeggiosabbiadoro.com
093 156 0000
www.campeggiosabbiadoro.com

Open (Touring Pitches):
All year.

This is truly one of Sicily's hidden gems and the Alia family will ensure your stay is pleasant and peaceful at this delightful campsite with 100 pitches. These are on terraces down towards the beach and there are stunning sea views. With over 100 different species of trees and flowers around the site, it is awash with colour and has good shade. A small, sandy beach complements the site's natural charm. When we arrived, a party was in progress to celebrate the natural products of the area and a huge copper pot was being used to make ricotta cheese, which within an hour was being distributed around the site, with local bread. It was delicious! Access would be difficult for larger motorcaravns.

An ultra modern, brand new toilet block is now open with facilities for disabled visitors. Motorcaravan services (automated and hands-free). Shop and bar (1/5-31/10). Restaurant (15/5-15/9). TV room. Sandy beach. Fishing. Sailing. WiFi over part of site (charged).

Ideal For...

 Beach

 Dogs

Year Round Camping

 Fishing

 Watersports

 Disabled Facilities

Scan me for more information.

140 accommodations
339 pitches
GPS: 40.6423, 8.1906
Post Code: I-07041

Alghero, Sardinia

Camping Torre del Porticciolo

www.alanrogers.com/it69950
info@torredelporticciolo.it
079 919 010
www.torredelporticciolo.it

Open (Touring Pitches):
15 May - 10 October.

Torre del Porticciolo is set high on a peninsula with fabulous views from some parts of the site over the sea and old fortifications. It is family owned with striking traditional old buildings, attractive landscaping and a large pool and paddling pool. Spread over a large area, the site is mostly under the shade of pine trees. A few pitches enjoy limited sea views through the trees. The attractive beach is accessed down a steep slope. The amenities are all by the entrance, with the restaurant and pool both very popular. We did notice a large number of intrusive stray cats on our visit.

The two mature sanitary blocks have exclusively Turkish style toilets. The few British style toilets are in locked cabins with a key on request. Hot showers are free. Washing machines. Motorcaravan services. Supermarket. Restaurant. Good supervised pool and paddling pool. Aerobics. Fitness centre. Play areas. Bicycle hire. Miniclub. Entertainment (July/Aug). Excursion service. Beach 100 m. down very steep slope. Excellent diving. WiFi in restaurant (charged).

Ideal For...

 Beach

 Dogs

 Watersports

 Play Area

 Pets Accepted

 Bar on Site

Scan me for more information.

LUXEMBOURG

The Grand Duchy of Luxembourg is a sovereign state, lying between Belgium, France and Germany. Divided into two areas: the spectacular Ardennes region in the north and the rolling farmlands and woodland in the south, bordered on the east by the wine growing area of the Moselle Valley.

Most attractions are within easy reach of Luxembourg's capital, Luxembourg-Ville, a fortress city perched dramatically on its rocky promontory overlooking the Alzette and Petrusse Valleys. The verdant hills and valleys of the Ardennes are a maze of hiking trails, footpaths and cycle routes – ideal for an activity holiday.

The Moselle Valley, famous for its sweet wines, is just across the river from Germany; its charming hamlets can be discovered by bicycle or by boat. Popular wine tasting tours take place from late spring to early autumn. Echternacht is a good base for exploring the Mullerthal region, known as 'Little Switzerland.' Lying on the banks of the River Sûre, its forested landscape is dotted with curious rock formations and castle ruins, notably those at Beaufort and Larochette. The pretty Schießentümpel cascade is worth a visit.

Language: Letzeburgesch is the national language, with French and German also being official languages
Capital: Luxembourg City
Currency: Euro (€)
Time Zone: Central European Time (GMT/UTC plus one hour)
Telephone Country Code: 00 352
Tourist Office: www.luxembourg.co.uk

Public Holidays
New Year; Carnival Day mid-Feb; Easter Mon; May Day; Ascension; Whit Mon; National Day 23 June; Assumption 15 Aug; Kermesse 1 Sept; All Saints; All Souls; Christmas 25, 26 Dec.

Motoring
Many holidaymakers travel through Luxembourg to take advantage of the lower fuel prices, thus creating traffic congestion at petrol stations, especially in summer. A Blue Zone area exists in Luxembourg City and various parts of the country (discs from tourist offices) but meters are also used.

161 pitches
GPS: 49.57180, 6.10900
Post Code: L-1899

Luxembourg, Luxembourg District

Camping Kockelscheuer

www.alanrogers.com/lu7660
caravani@pt.lu
471 815
www.camping-kockelscheuer.jimdo.com

Open (Touring Pitches):
Week before Easter - 31 October.

Camping Kockelscheuer is a municipal site owned by the city of Luxembourg and is 4 km. from its centre. It is managed by an enthusiastic couple and is quietly situated (although there can be some aircraft noise at times). On a slight slope, there are 161 individual pitches of good size, either on flat ground at the bottom of the site or on wide flat terraces with easy access, all with 16A electricity. There is also a special area for tents, with picnic tables and, in the reception building, a tent campers' lounge. For children, there is a large area with modern play equipment on safety tiles and next door to the site is a sports centre. There is a friendly welcome, charges are reasonable and English is spoken.

Two fully equipped, identical sanitary buildings, both very clean. Washing machines. Motorcaravan services. Shop (order bread the previous day). Snack bar. Restaurant in adjacent sports centre also with tennis, squash, pitch and putt and golf driving range. Rest room. No entry for vehicles (reception closed) 12.00-14.00. Free WiFi throughout.

Ideal For...

 Dogs

 Golf

 Play Area

 Disabled Facilities

 Pets Accepted

Scan me for more information.

27 accommodations
76 pitches
GPS: 50.00017, 5.99106
Post Code: L-9747

Enscherange, Diekirch

www.alanrogers.com/lu7770
valdor@pt.lu
920 691
www.valdor.lu

Open (Touring Pitches):
2 April - 29 October.

Camping Val d'Or

Camping Val d'Or is one of those small, family run, countryside sites where you easily find yourself staying longer than planned. Set in four hectares of lush meadowland under a scattering of trees, the site is divided into two by the tree-lined Clerve river as it winds its way slowly through the site. A footbridge goes some way to joining the site together and there are two entrances for vehicles. There are 76 marked, level grass touring pitches, all with electricity (6A Europlug) and with some tree shade. Cars are parked away from the pitches. There are open views of the surrounding countryside with its wooded hills. The site's Dutch owners speak good English.

Next to the reception is a heated sanitary block where some facilities are found, others including some showers are located under cover, outside. Showers are token operated. Laundry room. Gas supplies. Bar (all day in high season). Takeaway (high season except Sundays). Swimming and paddling in river. Three play areas (one with waterways, waterwheel and small pool). Bicycle hire. WiFi (free). Max. 1 dog.

Ideal For...

 Beach

 Dogs

Fishing

 Golf

 Play Area

 Pets Accepted

Scan me for more information.

18 accommodations
200 pitches
GPS: 49.95387, 6.0273
Post Code: L-9663

Kautenbach, Diekirch

Camping Kautenbach

www.alanrogers.com/lu7830
campkaut@pt.lu
00352950303
www.campingkautenbach.lu

Open (Touring Pitches):
20 January - 16 December

Kautenbach is situated in the heart of the Luxembourg Ardennes and was established over 60 years ago. Although in an idyllic location, it is less than a mile from a railway station with regular trains to Luxembourg City to the south. There are 200 touring pitches here, mostly of a good size and with reasonable shade. All pitches have electrical connections (10A). This is excellent walking country with many tracks around the site. The site managers will be happy to recommend walks for all abilities. Kautenbach has an attractive bistro style restaurant specialising in local cuisine, as well as a large selection of whiskies!

Three toilet blocks with open style washbasins and showers, baby changing. Facilities for disabled visitors (key). Laundry. Shop for basics (1/4-31/10, bread to order). Restaurant, bar/snack bar (all season). Direct river access. Fishing. Play area. Mobile homes, safari tents and camping pods for rent. Internet café.

Ideal For...

 Beach

 Dogs

 Fishing

 Walking

 Golf

 Play Area

Scan me for more information.

32 accommodations
359 pitches
GPS: 49.78472, 6.16519
Post Code: L-7465

Nommern, Luxembourg District

www.alanrogers.com/lu7620
info@nommerlayen-ec.lu
878 078
www.nommerlayen-ec.lu

Open (Touring Pitches):
1 March - 6 November.

Europacamping Nommerlayen

Situated at the end of its own road, in the lovely wooded hills of central Luxembourg, this is a top quality site with fees to match, but it has everything! A large, central building housing most of the services and amenities opens onto a terrace around an excellent swimming pool complex with a large fun pool and an imaginative water playground. The 359 individual pitches (100 sq.m) are on grassy terraces, all have access to electricity (2/16A) and water taps. Pitches are grouped beside age-appropriate play areas and the facilities throughout the campsite reflect the attention given to families in particular. Interestingly enough, the superb sanitary block is called Badtemple, (having been built in the style of a Greek temple). A member of Leading Campings group.

A large, high quality, modern sanitary unit provides some washbasins in cubicles, facilities for disabled visitors, family and baby rooms and a sauna. Twelve private bathrooms for hire. Laundry. Motorcaravan services. Supermarket. Restaurant. Snack bar. Bar (all 19/3-6/11). Excellent swimming pool complex and new heated pool with sliding roof (1/5-15/9). Fitness programmes. Bowling. Playground. Large screen TV. Entertainment in season. Bicycle hire. WiFi (free over part of site).

Ideal For...

 Kids

 Dogs

 Fishing

 Golf

 Play Area

 Disabled Facilities

Scan me for more information.

56 accommodations
280 pitches
GPS: 49.78508, 6.21033
Post Code: L-7633

Larochette, Luxembourg District

www.alanrogers.com/lu7610
info@irisparc.com
879 040
www.irisparc.co.uk/camping-birkelt

Camping Birkelt

Open (Touring Pitches):
27 March - 1 November.

This is very much a family site with a great range of facilities provided. It is well organised and well laid out, set in an elevated position in attractive, undulating countryside. A tarmac road runs around the site with 427 large grass pitches (280 for touring), some slightly sloping, many with a fair amount of shade, on either side of gravel access roads in straight rows and circles. Two hundred pitches have electricity, 134 serviced ones have 16A, the remainder 10A. An all-weather swimming pool complex is beside the site entrance (free for campers) and entertainment for children is arranged in high season. The site is very popular with tour operators (140 pitches).

Three modern heated sanitary buildings well situated around the site include mostly open washbasins (6 cabins in one block). Baby baths. Facilities (including accommodation to rent) for wheelchair users. Washing machines and dryers. Motorcaravan services. Shops. Coffee bar. Restaurant with terrace. Swimming pool with sliding cupola (heated all season). Outdoor pool for toddlers. Play areas. Trampolines. Volleyball. Minigolf. Tennis. Bicycle hire. Riding. Internet points. Free WiFi over site.

Ideal For...

 Kids

 Dogs

 Fishing

 Walking

 Golf

 Play Area

Scan me for more information.

200 pitches
GPS: 49.867608, 6.169467
Post Code: L-9201

Diekirch, Diekirch

Camping Op der Sauer

www.alanrogers.com/lu7430
info@campsauer.lu
80 85 90
www.campsauer.lu

Open (Touring Pitches):
1 April - 31 October

Op Der Sauer is by the river on the fringes of the town of Diekirch, a 15 minute walk away along a riverside path. The 200 large, grassy touring pitches have 10A electricity and views of the river. Reception and other buildings are set around a small courtyard, giving a village atmosphere to the site. Sebastiaan and Ellen, the enthusiastic new owners, are constantly making improvements. A wellness block with infra-red and traditional saunas, and a new bar and restaurant have been added this year, and they hold a national Eco-label award for their approach to recycling and the use of sustainable materials. Fishing is possible from the path adjacent to the site.

Modern heated sanitary blocks with hot showers. No shop, but bread can be ordered. Bar, restaurant and takeaway. Shallow (65 cm), unheated swimming pool. Play area. Boules pitch. Fishing. WiFi.

Ideal For...

 Beach

 Dogs

 Fishing

 Watersports

 Golf

 Disabled Facilities

Scan me for more information.

3 accommodations
112 pitches
GPS: 50.12340, 6.10517
Post Code: L-9972

Lieler, Luxembourg District

www.alanrogers.com/lu7880
info@troisfrontieres.lu
998 608
www.troisfrontieres.lu

Open (Touring Pitches):
All year.

Camping Trois Frontières

On a clear day, it is possible to see Belgium, Germany and Luxembourg from the campsite swimming pool, hence its name: Trois Frontières. Corinne and Erwin Levering own and manage the site themselves and all visitors receive a personal welcome and immediately become part of a large, happy family. There are 112 touring pitches on slightly sloping fields divided by pine trees which give some shade. All have 6-10A electricity. Most of the facilities are close to the entrance, leaving the camping area quiet, except for the play area. The restaurant/takeaway provides good quality food at reasonable prices, served either inside or on the pleasant terrace with flower borders, overlooking the pool which is covered and heated. The site is ideally situated for visits to Bitburg, Germany and spa towns in Belgium. A member of the TopCamp group.

Toilet block including suite for visitors with disabilities, plus baby bath and changing station, and family bathroom. More WCs in second building (down some steps). Laundry. Covered, heated swimming pool (1/4-31/10). Play area. Boules. Games room. Bicycle hire. WiFi (free).

Ideal For...

 Dogs

Year Round Camping

 Fishing

 Golf

 Play Area

 Disabled Facilities

Scan me for more information.

14 accommodations
98 pitches
GPS: 49.91015, 6.08635
Post Code: L-9164

Bourscheid, Diekirch

Camping Um Gritt

www.alanrogers.com/lu7930
umgritt@castlegarden.lu
990 449
www.umgritt.castlegarden.lu

Open (Touring Pitches):
25 March - 31 October.

Camping Um Gritt Castlegarden is a family run campsite with friendly Dutch owners. It is located at the foot of a castle in the heart of the Ardennes, in the beautiful wooded valley of Bourscheid. It has a long season, open from April until the end of October. There are 98 reasonably level, unmarked pitches, many with little shade, including about 40 long stay pitches. All have 10A Europlug. They are laid out in a sunny, grassy meadow along the banks of the shallow River Sûre. This is an ideal place to cool off on a hot day, bathing, fishing, messing around in small boats or having a drink in the small bar/ restaurant.

There are five modern toilet blocks with all necessary facilities. Washing machine and dryer. Bread delivery. Small bar, restaurant and takeaway. Club for children and some family entertainment (July/Aug). Small playground. Volleyball. Mountain bike hire. Walking and hiking maps. WiFi throughout (charged).

Ideal For...

 Beach

 Dogs

 Fishing

 Golf

 Play Area

 Pets Accepted

Scan me for more information.

NETHERLANDS

With vast areas of the Netherlands reclaimed from the sea, nearly half of the country lies at or below sea level. The result is a flat, fertile landscape criss-crossed with rivers and canals. Famous for its windmills and bulb fields, it also boasts some of the most impressive coastal dunes in Europe.

No visit to the Netherlands would be complete without experiencing its capital city, Amsterdam, with its maze of canals, bustling cafés, museums and summer festivals.

The fields of South Holland are an explosion of colour between March and May when the world's biggest flower auction takes place at Aalsmer.

The Vecht valley and its towns of Dalfsen, Ommen and Hardenberg are best explored by bicycle, while Giethoorn, justly dubbed the 'Venice of Holland' has to be seen from a boat. The Kinderdijk windmills on the Alblasserwaard polder are a UNESCO World Heritage Site. The islands of Zeeland are home to beautiful old towns such as Middelburg, the provincial capital, Zierikzee, with its old harbour and the quaint old town of Veere.

Language: Dutch. English and German are widely spoken. In Friesland a Germanic language, Frisian, is spoken
Capital: Amsterdam
Currency: Euro (€)
Time Zone: Central European Time (GMT/UTC plus one hour)
Telephone Country Code: 00 31
Tourist Office: www.holland.com/uk

Say Hello in Dutch
Hallo (hah-low)

Say Goodbye in Dutch
Tot ziens (tot seens)

Public Holidays
New Year; April Fools Day 1 April; Good Fri; Easter Mon; Queen's Birthday 30 April; Labour Day; Remembrance Day 4 May; Liberation Day 5 May; Ascension; Whit Mon; SinterKlaas 5 Dec; Kingdom Day 15 Dec; Christmas 25, 26 Dec.

Motoring
There is a comprehensive motorway system but all main roads can become very busy, particularly in the morning and evening rush hours. There are many bridges which can cause congestion. There are no toll roads but there are a few toll bridges and tunnels, notably the Zeeland Bridge, Europe's longest across the Oosterschelde.

7 accommodations
100 pitches
GPS: 51.57840, 3.69642
Post Code: NL-4493 NC

Kamperland, Zeeland

Camping De Molenhoek

www.alanrogers.com/nl5570
info@demolenhoek.com
0113 371 202
www.demolenhoek.com

Open (Touring Pitches):
19 March - 28 October.

This rural, family run site makes a pleasant contrast to the livelier coastal sites in this popular holiday area. There is an emphasis on catering for the users of the 300 permanent or seasonal holiday caravans and 100 tourers. Eighty of these have 6A electricity, water and drainage. The site is neat and tidy with surrounding hedges and trees giving privacy and some shade, and electrical connections are available. A large outdoor pool area has ample space for swimming, children's play and sun loungers. Entertainment, including dance evenings and bingo, is organised in season.

Two very clean and well appointed sanitary blocks include some washbasins in cabins and facilities for children. Toilet and shower facilities for disabled visitors and for babies. Laundry facilities. Motorcaravan services. Bar/restaurant with terrace and large TVs and LCD projection. Snack bar. Heated outdoor swimming pool (15/5-15/9). Playground. Bicycle hire. Pool tables. Sports field. Entertainment for children and teenagers. WiFi over site (charged).

Ideal For...

 Kids

 Beach

 Dogs

 Fishing

 Watersports

 Golf

Scan me for more information.

93 pitches
GPS: 51.36613, 3.38583
Post Code: NL-4525 LW

Retranchement, Zeeland

Camping Cassandria Bad

www.alanrogers.com/nl5502
info@cassandriabad.nl
0117 392 300
www.cassandriabad.nl

Open (Touring Pitches):
27 March - 30 October.

Cassandria Bad was established in 1992, lying very close to the Belgian border and the resort of Cadzand Bad, just under 2 km. from the nearest North Sea beach. Pitches are grassy and spacious; some are privately let for the full season. All pitches are equipped with 10A electricity and free cable TV connections. Except for loading and unloading, cars are not allowed in the camping area, but a large parking area is provided. On-site amenities include a bar, snack bar, shop services and games room. During the peak season, a variety of activities are organised, including karaoke, bingo and sports tournaments.

Two clean and well maintained sanitary units with free showers, and two family bathrooms in the main block. Good laundry facilities. Small shop (fresh bread daily). Bar with LCD projector and screen. Snack bar. Sports fields with volleyball and 2 football pitches. Games room with table football, air hockey and electronic games. Trampoline. Several well appointed and interesting play areas including an indoor play area. Bicycle hire. WiFi over site (charged). 1 dog allowed per pitch.

Ideal For...

 Dogs

 Play Area

 Pets Accepted

 Bar on Site

Scan me for more information.

48 accommodations
200 pitches
GPS: 52.20012, 4.45623
Post Code: NL-2231 NW

Rijnsburg, Zuid-Holland

Vakantiepark Koningshof

www.alanrogers.com/nl5630
info@koningshofholland.nl
0714 026 051
www.koningshofholland.nl

Open (Touring Pitches):
15 March - 31 October.

This popular site is run in a personal and friendly way. The 200 pitches for touring units (some with hardstandings for larger units) are laid out in small groups, divided by hedges and trees and all with 10A electrical connections. Cars are mostly parked in areas around the perimeter and 100 static caravans, confined to one section of the site, are entirely unobtrusive. Reception, a pleasant, good quality restaurant, bar and a snack bar are grouped around a courtyard-style entrance which is decorated with seasonal flowers. The site has a small outdoor, heated pool (13.5x7 m) with a separate paddling pool and imaginative children's play equipment. A member of the Holland Tulip Parcs Group.

Three good toilet blocks, two with underfloor heating, with washbasins in cabins and provision for disabled visitors. Laundry facilities. Motorcaravan services. Gas supplies. Shop (7/4-30/9). Bar (7/4-30/9). Restaurant (14/4-31/8). Snacks and takeaway (7/4-30/9). Small outdoor pool (unsupervised; 15/5-15/9). Indoor pool (18/3-31/10). Adventure playground and sports area. Outdoor gym and skateboard ramps. Tennis. Fishing pond (free). Bicycle hire. Entertainment in high season. Room for shows. Max. 1 dog, accepted in a limited area of the site. WiFi over site (free).

Ideal For...

 Beach

 Dogs

 Fishing

 Watersports

 Golf

 Play Area

Scan me for more information.

20 accommodations
100 pitches
GPS: 51.82943, 4.11618
Post Code: NL-3221 LJ

Hellevoetsluis, Zuid-Holland

www.alanrogers.com/nl6970
info@weergors.nl
0181 312 430
www.weergors.nl

Open (Touring Pitches):
18 March - 1 November.

Camping 't Weergors

A rustic style site built around old farm buildings, Camping Caravaning 't Weergors has a comfortable mature feel. At the front of the site is a well presented farmhouse which houses reception and includes the main site services. The sanitary blocks have been renewed recently as has the farm accommodating an attractive à la carte restaurant and pancake outlet. The reception has also been renewed including a new minimarket from where you can order fresh bread. There are currently 100 touring pitches (plus seasonal and static places), with another field at the back of the site which was recently developed to provide a further 70 or 80 touring places.

Three sanitary blocks have showers (by key), washbasins, some in cabins, children's showers and toilets plus baby baths. Laundry facilities. Motorcaravan services. Small shop. Restaurant and bar (snacks) and pancakes. Tennis. Internet access. Play area. Paddling pool (15/5-15/9). Organised entertainment in high season. Fishing pond. Bicycle hire. Rally field.

Ideal For...

 Beach

 Dogs

 Fishing

 Watersports

 Play Area

 Pets Accepted

Scan me for more information.

42 accommodations
160 pitches
GPS: 52.01767, 4.37908
Post Code: NL-2616 LJ

Delft, Zuid-Holland

Vakantiepark Delftse Hout

www.alanrogers.com/nl5600
info@delftsehout.nl
0152 130 040
www.delftsehout.nl

Open (Touring Pitches):
25 March - 1 November.

Pleasantly situated in Delft's park and forest area on the eastern edge of the city, is this well run, modern site. It has 160 touring pitches quite formally arranged in groups of four to six and surrounded by attractive trees and hedges. All have sufficient space and electrical connections (10A Europlug). Modern buildings near the entrance house the site amenities. A good sized first floor restaurant serves snacks and full meals and has an outdoor terrace overlooking the swimming pool and pitches. Walking and cycling tours are organised and there is a recreation programme in high season.

Modern, heated toilet facilities include a spacious family room and children's section. Facilities for disabled visitors. Laundry. Motorcaravan services. Shop for basic food and camping items (all season). Restaurant, takeaway and bar (1/4-1/10). Small heated outdoor swimming pool (mid May - mid Sept.) Adventure playground. Recreation room. Bicycle hire. Gas supplies. Max. 1 dog. WiFi (100mb/day included).

Ideal For...

Kids

Beach

Dogs

Fishing

Watersports

Golf

Scan me for more information.

93 accommodations
476 pitches
GPS: 51.33623, 5.29373
Post Code: NL-5521 RD

Eersel, Noord-Brabant

Recreatiepark TerSpegelt

www.alanrogers.com/nl6630
info@terspegelt.nl
0497 512 016
www.terspegelt.nl

Open (Touring Pitches):
18 March - 31 October.

Recreatiepark TerSpegelt is a large, attractively laid out site set around three (unsupervised) lakes used for sports, non-motorised boating, swimming and fishing. The site has 865 pitches, with 476 for touring units and tents, and 93 cabins, chalets and mobile homes for rent, plus various types of tent. All touring pitches have electricity (6-16A Europlug), 347 also have water and drainage and some have lakeside views. We can recommend this site to families with children (pushchairs useful) and people who like to participate in organised activities (sports and outdoor activities, campfires and themed dinners).

Five main toilet blocks, four heated by solar panels, provide toilets, washbasins (open and in cubicles) and showers. Washbasins for children. Heated baby rooms with changing mat and bath. Facilities for disabled visitors in one block. Laundry. Motorcaravan services. Supermarket, restaurant, bar, snack bar and swimming pools (all open as site). Entertainment and activities. Watersports, climbing wall and minigolf. Bicycle and go-cart hire. Tennis. Dogs are not accepted. WiFi over site (charged).

Ideal For...

 Kids

 Beach

 Fishing

 Watersports

 Golf

 Play Area

Scan me for more information.

5 accommodations
35 pitches
GPS: 51.377352, 4.336887
Post Code: NL-4641 SR

Ossendrecht, Noord-Brabant

www.alanrogers.com/nl5542
ossendrecht@naturisme-athena.org
0164 672 489
www.naturisme-athena.org

Open (Touring Pitches):
27 March - 4 November.

Athena Ossendrecht

This naturist site bordering the polders in a quiet location on heavily wooded undulating land; the attractive 14-hectare Athena Naturisten Ossendrecht site has over 300 pitches, 35 of which are reserved for touring units. Twenty-nine have electricity connections (6A) on grass/sand and are fairly level, with shade from trees in places. The reception, attractive clubhouse with bar and terrace, as well as the swimming pool, sports areas and car parks, are located towards the entrance to the site, leaving the camping area quiet and vehicle free.

Five well maintained sanitary buildings distributed over the site. Hot showers (€ 0.50). Good unit for disabled visitors. Laundry. Bread to order (July/Aug). Bar/café. Swimming pool. Paddling pool. Sauna. Beach volleyball. Pétanque. Badminton. Play areas. Social room with games and books. Activities for children in high season. All visitors must be in possession of an International Naturist licence. Dogs are not accepted. WiFi (free by reception).

Ideal For...

 Naturist

 Play Area

 Bar on Site

Scan me for more information.

36 accommodations
530 pitches
GPS: 51.33635, 5.35552
Post Code: NL-5571 TN

Bergeijk, Noord-Brabant

www.alanrogers.com/nl5970
info@depaal.nl
0497 571 977
www.depaal.nl

Open (Touring Pitches):
1 April - 31 October.

Camping De Paal

A really first class, family run campsite, ideal for families with children up to 12 years old, with activities on a grand scale, yet retaining a relaxed atmosphere. Situated in 42 hectares of woodland, it has 530 touring pitches (up to 150 sq.m). The pitches are numbered and in meadows, separated by trees, with cars parked mainly on dedicated parking areas. All have 6A electricity, TV, water, drainage and a bin. There are 60 pitches with private sanitary facilities some of which are partly underground and attractively covered with grass and flowers. Each group of pitches has a small playground. There are larger adventure-style play areas, one resembling a desert with water and other activities, in a 40,000 sq.m. dune-like setting.

High quality sanitary facilities are ultra modern, including washbasins in cabins, family rooms and baby baths, all with lots of space. Facilities for disabled visitors. Launderette. Motorcaravan services. Underground supermarket. Restaurant (high season), bar and snack bar (all season). Indoor pool (all season, supervised in high season). Outdoor pool (May-Sept). Tennis. Play areas. Theatre. WiFi (charged). Bicycle hire. Pet zoo.

Ideal For...

 Beach

 Dogs

 Fishing

 Golf

 Play Area

 Disabled Facilities

Scan me for more information.

4 accommodations
80 pitches
GPS: 51.469064, 4.322337
Post Code: NL-4625 DD

Bergen op Zoom, Noord-Brabant

Camping Uit en Thuis

www.alanrogers.com/nl5539
info@campinguitenthuis.nl
0164 233 391
www.campinguitenthuis.nl

Open (Touring Pitches):
1 April - 30 September.

Camping Uit en Thuis (home and away) is a friendly, family run site close to the town of Bergen op Zoom. There is a choice of 80 sunny or shady touring pitches including eight with hardstanding. Most pitches have electricity (6A), water, drainage and cable TV connections. A number of fully equipped mobile homes are available for rent, as well as a simply furnished hikers' cabin (maximum three nights). There are also several pitches for cycle campers. On-site amenities include a popular snack bar/restaurant which specialises in traditional Dutch cuisine (including frikandels and various schnitzels).

Three clean, modern toilet blocks have family showers, hot water (on payment) and dishwashing sinks. One block has facilities for disabled visitors and a small laundry. Shop, café/snack bar/ takeaway (all season). Half-size billiard tables. Play area. Football pitch. Tennis. Volleyball. Minigolf. Activities for children up to 12 yrs. (high season). Bicycle hire. WiFi throughout (charged).

Ideal For...

 Beach

 Dogs

 Watersports

 Walking

 Play Area

 Disabled Facilities

Scan me for more information.

34 accommodations
66 pitches
GPS: 50.92113, 5.95719
Post Code: NL-6413 TC

Heerlen, Limburg

Camping Hitjesvijver

www.alanrogers.com/nl6578
info@hitjesvijver.nl
0455 211 353
www.hitjesvijver.nl

Open (Touring Pitches):
All year.

Just five kilometres from the centre of Heerlen, and within easy reach of Maastricht, Liège and Aachen, Camping Hitjesvijver is an ideal choice for visitors who appreciate a natural setting, but wish to be close to the commercial and cultural attractions of towns and cities. This friendly, 4.5-hectare site has 66 touring pitches, mainly on grass, but with a number of hardstandings, most with electricity (6A Europlug) and water connections for motorcaravans. Some pitches are shaded, while others are more open. There are some chalets and mobile homes for hire. The site is very suitable for couples and families who wish to enjoy the miles of cycle routes locally, some of which begin at the site. There may be some noise from the nearby road.

Two heated sanitary blocks, one rather dated, with hot showers, some washbasins in cubicles, and a baby room. Washing machine and dryer. Motorcaravan services. Bar with fireplace. Heated outdoor swimming and paddling pools (15/5-1/9). Play area. Bocce courts. Badminton courts. Activities and entertainment including night swimming (adults only), disco nights and competitions (July/Aug). Games room. WiFi free on covered terrace, charged on pitches.. Accommodation to rent. Max. 1 dog per unit.

Ideal For...

 Dogs

Year Round Camping

 Fishing

 Golf

 Play Area

 Pets Accepted

Scan me for more information.

26 accommodations
137 pitches
GPS: 50.86012, 5.83102
Post Code: NL-6301 BN

Valkenburg, Limburg

Camping Den Driesch

www.alanrogers.com/nl6565
info@campingdendriesch.nl
0436 012 025
www.campingdendriesch.nl

Open (Touring Pitches):
27 March - 23 December.

Den Driesch is an attractive site just 500 m. from the centre of the historic town of Valkenburg. Pitches here are grassy with reasonable shade and are all supplied with 10A electricity. A number of semi-asphalted pitches are particularly suitable for motorcaravans. On-site amenities include the site restaurant, De Zachte Gee, and a snack bar. There is also a well stocked shop with freshly baked bread every day. The southern Limburg region is very popular for outdoor activities and Den Driesch is well placed to take advantage of these. This is excellent walking country and the long distance walks, Krijtlandpad and Pieterpad both start nearby.

Two heated toilet blocks with hot showers (€ 0.70/5 mins). Launderette. Shop. Fresh bread and newspapers daily. Restaurant. Snack bar. Internet café. Free use of local gym. Bicycle hire. Play area.

Ideal For...

Dogs

Pets Accepted

Scan me for more information.

9 accommodations
88 pitches
GPS: 51.19195, 5.94942
Post Code: NL-6041 TR

Roermond, Limburg

www.alanrogers.com/nl6515
info@oolderhuuske.nl
0475 588 686

Open (Touring Pitches):
All year.

Resort Marina Oolderhuuske

When staying on this interesting site, which is part of a resort complex, you know you are on holiday. The site is situated at the end of a peninsula, on a low lying spit of land and overlooks wild stretches of open water and the River Maas. There are 220 pitches, 88 of which are for touring. All have electricity (6-16A), water and drainage, are level, grassed and many are waterside - no pitch lies more than 60 m. from the water. There are numerous cycling routes from the site, either directly overland or via the passenger/cycle ferry that crosses the Maas.

One floating block and two prefabricated sanitary units provide toilets, free showers, washbasins and outside sinks. Motorcaravan services. Shop and bar (weekends and high season), restaurant with terrace (all season), snacks and takeaway. Small indoor swimming pool, gym, sauna, steam bath, solarium. Sports fields. Tennis. Playgrounds. Bicycle hire. Boat launching. High season entertainment. Many possibilities for boating, sailing, swimming and fishing. Barrier deposit € 50. WiFi over site.

Ideal For...

 Beach

 Dogs

Year Round Camping

 Fishing

 Watersports

 Play Area

Scan me for more information.

21 accommodations
550 pitches
GPS: 51.382964, 5.976147
Post Code: NL-5975 MZ

Sevenum, Limburg

www.alanrogers.com/nl6510
info@schatberg.nl
0774 677 777
www.schatberg.nl

Open (Touring Pitches):
All year.

De Schatberg

In a woodland setting of 96 hectares, this friendly, family run campsite is more reminiscent of a holiday village, with a superb range of activities that make it an ideal venue for families. Look out for the deer! A large site with 1,100 pitches and many mobile homes and seasonal or weekend visitors, there are 550 touring pitches. All have electricity (10/16A Europlug), cable, water and drainage and average 100-150 sq.m. in size. They are on rough grass terrain, mostly with shade, but not separated. Seventy two pitches have private sanitary facilities, of which 32 also have dishwashing, fridge and gas ring, and two have a sauna and jacuzzi.

Five modern, fully equipped toilet blocks, supplemented by three small wooden toilet units to save night-time walks. Family shower rooms, baby baths and en-suite units for disabled visitors. Washing machines and dryers. Motorcaravan services. Supermarket. Restaurant, bar and takeaway. Pizzeria. Pancake restaurant. Indoor pool. Outdoor pool. Multisport play areas. Air trampolines. Fishing. Watersports. Bicycle hire. Games room. Bowling. Climbing park. Indoor playground. Entertainment weekends and high season. Theatre for small children. Water-ski track. Charcoal barbecues not permitted. WiFi (free).

Ideal For...

 Beach

 Dogs

Year Round Camping

 Fishing

 Golf

 Play Area

Scan me for more information.

Roller coaster at Toverland - By Stefan Scheer - CC BY-SA 3.0

23 pitches
GPS: 52.12898, 4.96869
Post Code: NL-3628 GC

Kockengen, Utrecht

Mini-Camping Hazenveld

www.alanrogers.com/nl6831
camping@boerderijhazenveld.nl
30 666 3372
www.boerderijhazenveld.nl

Open (Touring Pitches):
25 March - 1 October.

This peaceful country campsite is in a picturesque location between Amsterdam and Utrecht. It is adjacent to a small dairy farm and is a traditional rural site without permanent units. There are just 23 grass pitches (110 sq.m), all for tourers, serviced with electricity (6A, Europlug), water and drainage. Four hardstanding motorcaravan pitches are available all year. Younger children will enjoy the animals and the opportunity play in a safe, car-free area (parents should note that there are areas of open water). There are plenty of attractions within an hour's drive of the site, including Amsterdam, The Hague, Texel and the Efteling amusement park. Bikes can be hired on site and it is an easy, three-kilometre ride to De Haar castle.

Newly renovated (2015), heated sanitary block with spacious hot showers and washbasins in cubicles. Baby changing. Laundry. Microwave. Bread service. TV room and library. Playground. Bicycle hire. WiFi (charged).

Ideal For...

 Beach

 Dogs

 Fishing

 Watersports

 Golf

 Play Area

Scan me for more information.

154 accommodations
850 pitches
GPS: 52.44671, 5.79223
Post Code: NL-8256 RJ

Biddinghuizen, Flevoland

Rivièra Parc

www.alanrogers.com/nl6195
info@riviera.nl
0321 331 344
www.en.oostappenvakantieparken.nl

Open (Touring Pitches):
30 March - 28 October.

This Dutch Rivièra at the Veluwe Lake is two square kilometres, with Camping Rivièra Beach beyond the dykes, close to the water and the beach, and the bigger Rivièra Parc within the dykes. This family site has 1,195 pitches, 850 for touring, all on grass and all with 4/10A electricity. There are also 450 serviced pitches (large with water, drainage and TV connection) and 12 pitches with private sanitary facilities. The site boasts a very impressive range of facilities, including a covered play area and indoor swimming pool with restaurant (all decorated with a pirate theme) in the main building behind reception. The site is perfect for children and pre-teens.

Good heated toilet blocks with separate facilities for babies and disabled visitors. Family rooms. Restaurants. Café. Snack bar. Takeaway. Supermarket. Swimming pool with slide. Covered play area. Laser games. Bowling. Bicycle and go-kart hire. Fishing. Amusement arcade. Internet access. Around 54 mobile homes and bungalows for hire.

Ideal For...

 Kids

 Beach

 Dogs

 Fishing

 Watersports

 Golf

Scan me for more information.

18 accommodations
240 pitches
GPS: 52.841381, 4.719001
Post Code: NL-1759 JD

Callantsoog, Noord-Holland

Camping De Nollen

www.alanrogers.com/nl6888
info@denollen.nl
0224 581 281
www.denollen.nl

Open (Touring Pitches):
19 March - 23 October.

De Nollen is a comfortable, nine-hectare site, ideal for couples, seniors and families with younger children. There is a variety of pitches (60-120 sq.m) some basic without connections, most with 10A electricity and comfort pitches also with water, drainage and cable TV. There is plenty to keep children occupied, with several playgrounds across the site, one with a large inflatable. The two nature reserves adjacent give the site a tranquil atmosphere. The Eetboey restaurant and snack bar offers simple meals and takeaway dishes. You can also eat outside on the terrace and there is a play corner for younger children.

Two modern toilet blocks with underfloor heating. Separate facilities for children. En-suite unit for disabled visitors. Launderette. Dog shower. Motorcaravan services. Microwave. Freezer. Supermarket (as site). Cafeteria/snack bar and takeaway service (Thu-Sun; daily in July/Aug). Play areas. Bouncy castle. Football. Basketball. Beach volleyball. Fishing. Fridge hire. Bicycle hire. WiFi over site (free).

Ideal For...

 Beach

 Dogs

 Fishing

 Golf

 Play Area

 Disabled Facilities

Scan me for more information.

100 pitches
GPS: 52.36532, 4.95871
Post Code: NL-1095 KN

Amsterdam, Noord-Holland

Camping Zeeburg

www.alanrogers.com/nl5665
info@campingzeeburg.nl
206 944 430
www.campingzeeburg.nl

Open (Touring Pitches):
All year.

Camping Zeeburg is a welcoming site attractively located to the east of Amsterdam on an island in the IJmeer and, unusually, combines a sense of nature with the advantage of being just 20 minutes (5 km) from the city centre. In a sense, Zeeburg reflects the spirit of Amsterdam, claiming to be open, friendly and tolerant. The site provides 400 pitches, 350 for tents (no electricity) and 100 pitches with 10A electricity for caravans and motorcaravans, most on hardstandings and with views over the IJmeer. Tent pitches cannot be booked in advance and the maximum duration allowed on site is 14 days. Zeeburg also offers a number of colourful eco-cabins and Romany-style wagons or 'pipowagens.'

Three toilet blocks are generally simple and well used, but clean. Although adequate, facilities may be stretched at peak times. Facilities for disabled visitors (key access). Shop (all year). Café/restaurant (1/4-11/11). Very small playground. Games room. Bicycle hire. Motorcaravan services. Children's petting farm. Canoe hire. Eco-cabins and wagons to rent. Free WiFi throughout.

Ideal For...

 Beach

 Dogs

 Year Round Camping

 Watersports

 Disabled Facilities

 Pets Accepted

Scan me for more information.

350 pitches
GPS: 52.312222, 4.991389
Post Code: NL-1108 AZ

Amsterdam, Noord-Holland

Gaasper Camping

www.alanrogers.com/nl5670
info@gaaspercamping.nl
0206 967 326
www.gaaspercamping.nl/en

Open (Touring Pitches):
15 March - 1 November.

Amsterdam is probably the most popular destination for visits in the Netherlands and Gaasper Camping Amsterdam is on the southeast side, a short walk from a Metro station with a direct 20-minute service to the centre. The site is well kept and neatly laid out on flat grass with attractive trees and shrubs. There are 350 touring pitches in two main areas – one more open and grassy, mainly kept for tents (30 pitches with 10A connections), the other more formal with numbered pitches mainly divided by shallow ditches or good hedges. Areas of hardstanding are available and all caravan pitches have electrical connections (10A).

Three modern, clean toilet blocks (one unisex) for the tourist sections are an adequate provision. A number of cabins with basin and shower. Hot water for showers and some dishwashing sinks on payment. Facilities for babies. Washing machine and dryer. Motorcaravan services. Gas supplies. Supermarket, café/bar/restaurant plus takeaway (all 1/4-1/11). Play area on grass. WiFi over site (charged).

Ideal For...

 Beach

 Dogs

 Fishing

 Golf

 Play Area

 Pets Accepted

Scan me for more information.

16 accommodations
165 pitches
GPS: 51.76915, 5.82050
Post Code: NL-6582 BR

Heumen, Gelderland

Camping Heumens Bos

www.alanrogers.com/nl5950
info@heumensbos.nl
0243 581 481
www.heumensbos.nl

Open (Touring Pitches):
All year.

Recreatiecentrum Heumens Bos covers 17 hectares of woodland and grassed fields providing 162 level touring pitches arranged in groups of ten or twelve. All pitches have electricity (6A) and cable connections, and cars are parked away from the units allowing plenty of recreational space. The site is situated beside miles of beautiful woods, criss-crossed by cycle paths, in a tranquil, rural setting. Heumens Bos is open all year for touring families and all year for bungalows. One small section for motorcaravans has some hardstandings.

The main, good quality sanitary building, plus another new block, are modern and heated, providing showers on payment. Rooms for families and disabled visitors. Smart launderette. Motorcaravan services. Gas supplies. Shop. Bar, restaurant and snack bar. Heated outdoor swimming pool (1/5-30/9). Bicycle hire. Tennis. Boules. Glade area with play equipment on sand and grass. Activity and excursion programme (high season). Large wet weather room. WiFi over site (charged).

Ideal For...

 Beach

 Dogs

Year Round Camping

 Fishing

 Watersports

 Golf

Scan me for more information.

4 accommodations
90 pitches
GPS: 52.0072, 5.87135
Post Code: NL-6816 PB

Arnhem, Gelderland

www.alanrogers.com/nl5830
info@campingwarnsborn.nl
0264 423 469
www.campingwarnsborn.nl

Open (Touring Pitches):
4 May - 30 October (accommodation from 3 April).

Camping Warnsborn

Camping Warnsborn is a small, well maintained site set in the grounds of an attractive estate owned by the Gelderland Trust for natural beauty. Located on the outskirts of the historical city of Arnhem and set amongst 3.5 hectares of undulating woodland, this site really has something for everyone. There are 90 hardstanding pitches for tourers (6A electricity) arranged in either open grassy fields or surrounded by trees, with a separate secluded area for backpackers and small tents. On-site facilities include a good play area with a large sandpit and guided walks through the surrounding countryside, taking in local historical points of interest. This is an ideal site for those seeking tranquillity in a delightful natural setting.

Modern heated toilet block including facilities for babies, families and disabled visitors. Washing machines and dryers. Well stocked shop, bread to order. TV room/library. Playground with large sandpit. Bicycle hire. Boules. Hikers' cabins. WiFi over site (charged).

Ideal For...

 Beach

 Dogs

 Fishing

 Walking

 Golf

 Play Area

Scan me for more information.

80 accommodations
200 pitches
GPS: 52.02848, 6.16292
Post Code: NL-6984 AG

Doesburg, Gelderland

Camping IJsselstrand

www.alanrogers.com/nl6332
info@ijsselstrand.nl
0313 472 797
www.ijsselstrand.nl

Open (Touring Pitches):
All year.

This campsite calls itself a recreation village on the river, and the name suits it perfectly. It has 700 pitches in total, with a mix of permanent and touring pitches. The 200 touring pitches are set on sunny, grassy fields and around the marina and beach area. There are 46 pitches with private sanitary facilities (shower, washbasin, toilet) and 18 hardstandings for motorcaravans. Central to the campsite is a new, covered water complex, including a pool, a jacuzzi and slide. This can be opened in summer. There is a large play area and, for bad weather, there is enough room for all in a pleasant indoor playground.

Modern sanitary facilities are plentiful. Supermarket (15/3-2/11). Covered swimming pool. Large indoor and outdoor play areas. Riding. Sandy beach. Marina and floating restaurant. Pedalos and canoes for hire. Professional entertainment team. Free WiFi. Chalets, lodges and tents for hire.

Ideal For...

 Beach

 Dogs

 Year Round Camping

 Fishing

 Watersports

 Golf

Scan me for more information.

1 accommodations
140 pitches
GPS: 52.09221, 5.66294
Post Code: NL-6741 KG

Lunteren, Gelderland

Camping De Rimboe

www.alanrogers.com/nl6331
info@campingderimboe.com
0318 482 371
www.campingderimboe.com

Open (Touring Pitches):
1 March - 27 October.

Camping De Rimboe is set in 10.5 hectares of sloping fields and mature woodland. The 140 touring pitches (90-150 sq.m) are either on grass, which has both sun and shade, or in the woods where there is an opportunity for free camping. All have a water point and 4/6A electricity. This is a peaceful site where visitors can relax, appreciate the natural environment and explore the area by foot or bicycle. As a contrast, the lively resort towns of Lunteren, Ede and Bardeveld are a short distance away. The site's recreational space provides opportunities for a variety of games and sports, and there is also a clubhouse and two play areas.

Heated sanitary facilities. Washing machines and dryers. Clubhouse. Picnic tables. Recreation space. Volleyball. Sand quarry nature reserve. Bicycle hire. WiFi (charged).

Ideal For...

 Dogs

 Fishing

 Golf

 Play Area

 Pets Accepted

Scan me for more information.

10 accommodations
190 pitches
GPS: 52.46711, 6.42478
Post Code: NL-8148 PC

Lemele, Overijssel

De Lemeler Esch

www.alanrogers.com/nl6460
info@lemeleresch.nl
0572 331 241
www.lemeleresch.nl

Open (Touring Pitches):
24 March - 22 October.

Natuurcamping De Lemeler Esch is reminiscent of camping as it used to be, but with modern facilities including 190 spacious grass pitches for touring units, 114 with all comforts such as water, drainage, electricity, cable TV, WiFi and even a private bathroom if desired. The pitches are arranged on large grass meadows, some with shade from tall trees, others more in the open. The natural woodland setting gives this site a special atmosphere that allows children to explore and make friends. The good playground and a heated swimming pool are additional fun for children. This site will also appeal to adults as there are kilometres of cycling and walking tracks in the woods and across the moors.

Good modern toilet block with hot, controllable showers, open style washbasins and well decorated facilities for children. Baby room and family shower rooms. Facilities for disabled visitors. Private sanitary facilities for rent. Laundry with washing machines and dryers. Shop for basics. Bar/restaurant. Heated outdoor swimming pool with paddling pool. Playing field. Indoor play hall. Bicycle hire. WiFi over site (charged). Entertainment team. Accommodation to rent. Dogs are not accepted.

Ideal For...

 Fishing

 Play Area

 Disabled Facilities

 Bar on Site

Scan me for more information.

60 accommodations
550 pitches
GPS: 52.51139, 6.54618
Post Code: NL-7736 PK

Beerze-Ommen, Overijssel

Vrijetijdspark Beerze Bulten

www.alanrogers.com/nl5985
info@beerzebulten.nl
0523 251 398
www.beerzebulten.nl

Open (Touring Pitches):
April - November (accommodation all year).

Beerze Bulten is a large leisure park with superb indoor and outdoor amenities, so you can enjoy yourself whatever the weather. A large, partly underground 'rabbit hole' provides a big indoor playground for children, a theatre for both indoor and outdoor shows, a buffet, a superb full wellness spa and a very large, specially designed indoor pool. Beerze Bulten has 550 pitches, mainly for touring units, but also accommodation for hire (all year). In the shade of mature woodland, all the pitches are level and numbered, and all have 10A Europlug electricity, water, drainage and TV connections. To the rear of the site is a large lake area with a sandy beach and new, exciting adventure play equipment.

Several toilet blocks are well placed around the site, with washbasins in cabins and hot showers. Laundry. Shop. Bar and snack bar/restaurant with open-air terrace. Heated indoor and outdoor pool complex and spa centre. Multisports court. Bicycle hire. Indoor playground and theatre. Playgrounds. WiFi over site (charged). Full entertainment team in season and school holidays. Dogs only allowed on some fields.

Ideal For...

 Kids

 Beach

 Dogs

 Fishing

 Play Area

 Disabled Facilities

Scan me for more information.

100 pitches
GPS: 52.65664, 6.30191
Post Code: NL-7955 PT

IJhorst, Overijssel

www.alanrogers.com/nl6502
info@devossenburcht.nl
052 244 1626
www.devossenburcht.nl

Open (Touring Pitches):
All year.

Camping De Vossenburcht

A pleasant, wooded family campsite in a rural location in the north of the country, Familiecamping De Vossenburcht has 370 pitches of which many are seasonal, with 100 available for tourers and some accommodation for hire. They are level, a few in the open but mainly among the trees, and with electrical connections available. This is one of the most beautiful parts of Overijssel where you can still enjoy the beautiful forests and farmland. Nearby are moors, fens and attractive old farmhouses. The village of IJhorst has a few shops whilst the neighbouring towns of Meppel, Hoogeveen and Zwolle offer a wider choice of shops, bars and restaurants.

Heated sanitary block with provision for babies, children and disabled visitors. Washing machines and dryers. Motorcaravan service point. Bar with pool table and TV, snack bar with takeaway provision (1/4-1/11). Heated outdoor swimming and children's pools (1/5-15/9). Large children's playground. Children's entertainment in high season. Table tennis and table football. WiFi throughout (charged).

Ideal For...

 Beach

 Dogs

Year Round Camping

 Fishing

 Watersports

 Golf

Scan me for more information.

85 pitches
GPS: 52.36352, 6.08823
Post Code: NL-8121 SK

Olst, Overijssel

Camping 't Haasje

www.alanrogers.com/nl6493
info@kampeeridee.eu
0570 56 12 26
www.kampeeridee.eu

Open (Touring Pitches):
1 April - 30 September.

On the bank of the River IJsel, in an attractive rural location roughly half-way between Amsterdam and the German border, Camping 't Haasje has 285 pitches, 85 for touring (100 sq.m) all with 4-6A electricity. It is within striking distance of three motorways and could be a convenient stop-over on a journey to or from Denmark or northern Gemany. It would, however, repay a longer visit by nature-lovers, walkers and cyclists: the western IJsel valley has a unique flora, has several Nature Reserves and is popular as a nesting area for birds. A number of small towns and villages are nearby, the historical city of Zwolle is an easy drive away, whilst IJselmeer is a possible destination for a day out.

Modern sanitary facilities. Launderette with dryer and ironing facilities. Outdoor heated pool with terrace (15/5-7/9). Holiday shop in reception, selling fresh bread, newspapers and basic supplies. Cafeteria serving snacks, meals, soft drinks and beer (1/5-15/9). Taverne O'Lagos restaurant offering Greek food as well as local delicacies on Sundays. Programme of activities and entertainment for children and families in high season. Swimming and fishing in River IJsel. Water-ski school and wakeboarding. Bicycle hire. Communal barbecue. WiFi throughout (charged). Torches required.

Ideal For...

 Kids

 Beach

 Dogs

 Fishing

 Watersports

 Golf

Scan me for more information.

3 accommodations
141 pitches
GPS: 52.93492, 5.40430
Post Code: NL-8713 JA

Hindeloopen, Friesland

Camping Hindeloopen

www.alanrogers.com/nl6050
info@campinghindeloopen.nl
0514 521 452
www.campinghindeloopen.nl

Open (Touring Pitches):
26 March - 1 November.

Hindeloopen is one of the 11 historic cities of Friesland and this site is nearby. The delightful city retains plenty of old maritime charm. Situated directly behind the embankment of the IJsselmeer, the site has 141 touring pitches (out of a total of 640), all of which have 6/16A electricity (Europlug), water and drainage. There are 15 hardstandings for motorcaravans and large caravans. The pitches are 90-100 sq.m. in size and are arranged in groups that are separated from each other by high hedges. The lake here is not deep and from its banks there are wonderful views of the town of Hindeloopen and the surrounding countryside.

Two basic toilet blocks include showers and washbasins in cabins. Facilities for children. Baby room. Facilities for disabled visitors. Laundry. Freezer for ice packs. Motorcaravan services. Shop (daily in July/Aug). Café/restaurant and snack bar (daily in July/Aug). Play area with bike course. Football pitch. Tennis. Bicycle hire. Fishing. Surfing school. Boat launching and boat rental. Children's club (open 6 weeks during July/Aug). Free WiFi over site. Dogs are not accepted.

Ideal For...

 Beach

 Fishing

 Watersports

 Golf

 Play Area

 Disabled Facilities

Scan me for more information.

60 pitches
GPS: 52.87174, 5.46891
Post Code: NL-8574 VC

Bakhuizen, Friesland

Recreatiepark De Wite Burch

www.alanrogers.com/nl6033
info@witeburch.nl
0514 581382
www.witeburch.nl

Open (Touring Pitches):
15 March - 31 October.

In the southwest corner of Friesland, close to the northern shore of the IJsselmeer, Camping De Wite Burch underwent major rebuilding and remodelling for the 2014 season. Improvements include a new restaurant, shop and an excellent indoor play pavilion. There are 300 pitches, of which 60 are for tourers, all equipped with electricity connections (10A), water, waste water, TV connection and free WiFi. There are 12 chalets and three trekkers cabins for hire, the remaining pitches being occupied by seasonal units. The nearby coastal village of Stavoren is a watersports centre and has a few restaurants.

Modern, heated Sanitary block includes showers and dishwashing (on payment), facilities for babies and disabled visitors, laundry room with washing machine and dryer. Shop (15/3-31/10). Restaurant serving reasonably priced hot and cold dishes. Large playground with new adventure equipment. Table tennis. Sports field. Animal corner. Bicycle hire. Organised activities for children and families in high season.

Ideal For...

 Beach

 Dogs

 Fishing

 Watersports

 Golf

 Play Area

Scan me for more information.

129 pitches
GPS: 53.37909, 6.162332
Post Code: NL-9133 DT

Anjum, Friesland

Landal Esonstad

www.alanrogers.com/nl6051
esonstad@landal.nl
0519 329 555
www.landalcampings.nl

Open (Touring Pitches):
27 March - 2 November.

Esonstad is a member of the Landal group and is attractively located on the Lauwersmeer, close to the Schiermonnikoog ferry. There is an impressive range of facilities, including an all-weather tennis court, indoor pool and indoor play barn. This open site is situated on the edge of the National Park, in a landscape of lakes, forests and dykes – ideal for wildlife and watersports enthusiasts. It extends over five hectares and comprises 129 spacious pitches (100 sq.m) all with 16A electricity and a private water supply close by. Many pitches are close to the water. There are some tent pitches on a separate field and a few hardstandings.

The modern, clean toilet block has vanity-style washbasins, preset hot showers, a baby room and facilities for disabled visitors. Washing machine. Shop, restaurant/bar (all 25/3-31/10). Indoor heated swimming pool with separate paddling pool (25/3-31/10). Whirlpool. Solarium. Sauna and Turkish bath. Indoor play barn. Games room. Tennis. Golf. Site ferry to Schiermonnikoog. WiFi (charged).

Ideal For...

 Beach

 Dogs

 Fishing

 Watersports

 Golf

 Play Area

Scan me for more information.

3 accommodations
27 pitches
GPS: 52.88000, 6.44200
Post Code: NL-9411 VP

Beilen, Drenthe

www.alanrogers.com/nl6134
info@campingvorrelveen.nl
0593 527 261
www.campingvorrelveen.nl

Open (Touring Pitches):
1 April - 30 September.

Camping Vorrelveen

In comparison with the larger (and justifiably popular) campsites in Drenthe, Camping Vorrelveen is a small site which reflects the pleasant countryside. It is located next to a working farm and enjoys beautiful views. There are just 27 spacious pitches, all with 6A electricity, and the owners do their best to ensure a very personal, tranquil atmosphere. For example, your bread for breakfast will be delivered to your pitch and, in the evening, you can order home made pizzas. This is a prime example of a small, uncomplicated rural campsite.

Single toilet block includes a family shower. The same building houses a large room for meals and socialising. Essential supplies kept at the farmhouse. Motorcaravan services (with pitches on hardstanding). Play area with cable track and children's fort. Pétanque. Bicycle hire. WiFi throughout. Three new chalets for hire.

Ideal For...

 Beach

 Dogs

 Fishing

 Play Area

 Pets Accepted

Scan me for more information.

20 accommodations
500 pitches
GPS: 52.9802, 6.5053
Post Code: NL-9405 VE

Assen, Drenthe

www.alanrogers.com/nl6153
info@witterzomer.nl
0592 393 535
www.witterzomer.nl

Open (Touring Pitches):
All year.

Vakantiepark Witterzomer

Attractively located in a century old area of woodland and fields in the province of the Hunebedden, this is an attractive, large and well organised site. The Hunebedden are prehistoric monuments, built of enormous granite boulders and older than Stonehenge. The 600 touring pitches at Witterzomer are on grass with a woodland setting, with varying degrees of shade and 4-10A electricity. Most also have water, a drain and TV connections and some have private sanitary facilities. All of the amenities here are of excellent quality and are particularly targeted at families. They include a well stocked shop and a bar/restaurant with a good menu and takeaway meals.

Good heated toilet blocks include separate facilities for babies and disabled visitors, as well as family bathrooms. Laundry. Shop (1/4-30/9). Restaurant/bar and takeaway (1/4-28/10). Heated outdoor swimming pool (25/4-2/9). Sports field and games room. Tennis. Bicycle hire. Minigolf. Lake with beach and fishing. Internet and WiFi throughout (charged). Max. 2 dogs.

Ideal For...

 Beach

 Dogs

 Year Round Camping

 Fishing

 Golf

 Play Area

Scan me for more information.

5 accommodations
100 pitches
GPS: 53.0093, 7.1844
Post Code: NL-9545 VJ

Bourtange, Groningen

Camping 't Plathuis

www.alanrogers.com/nl6110
info@plathuis.nl
0599 354 383
www.plathuis.nl

Open (Touring Pitches):
1 April - 31 October.

Camping 't Plathuis is beautifully located in the fortified village of Bourtange. This small town dates back to the times of the invasion of the Bishop of Münster in the 1600s. The site has 100 touring pitches, most on well established grass fields with shade from the mature trees that surround the site. On the newest area at the back of the site there are 25 serviced pitches with 10A electricity, water and drainage. There are ten hardstandings available for motorcaravans. To the front of the site is a lake for swimming and fishing with a sandy beach.

Modern heated sanitary block with washbasins (open style and in cabins), coin-operated, controllable, hot showers and facilities for disabled visitors. Second prefabricated block in the new field. Family shower rooms. Baby room. Laundry facilities. Shopping service for basics. Bar. Snack bar. Lake for swimming and fishing. Canoe hire. Playground. Bicycle hire. Cable TV box rental. WiFi (free).

Ideal For...

 Beach

 Dogs

 Fishing

 Play Area

 Disabled Facilities

 Pets Accepted

Scan me for more information.

15 accommodations
200 pitches
GPS: 53.14316, 6.68916
Post Code: NL-9606 PR

Kropswolde, Groningen

www.alanrogers.com/nl5775
info@meerwijck.nl
0598 323 659
www.meerwijck.nl

Open (Touring Pitches):
25 March - 4 October.

Camping Meerwijck

This large lakeside site (23 hectares) has 500 pitches (200 for touring units), 11 of them on hardstanding, and is beautifully located on the beaches of the Zuidlaardermeer. The touring pitches are arranged on several separate fields away from the mobile homes and seasonal guests, either in circular bays or in long rows from paved access lanes. All touring pitches have electricity (6A), water, waste water and cable TV connections. This site is ideal for youngsters as there is direct access to the sandy beaches in addition to an indoor heated swimming pool with a paddling pool. In high season, an entertainment team provides games and excursions for youngsters and adults.

Four modern and clean toilet blocks for touring units with free hot showers (six minutes), washbasins (open style and in cabins), family shower rooms, baby rooms and facilities for disabled visitors. Laundry facilities. Small supermarket. Bar and snack bar. Indoor pool (15x20 m) with paddling pool. Playing field. Multisports court. Playgrounds. Animal farm. Tennis. Fishing. Bicycle hire. Marina. Activity team in high season. Lake with sandy beaches. WiFi throughout (charged).

Ideal For...

 Kids

 Beach

 Dogs

 Fishing

 Watersports

 Golf

Scan me for more information.

PORTUGAL

Portugal is the westernmost country of Europe, situated on the Iberian peninsula, bordered by Spain in the north and east, with the Atlantic coast in the south and west. In spite of its relatively small size, the country offers a tremendous variety, both in its way of life and in its history and traditions.

Every year the Algarve is the destination for some ten million sunseekers and watersports enthusiasts who love its sheltered sandy beaches and clear Atlantic sea. In contrast, the lush hills and forests of central Portugal are home to historic buildings and monuments, in particular the capital city of Lisbon, adjacent to the estuary of the River Tagus. Lisbon's history can still be seen in the Alfama quarter, which survived the devastating earthquake of 1755; at night the city comes alive with vibrant cafés, restaurants and discos.

Moving south east of Lisbon, the land becomes rather impoverished, consisting of stretches of vast undulating plains, dominated by cork plantations. Most people head for Evora, a medieval walled town and UNESCO World Heritage Site. The Minho area in the north is said to be the most beautiful part of Portugal, home to the country's only National Park, and vineyards producing the famous Port wine.

Language: Portuguese
Capital: Lisbon
Currency: Euro (€)
Time Zone: Western European Time (no GMT/UTC offset)
Tourist Office: www.visitportugal.com

Say Hello
'Ola' (o-laa)

Say Goodbye
Adeus (ah-deuzh)

Public Holidays
New Year; Carnival (Shrove Tues); Good Fri; Liberty Day 25 Apr; Labour Day; Corpus Christi; National Day 10 June; Saints Days; Assumption 15 Aug; Republic Day 5 Oct; All Saints 1 Nov; Immaculate Conception 8 Dec; Christmas 24-26 Dec.

Motoring
The standard of roads is very variable, even some of the main roads can be very uneven. Tolls are levied on certain motorways (auto-estradas) out of Lisbon, and upon southbound traffic at the Lisbon end of the giant 25th Abril bridge over the Tagus. Parked vehicles must face the same direction as moving traffic.

12 accommodations
186 pitches
GPS: 41.7631, -8.1905
Post Code: P-4840 030

Braga, Porto and The North

Parque Cerdeira

www.alanrogers.com/po8370
info@parquecerdeira.com
253 351 005
www.parquecerdeira.com

Open (Touring Pitches):
All year.

Located in the Peneda-Gerês National Park, amidst spectacular mountain scenery, this excellent site offers modern facilities in a truly natural area. The national park is home to all manner of flora, fauna and wildlife, including the roebuck, wolf and wild boar. The well fenced, professional and peaceful site offers 186 good sized, unmarked, mostly level, grassy pitches in a shady woodland setting. Electricity (5/10A) is available for the touring pitches, though some long leads may be required. A very large timber complex, tastefully designed with the use of noble materials - granite and wood - provides a superb restaurant with a comprehensive menu.

Three very clean sanitary blocks provide mixed style WCs, controllable showers and hot water. Good facilities for disabled visitors. Laundry. Gas supplies. Shop. Restaurant/bar. Outdoor pool (15/6-15/9). Playground. TV room (satellite). Medical post. Good tennis courts. Minigolf. Adventure park. Car wash. Barbecue areas. Torches useful. English spoken. Attractive bungalows to rent. WiFi in reception/bar area.

Ideal For...

 Beach

 Dogs

 Year Round Camping

 Fishing

 Walking

 Play Area

Scan me for more information.

96 accommodations
400 pitches
GPS: 38.72117, -9.46667
Post Code: P-2750-053

Lisbon, Lisbon and Vale do Tejo

Orbitur Guincho

www.alanrogers.com/po8130
infoguincho@orbitur.pt
214 870 450
orbitur.pt/en/destinations/region-lisboa/orbitur-guincho

Open (Touring Pitches):
All year.

Attractively laid out among low pine trees, some twisted by the wind into interesting shapes, Orbitur Camping Guincho is located behind sand dunes and a wide, sandy beach. With railway and motorway connection to Lisbon, the site provides a good base for combining a seaside holiday with a sightseeing visit to Portugal's fascinating capital. There is space for well over 400 touring units alongside seasonal pitches and rental accommodation. They are generally small, although larger units can be accommodated. Manoeuvring amongst the trees may be tricky, particularly when the site is full. Electrical connections (6A) are available throughout. Cascais is an interesting seaside town with plenty of shops, supermarkets, bars and restaurants.

Three sanitary blocks, one refurbished, are in the older style and could do with some refurbishment, but are clean and tidy. Open-style washbasins with cold water but hot showers. Facilities for disabled visitors. Washing machines and dryers. Motorcaravan services. Gas. Supermarket. Bar with excellent restaurant and takeaway (all year). Terrace. Swimming pool (5/4-30/9). General room with TV. Tennis. Playground. Entertainment in summer. WiFi on part of site (free). Chalets to rent.

Ideal For...

 Beach

 Dogs

Year Round Camping

 Fishing

 Watersports

 Golf

Scan me for more information.

100 accommodations
400 pitches
GPS: 39.75806, -9.02588
Post Code: P-2430

Leiria, Lisbon and Vale do Tejo

Orbitur São Pedro de Moel

www.alanrogers.com/po8100
infospedro@orbitur.pt
244 599 168
orbitur.com/en/destinations/region-center/orbitur-s-pedro-de-moel

Open (Touring Pitches):
All year.

This very attractive and well kept site is situated under tall pines on the edge of the rather select, small resort of São Pedro de Moel. It is a shady and peaceful place in low season, but can be crowded in July and August. There is space for some 400 touring units, including a few small marked pitches; otherwise you choose a place between the trees in one of two large camping areas; one has plentiful 6/10A electrical connections, the other a very limited provision. A few pitches are used for permanent units and an area to one side has 120 chalets and mobile homes, mostly for hire. The attractive, sandy beach is a short walk downhill from the site (you can take the car, although parking may be difficult in the town) and is sheltered from the wind by low cliffs.

Four clean toilet blocks (not all opened in low season) have mainly British style toilets, hot showers and mainly open-style washbasins (some with hot water). Washing machines and dryer. Motorcaravan services. Gas supplies. Simple shop (1/10-31/5). Supermarket, restaurant and bar with terrace (1/6-30/9). Excellent pool complex with paddling pool and large slide (1/6-30/9). Satellite TV. Games room. Playground. Tennis. WiFi in some areas (free).

Ideal For...

 Beach

 Dogs

 Year Round Camping

 Fishing

 Watersports

 Play Area

Scan me for more information.

70 accommodations
171 pitches
GPS: 38.72477, -9.20737
Post Code: P-1400-061

Lisbon, Lisbon and Vale do Tejo

Lisboa Camping & Bungalows

www.alanrogers.com/po8140
info@lisboacamping.com
217 628 200
www.lisboacamping.com

Open (Touring Pitches):
All year.

Arriving at this large site in the suburbs of Lisbon, first impressions are good. Beyond the wide entrance with its ponds and fountains, the trees, lawns and flowering shrubs lead up to the attractive swimming pool area. Positive impressions continue: on sloping ground, the site's many terraces are well shaded by trees and shrubs and all 171 touring pitches are on concrete hardstandings with grass and a picnic table. All have 10A electricity connections, water and a drain. There is a huge separate area for tents and 70 chalet-style bungalows are for hire. Central Lisbon is easily reached by bus with a regular service from near the gate.

Eight solar-powered toilet blocks are well equipped and kept clean, although in need of some refurbishment. Controllable showers and hot water to open style washbasins. Facilities for disabled visitors. Launderette. Motorcaravan services. Shop, bar and self-service restaurant with takeaway (all year). Swimming and paddling pools (lifeguard June-Sept). Tennis. Minigolf. Sports field. Playgrounds. Amphitheatre. Entertainment in high season. Games and TV rooms. Bicycle hire. Booking service for excursions. WiFi in restaurant area (free).

Ideal For...

 Beach

 Dogs

Year Round Camping

 Fishing

 Watersports

 Golf

Scan me for more information.

52 accommodations
190 pitches
GPS: 39.62028, -9.05639
Post Code: P-2450-138

Leiria, Lisbon and Vale do Tejo

Vale Paraiso Natur Park

www.alanrogers.com/po8460
info@valeparaiso.com
262 561 800
www.valeparaiso.com

Open (Touring Pitches):
All year excl.20-27 December.

A pleasant, well managed site, Vale Paraiso continues to improve. Its reception and amenities buildings create a good impression and a warm welcome is offered. Occupying eight hectares of undulating pine woods, the site has 650 shady pitches, mainly in the valley and on terraces either side. Many are occupied by seasonal units, but there are around 190 marked pitches of varying size with 6/10A electricity available. Others on sandy ground are suitable for tents and there are areas occupied by chalets, canvas bungalows and teepees for rent. Twelve pitches on a terrace below the amenities area have electricity, water and waste water/chemical disposal.

Main toilet block has controllable showers, two other blocks have pushbutton showers. Hot water to all washbasins and sinks. Facilities for disabled visitors. Baby baths. All facilities are kept very clean. Washing machines and dryer. Motorcaravan services. Small supermarket, restaurant and café/bar with satellite TV (currently all year). Swimming and paddling pools (1/5-30/9; adults charged in high season). Pétanque. Amusement hall. Entertainment for children and evening entertainment in high season. Safety deposit. Gas supplies. WiFi in amenities area. Apartments, chalets, canvas bungalows and teepees to rent.

Ideal For...

 Beach

 Dogs

 Fishing

 Watersports

 Golf

 Play Area

Scan me for more information.

42 accommodations
540 pitches
GPS: 37.7319, -8.78301
Post Code: P-7645-300

Beja, Alentejo

Camping Milfontes

www.alanrogers.com/po8180
geral@campingmilfontes.com
283 996 140
www.campingmilfontes.com

Open (Touring Pitches):
All year.

This popular site, with good facilities, has the advantage of being open all year and is within walking distance of the town and beach. As such, it makes a perfect base for those visiting out of main season, or for long winter stays when fees are heavily discounted. Well lit and fenced, it has around 500 shady pitches for touring units on sandy terrain, many marked out and divided by hedges. There is an area, mainly for motorcaravans, where you just park under the trees. Some pitches are small and cars may have to be parked in an internal car park. Electricity (6A) is available throughout.

Four clean and well maintained toilet blocks. Two have en-suite units for disabled visitors with ramped entrances. Mainly British style WCs, bidets, washbasins (some with hot water), controllable showers and limited facilities for children. Laundry. Motorcaravan services. Supermarket, bar, snacks and takeaway (all 15/4-30/9). Outdoor pool (15/6-30/9). TV room. Playground. Car wash. Gas supplies. WiFi throughout (free).

Ideal For...

 Beach

 Dogs

Year Round Camping

 Fishing

 Watersports

 Play Area

Scan me for more information.

130 pitches
GPS: 37.60422, -8.73142
Post Code: P-7630-011

Beja, Alentejo

Zmar Eco Campo

www.alanrogers.com/po8175
reservas@zmar.eu
283 690 010
www.zmar.eu

Open (Touring Pitches):
All year (facilities all closed in January).

Zmar is an exciting project which was set up in 2009. The site is located near Zambujeira do Mar, on the Alentejo coast. It is a highly ambitious initiative developed along very strict environmental lines. Renewable resources such as locally harvested timber and recycled plastic are used wherever possible and the main complex of buildings is clean cut and impressive. A terrace overlooks an open-air pool that seems to go on forever. The 132 pitches are 90 sq.m. and some, mainly for tents or smaller caravans and motorcaravans, benefit from artificial shade. All have 16A electricity. Caravans and wood-clad mobile homes are also available to rent.

Eight toilet blocks provide comprehensive facilities, including for children and disabled visitors. Washing machine. Large supermarket. Bar. Restaurant. Crêperie. Takeaway. Outdoor swimming pool (April-Oct). Covered pool and wellness centre (Feb-Dec). Sports field. Games room. Play area, farm and play house. Tennis. Bicycle hire. Activity and entertainment programme. Mobile homes and caravans to rent. Caravan repair and servicing. The site's own debit card system is used for payment at all facilities. WiFi around central complex (free),

Ideal For...

 Kids

 Beach

Dogs

 Fishing

 Watersports

 Walking

Scan me for more information.

130 pitches
GPS: 38.1812, -8.10293
Post Code: P-7920-999

Beja, Alentejo

www.alanrogers.com/po8350
markadia@hotmail.com
284 763 141
www.markadia.net

Open (Touring Pitches):
All year.

Camping Markádia

A tranquil, lakeside site in an unspoilt setting, this will appeal most to those nature lovers who want to 'get away from it all' and to those who enjoy country pursuits such as walking, fishing and riding. There are 130 casual unmarked pitches on undulating grass and sand with ample electricity connections (16A). The site is lit but a torch is required. The friendly Dutch owner has carefully planned the site so each pitch has its own oak tree to provide shade. The open countryside and lake provide excellent views and a very pleasant environment.

Four toilet blocks built in traditional Portuguese style are kept very clean and provide spacious, controllable showers, open-style washbasins, dishwashing and laundry sinks under cover, with hot water throughout. Washing machines. Basic motorcaravan services and car wash. Bar/restaurant with terrace overlooking lake (1/4-30/9). Shop (all year, bread to order). Playground. Fishing, swimming and boating in the lake. Boat hire. Tennis. Riding. Dogs are not accepted in Aug. Facilities and amenities may be reduced outside the main season.

Ideal For...

 Beach

 Dogs

 Year Round Camping

 Fishing

 Watersports

 Walking

Scan me for more information.

1 accommodations
30 pitches
GPS: 39.008326, -7.048384
Post Code: P-7371-909

Portalegre, Alentejo

Camping Rural Os Anjos

www.alanrogers.com/po8356
info@campingosanjos.com
268 688 138
www.campingosanjos.com

Open (Touring Pitches):
All year.

This really is rural Portugal. Set in rolling countryside in a working olive grove, Os Anjos (The Angels) is an ideal spot from which to explore this lesser-known corner of the Alentejo. The white fortified town of Campo Maior is within walking distance and the historic town of Elvas, now a UNESCO World Heritage Site, is a short drive away. Solange and Joris will provide a warm welcome and as much advice as you need on where to go on foot, by bike or by car, with appropriate route sheets. The site has 30 terraced pitches accessed by a circular track, with twelve electrical connections (6A) available.

Central toilet block has preset showers, some washbasins in cubicles with hot and cold water, and a unit for disabled visitors (which in winter is heated and available to all). Note: the terrain generally might cause problems for wheelchair users. Small bar with seating on terrace and in reception lounge. Pleasant little swimming pool with attractively equipped terrace. Boules. Bicycle hire. Barbecue evening on Fridays (BYO meat). WiFi throughout (charged).

Ideal For...

 Beach

 Dogs

Year Round Camping

 Fishing

 Watersports

 Golf

Scan me for more information.

24 accommodations
900 pitches
GPS: 37.10639, -8.25361
Post Code: P-8200-555

Faro, Algarve

www.alanrogers.com/po8210
geral@campingalbufeira.net
289 587 629
www.campingalbufeira.net

Open (Touring Pitches):
All year.

Camping Albufeira

The spacious entrance to this site will accommodate the largest of units. A very pleasant, well run site, it has space for 900 touring units on generally flat ground with some terracing on the upper area: trees and shrubs giving reasonable shade in most parts. Pitches are not marked or numbered and you can take as much space as you wish. Electrical connections (10A) are available throughout. Winter stays are encouraged with the main facilities remaining open, including a pool. An attractively designed complex of traditional Portuguese-style buildings on the hill houses the impressive range of restaurants and bars with the pool complex adjacent.

Very clean and spacious toilet blocks include hot showers and open-style washbasins (hot water to some). Launderette. Motorcaravan services. Very large supermarket. Kiosk (English papers). Waiter and self-service restaurants. Pizzeria. Bars. The main facilities are open all year. Swimming pools. Satellite TV. Soundproofed disco. Tennis. Playground. Bicycle hire. WiFi over part of site (charged). First aid post with doctor nearby. Car wash. ATM. Car hire.

Ideal For...

 Beach

 Dogs

 Year Round Camping

 Fishing

 Watersports

 Golf

Scan me for more information.

108 accommodations
240 pitches
GPS: 37.10111, -8.73278
Post Code: P-8600-109

Faro, Algarve

Turiscampo Algarve

www.alanrogers.com/po8202
info@turiscampo.com
282 789 265
www.turiscampo.com/en

Open (Touring Pitches):
All year.

Yelloh! Village Turiscampo is an outstanding site which has been thoughtfully refurbished and updated since it was purchased by the friendly Coll family in 2003. The site provides 240 pitches for touring units, mainly in rows of terraces, 197 of which have 6/10A electricity, some with shade. There are 43 deluxe pitches with water and drain. The upper terraces are occupied by 132 bungalows for rent. Just down the road is the fashionable resort of Praia de Luz with a beach, shops, bars and restaurants. Head west and the road takes you to Sagres and the western tip of the Algarve. Portugal's 'Land's End' remains unspoilt and there are numerous rocky coves and little sandy beaches to explore. A member of Leading Campings group.

Two heated toilet blocks provide outstanding facilities. There is a third facility beneath the pool. Spacious controllable showers, hot water throughout. Children & baby room. Facilities for disabled visitors. Dog shower. Laundry facilities. Shop. Gas supplies. Modern restaurant/bar with buffet & mexican-style meals. Pizza bar & takeaway. Swimming pools (all year) with extensive terrace & Jacuzzi. Aquagym. Wellness facility. Bicycle hire. Entertainment on the bar terrace. Miniclub. Two playgrounds. Boules. Archery. Multisports court. Cable TV. Internet and WiFi (partial coverage) on payment.

Ideal For...

 Kids

 Beach

 Dogs

Year Round Camping

 Fishing

 Watersports

Scan me for more information.

Open all year!
2018: HEATED SWIMMING POOL
PITCHES WITH WATER AND DRAINAGE
INDIVIDUAL CABINES IN SHOWER BLOCK
2017: NEW - SPA, BEAUTY & SPORT
Turiscampo
camping bungalow park
LeadingCampings
yelloh! VILLAGE
N. 125, Km17 Espiche 8600-109 Lagos-Algarve-Portugal | T. +351 282 789 265 | info@turiscampo.com | www.turiscampo.com

35 accommodations
800 pitches
GPS: 37.03528, -7.8225
Post Code: P-8700

Faro, Algarve

Camping Olhão

www.alanrogers.com/po8230
parque.campismo@sbsi.pt
289 700 300
www.sbsi.pt/atividadesindical/
Servicos/ParquedeCampismo

Open (Touring Pitches):
All year.

The large, sandy beaches in this area are on offshore islands reached by ferry and are, as a result, relatively quiet. This site, on the edge of town, has around 800 pitches, all with 6A electrical connections available. Its many mature trees provide good shade. The pitches are marked in rows divided by shrubs, although levelling will be necessary in places and the trees make access tricky on some. There is a separate area for tents and places for very large motorcaravans. Seasonal units take up one fifth of the pitches, the touring pitches filling up quickly in July and August, so arrive early. The site has a relaxed, casual atmosphere, though there is some subdued noise in the lower area from an adjacent railway.

Eleven sanitary blocks are adequate, kept clean even when busy and are well sited so that any pitch is close to one. Two blocks have facilities for disabled visitors. Laundry. Excellent supermarket. Kiosk. Restaurant/bar. Café and general room with cable TV. Playgrounds. Swimming pools (all year, charged in season). Tennis courts. Bicycle hire. Internet at reception.

Ideal For...

 Beach

 Dogs

Year Round Camping

 Fishing

 Watersports

 Golf

Scan me for more information.

Traditional portuguese architecture in Olhao

SLOVENIA

What Slovenia lacks in size it makes up for in exceptional beauty. Situated between Italy, Austria, Hungary and Croatia, it has a diverse landscape with stunning Alps, rivers, forests and the warm Adriatic coast.

From the Alps down to the Adriatic coast, the Karst region is home to the famous Lipizzaner horses, vineyards and myriad underground caves, including the Portojna and Skocjan caves.

The Adriatic coast has several bustling towns including Koper, Slovenia's only commercial port, whose 500 years of Venetian rule is evident in its Italianate style. Ljubljana, one of Europe's smallest capitals with beautiful baroque buildings, lies on the Ljubljanica river, spanned by numerous bridges, including Jože Plečnik's triple bridge.

The old city and castle sit alongside a thriving commercial centre. Heading eastwards, the hilly landscape is dotted with monasteries, churches and castles, including the 13th century Zuzemberk castle, one of Slovenia's most picturesque. The Posavje region produces cviček, a famous blend of white and red wines.

Language: Slovene
Capital: Ljubljana
Currency: Euro (€)
Time Zone: Central European Time (GMT/UTC plus one hour)
Telephone Country Code: 00 386
Tourist Office: www.slovenia.info

Say Hello
Zdravo (ZDRAH-voh)

Say Goodbye
Nasvidenje (nahs-VEE-deh-nyeh)

Public Holidays
New Year's Day 1 Jan; Culture Day 8 Feb; Easter Monday; Resistance Day 27 Apr; Labour Day 1-2 May; National Day 25 Jun; People's Day 22 July; Assumption; Reformation Day 31 Oct; All Saints Day; Christmas Day; Independence Day 26 Dec.

Motoring
A 'vignette' system for motorway travel is in place. The cost is around €35 (for a six month vignette) and they can be purchased at petrol stations and DARS offices in Slovenia and near the border. Winter driving equipment (winter tyres and snow chains) is mandatory between 15 Nov and 15 March. Headlights must be on at all times. You are also required to carry a reflective jacket, warning triangle and first aid kit in the vehicle. Do not drink and drive.

25 pitches
GPS: 45.88994, 13.74745
Post Code: SLO-5294

Dornberk, Slovenia

Camping Saksida

www.alanrogers.com/sv4320
info@vinasaksida.com
053 017 853
www.vinasaksida.com

Open (Touring Pitches):
All year.

Camping Saksida is a very small campsite, open all year in a rural setting in the Vipava Valley. It is set in the grounds of a restaurant which has its own vineyard and it is surrounded by vineyards and orchards. There are 25 pitches for all units, including 12 hardstandings, most with electricity (10A, Europlug). There is a large, covered picnic area and a communal area for barbecues. The price of one night's stay includes wine tasting from three local wines. There is a small, heated swimming pool where one can relax and the campsite restaurant offers an extensive menu of genuine Vipava dishes.

Heated sanitary facilities. Motorcaravan service point. Restaurant. Heated outdoor swimming pool (15/5-30/9). Large covered picnic area. Communal barbecue area. WiFi throughout (free).

Ideal For...

 Beach

 Dogs

 Year Round Camping

 Fishing

 Play Area

 Pets Accepted

Scan me for more information.

6 accommodations
90 pitches
GPS: 46.25075, 13.58658
Post Code: SLO-5222

Kobarid, Slovenia

www.alanrogers.com/sv4270
info@kamp-koren.si
053 891 311
www.campingslovenia.com

Open (Touring Pitches):
9 May - 31 December

Kamp Koren Kobarid

Kamp Koren, Slovenia's first ecological site, is in a quiet location above the Soca river gorge, within easy walking distance of Kobarid. The site has 50 slightly sloping pitches, all with 6/16A electricity and ample tree shade. It is deservedly very popular with those interested in outdoor sports, be it on the water, in the mountains or in the air. At the same time, its peaceful situation makes it an ideal choice for those seeking a relaxing break. At the top of the site there are also six well equipped chalets and a shady area, mainly for tents.

Three attractive and well maintained log-built toilet blocks, two recently renovated. Facilities for disabled visitors. Laundry facilities. Motorcaravan services. Shop (March-Nov). Café serves light meals, snacks and drinks apparently with flexible closing hours. Play area. Volleyball. Table tennis. Bowling. Fishing. Bicycle hire. Canoe hire. Climbing walls. Adventure park. Communal barbecue. WiFi. Sauna.

Ideal For...

 Kids

 Beach

 Dogs

Year Round Camping

 Fishing

 Walking

Scan me for more information.

13 accommodations
19 pitches
GPS: 46.35336, 14.81555
Post Code: SLO-3333

Ljubno ob Savinji, Slovenia

www.alanrogers.com/sv4460
info@naturavantura.com
051 235 215
www.naturavantura.com

Open (Touring Pitches):
25 April - 1 October.

Camp NaturPlac

Camp NaturPlac is a small, quiet and peaceful rustic campsite located beside the river Savinja close to the Logar Valley. The site is run by a group of very friendly enthusiasts who will advise you about many organised trips on land or water. This is a great place for the more active families who enjoy nature and who are seeking a quiet site where they can entertain themselves. The site caters for those with their own tents, though small tents in ten wooden shelters are available to rent. Guests have access to a kitchen, a shared dining area and an outside fire pit, very popular for evening meals and social events such as sampling the local specialities.

Simple heated toilet block with hot showers. Some meals. Badminton and beach volleyball. Kitchen and shared dining area. Play area. Library under the trees. Bicycle hire. Themed workshops for adults and children. Hammocks and sleeping bags for hire. Communal barbecue. River swimming. WiFi thoughout (free).

Ideal For...

 Beach

 Dogs

 Fishing

 Play Area

 Pets Accepted

Scan me for more information.

8 accommodations
280 pitches
GPS: 46.36155, 14.08075
Post Code: SLO-4260

Bled, Slovenia

Camping Bled

Camping Bled is situated on the western tip of Lake Bled. The waterfront here has a small public beach, immediately behind which runs a gently sloping narrow wooded valley. There are wonderful views across the lake towards its famous island. Pitches at the front, used mainly for overnighters, are now marked, separated by trees and enlarged, bringing the total number to 280. All are on gravel/grass with 16A electricity. A railway line passes close by but it is only a local line with few trains and they do not disturb the peacefulness of the site.

Toilet facilities in five blocks are of a high standard (with free hot showers). Three blocks are heated. Private bathrooms for rent. Solar energy used. Washing machines and dryers. Motorcaravan services. Gas supplies. Fridge hire. Supermarket. Restaurant. Play area and children's zoo. Games area. Trampolines. Organised activities in July/Aug including children's club, excursions and sporting activities. Mountain bike tours. Live entertainment. Fishing. Bicycle hire. Free WiFi over site.

www.alanrogers.com/sv4200
info@camping-bled.com
045 752 000
www.camping-bled.com

Open (Touring Pitches):
25 March - 15 October, 20 December - 6 January.

Ideal For...

 Beach

 Dogs

 Fishing

 Watersports

 Walking

 Golf

Scan me for more information.

472 accommodations
250 pitches
GPS: 45.89137, 15.62598
Post Code: SLO-8251

Catez ob Savi, Slovenia

Camping Terme Catez

www.alanrogers.com/sv4415
info@terme-catez.si
074 936 700
www.terme-catez.si

Open (Touring Pitches):
All year.

Terme Catez is part of the modern Catez thermal spa, which includes very large and attractive indoor (31°C) and outdoor swimming complexes, both with large slides and waves. The campsite has over 700 pitches, with 250 places for tourers, arranged on one large, open field with some young trees – a real sun trap – and provides level, grass pitches, which are numbered by markings on the tarmac access roads. All have 10A electricity connections. Although the site is ideally placed for an overnight stop when travelling on the E70, it is well worthwhile planning to spend some time here to take advantage of the excellent facilities that are included in the overnight camping charges.

Two modern toilet blocks with British style toilets, washbasins in cabins, large and controllable hot showers. Washbasins for children. Facilities for disabled visitors. Laundry facilities. Motorcaravan services. Supermarket. Kiosks for fruit, newspapers, souvenirs and tobacco. Attractive restaurant with buffet. Bar with terrace. Large indoor and outdoor (20/4-15/10) swimming complexes. Sauna. Solarium. Rowing boats. Jogging track. Fishing. Golf. Riding. Organised activities. Video games. Bicycle hire. WiFi throughout (free).

Ideal For...

 Dogs

 Year Round Camping

 Fishing

 Golf

 Play Area

 Disabled Facilities

Scan me for more information.

12 accommodations
177 pitches
GPS: 46.09752, 14.5187
Post Code: SLO-1000

Ljubljana, Slovenia

www.alanrogers.com/sv4340
resort@gpl.si
015 890 130
www.ljubljanaresort.si

Open (Touring Pitches):
All year.

Camping Ljubljana Resort

Located only five kilometres north of central Ljubljana, on the relatively quiet bank of the River Sava, Ljubljana Resort is an ideal city campsite. This relaxed site is attached to, but effectively separated from, the sparklingly modern Laguna swimming pool complex. This is open between mid June and the beginning of September and a small, discounted charge is made in order for campers to gain access. The site has 177 pitches, largely situated between mature trees and all with 16A electricity connections (16A). The main building and the pool complex provide several bars, restaurants and takeaways to cater for the campsite guests and day visitors.

The modern toilet block includes facilities for disabled campers, a baby room and children's toilet and shower. Motorcaravan services. Laundry room. Restaurant and bar with terrace. Spa and outdoor swimming pool (13/6-31/8). Play area. Entertainment for children in July/Aug. TV lounge. Barbecue area. Fitness centre. Beach volleyball. Bicycle hire. Airport transfer service. WiFi throughout (free in reception).

Ideal For...

 Beach

 Dogs

Year Round Camping

 Fishing

 Golf

 Play Area

Scan me for more information.

SPAIN

One of the largest countries in Europe with glorious beaches, vibrant towns and sleepy villages, plus a diversity of landscape, culture and artistic traditions, Spain has all the ingredients for a great holiday.

Spain's vast and diverse coastline is a magnet for visitors; glitzy, hedonistic resorts packed with bars and clubs are a foil to secluded coves backed by wooded cliffs. Yet Spain has much more to offer – the verdant north with its ancient pilgrimage routes where the Picos de Europa sweep down to the Atlantic gems of Santander and Bilbao. Vibrant Madrid in the heart of the country boasts the Prado with works by Velázquez and Goya, the beautiful cobbled Plaza Major, plus all the attractions of a capital city.

Andalucía in the south dazzles with the symbolic arts of bullfighting and flamenco. It offers the cosmopolitan cities of Córdoba, Cádiz and Málaga, alongside magnificent examples of the past such as the Alhambra at Granada.

On the Mediterranean east coast, Valencia has a wealth of monuments and cultural sites, including the magnificent City of Arts and Science.

Language: Castilian Spanish is spoken by most people with Catalan (north east), Basque (north) and Galician (north west) used in their respective areas.
Capital: Madrid
Currency: Euro (€)
Time Zone: Central European Time (GMT/UTC plus one hour)
Telephone Country Code: 00 34
Tourist Office: www.tourspain.co.uk

Say Hello
Hola (OH-lah)

Say Goodbye
Adiós (ah-DYOHS)

Public Holidays
New Year; Epiphany; Saint's Day 19 Mar; Maundy Thurs; Good Fri; Easter Mon; Labour Day; Saints Day 25 July; Assumption 15 Aug; National Day 12 Oct; All Saints' Day 1 Nov; Constitution Day 6 Dec; Immaculate Conception 8 Dec; Christmas Day.

Motoring
The surface of the main roads is on the whole good, although secondary roads in some rural areas can be rough and winding. Tolls are payable on certain roads and for the Cadi Tunnel, Vallvidrera Tunnel and the Tunnel de Garraf on the A16.

72 accommodations
612 pitches
GPS: 41.71292, 2.906465
Post Code: E-17320

Girona, Cataluña-Catalunya

Camping Cala Llevadó

www.alanrogers.com/es82000
info@calallevado.com
972 340 314
www.calallevado.com

Open (Touring Pitches):
26 March - 26 September

Cala Llevado is a beautifully situated and quiet (although popular), cliff-side site, enjoying fine views of the sea and coast below. It is shaped around a wooded valley with steep access roads and terracing. High up on the site, with a superb aspect, is the attractive restaurant/bar with a large terrace overlooking the pleasant swimming pool directly below. There are 612 terraced, level touring pitches (489 with 10/16A electricity) on the upper levels of the two slopes, with a great many individual pitches for tents scattered around the site. Many of these pitches have fantastic settings and views. The site is unsuitable for campers with disabilities. In some areas cars may be required to park separately.

Four very well equipped toilet blocks are immaculately maintained and well spaced around the site. Baby baths. Laundry facilities. Motorcaravan services. Gas supplies. Fridge hire. Large supermarket. Restaurant/bar, swimming and paddling pools (all season). Three play areas. Small botanical garden. Entertainment for children and adults (July/Aug). Sports courts. Sailing, water-skiing, windsurfing, diving, canoe hire. Fishing. Bicycle hire. Excursions. ATM. Internet access and WiFi over part of site (part free/charged). Torches required in some areas. Doctor service in high season. Only electric barbecues allowed, communal available.

Ideal For...

 Beach

 Dogs

 Fishing

 Watersports

 Golf

 Play Area

Scan me for more information.

140 accommodations
747 pitches
GPS: 42.18147, 3.10405
Post Code: E-17470

Girona, Cataluña-Catalunya

Camping l'Amfora

www.alanrogers.com/es80350
info@campingamfora.com
972 520 540
www.campingamfora.com

Open (Touring Pitches):
23 April 2018 - 28 September 2018

This spacious, friendly site is run by Michelle, Josep and their daughter. It is spotlessly clean and well maintained and the owners operate the site in an environmentally friendly way. There are 830 level, grass pitches (741 for touring units) laid out in a grid system, all with 10A electricity. Attractive trees and shrubs have been planted around each pitch. There is good shade in the more mature areas, which include 64 large pitches (180 sq.m), each with an individual sanitary unit (toilet, shower and washbasin). The newer area is more open with less shade and you can choose which you would prefer.

Three excellent sanitary blocks, one heated, provide washbasins in cabins and roomy free showers. Baby rooms. Laundry facilities and service. Motorcaravan services. Supermarket. Terraced bar, self-service and waiter-service restaurants. Pizzeria/takeaway. Restaurant and bar on the beach with limited menu (high season). Disco bar. Swimming pools with 2 new long waterslides for the 2017 season (1/5-27/9) as also SPA area. Pétanque. Tennis. Minigolf. Play area. Miniclub. Entertainment and activities. Windsurfing. Kite surfing (low season).Sailing, kayak, fishing. Games rooms. Bicycle hire. Internet room and WiFi over site (charged). Car wash. Torches required in most areas.

Ideal For...

 Kids

 Beach

 Dogs

 Fishing

 Watersports

 Golf

Scan me for more information.

7 accommodations
445 pitches
GPS: 42.17728, 3.10793
Post Code: E-17470

Girona, Cataluña-Catalunya

www.alanrogers.com/es80500
reservas@aquarius.es
972 520 101
www.aquarius.es/en

Open (Touring Pitches):
15 March - 31 October

Camping Aquarius

This is a welcoming and organised family site approached by an attractive road flanked by orchards. Aquarius has direct access to a quiet, sandy beach that slopes gently and provides good bathing. Watersports are popular, particularly windsurfing (a school is provided). One third of the site has good shade with a park-like atmosphere. There are 445 touring pitches, all with electricity (6/16A and 6 caravans for hire). Markus Rupp and his wife are keen to make every visitor's experience a happy one. The site is ideal for those who really like sun and sea, with a quiet situation.

Attractively tiled, fully equipped, toilet blocks provide some cabins for each sex. Excellent facilities for disabled visitors, plus baths for children. One block has underfloor heating and family cabins with showers and washbasins. Laundry facilities. Gas supplies. Motorcaravan services. Full size refrigerators. Supermarket. Pleasant restaurant and bar with 'chill-out' terrace. Takeaway. Purpose built play centre (with qualified attendant). Playground. TV room. Surf Centre. Yoga and fitness classes. Water playground for children with water slides. Fishing and sailing. Minigolf. Bicycle hire. Guided excursions (e-bikes, bikes and trekking). Live music (twice weekly in high season, once a week low season). ATM. Internet. WiFi over site (charged). Charging station for e-vehicles. Dogs are accepted in one section.

Ideal For...

 Kids

 Beach

 Dogs

Fishing

 Watersports

 Walking

Scan me for more information.

30 accommodations
230 pitches
GPS: 42.18805, 3.1027
Post Code: E-17470

Girona, Cataluña-Catalunya

Camping Las Palmeras

www.alanrogers.com/es80330
info@campinglaspalmeras.com
972 520 506
www.campinglaspalmeras.com

Open (Touring Pitches):
24 March - 27 October

A very welcoming, open site, which is attractively laid out and cared for. The 230 grass pitches are flat and well maintained, with some shade and 10A electricity. Ten pitches also have water and drainage. Thirty smart mobile homes are placed unobtrusively at one end of the site. A very pleasant pool complex has a lifeguard and the brightly coloured play areas are clean and safe. A great beach, noted for watersports, is a 200 m. walk through a gate at the rear of the site.

Two excellent, very clean, solar powered toilet blocks include first class facilities for disabled campers. Baby rooms. Facilities may become a little busy at peak periods. Washing machines. Motorcaravan services. Supermarket, restaurant/bar/takeaway open all season (children's menu). Swimming pools (heated). Play areas. Tennis. Five-a-side. Fronton. Boules. Gym. Barbecue. Bicycle hire. Miniclub. Entertainment. Satellite TV. Internet. WiFi over site (charged). ATM. Torches useful.

Ideal For...

 Beach

 Dogs

 Fishing

 Watersports

 Golf

 Play Area

Scan me for more information.

100 accommodations
1500 pitches
GPS: 42.16098, 3.107774
Post Code: E-17470

Girona, Cataluña-Catalunya

Camping Las Dunas

www.alanrogers.com/es80400
info@campinglasdunas.com
972 521 717
www.campinglasdunas.com

Open (Touring Pitches):
20 May - 15 September.

Las Dunas is an extremely large, impressive and well organised resort-style site with many on-site activities and an ongoing programme of improvements. It has direct access to a superb sandy beach that stretches along the site for nearly a kilometre with a windsurfing school and beach bar. There is also a much used, huge swimming pool, plus a large double pool for children which opened in 2015. Las Dunas has 1,700 individual hedged pitches (1,500 for touring units) of around 100 sq.m. laid out on flat ground in long, regular parallel rows. All have electricity (6/10A) and 400 have water and drainage.

Five excellent large toilet blocks with electronic sliding glass doors. Toilets without seats, controllable hot showers and washbasins in cabins. Excellent facilities for children, babies and disabled campers. Laundry facilities. Motorcaravan services. Supermarket, boutique and other shops. Large bar with terrace. Large restaurant & takeaway. Ice cream parlour. Beach bar (seasonal). Disco club. Swimming pools. Adventure crazy golf. Playgrounds. Tennis. Minigolf. Sailing/windsurfing school and other watersports. Programme of sports, games, excursions and entertainment, partly in English. Exchange facilities. ATM. Safety deposit. Internet café. WiFi over site (charged). Dogs taken in one section. Torches required in some areas.

Ideal For...

 Kids

 Beach

 Dogs

 Fishing

 Watersports

 Play Area

Scan me for more information.

CAMPING LAS DUNAS

50 ANYS DES DE 1968

COSTA BRAVA
SPAIN

CAMPING BUNGALOWPARK

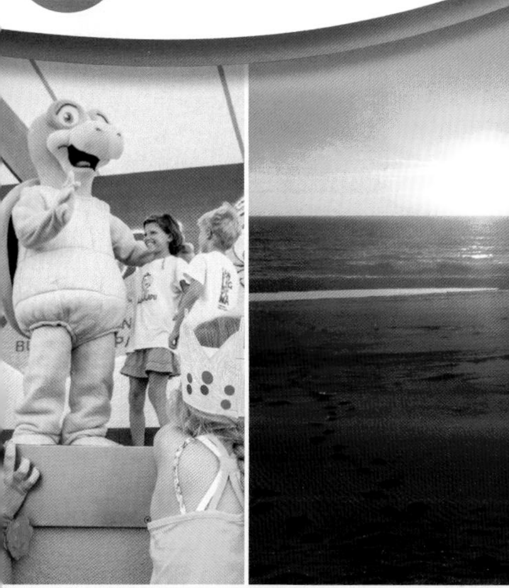

LAS Dunas CAMPING BUNGALOW PARK

Seaside holiday paradise for the whole family!

Camping & Bungalow Park located right at one of the most beautiful beaches in the Bay of Rosas. Offers a large variety of entertainment and activities for all ages, state-of-the-art sanitary facilities and a large shopping centre. Newly inaugurated AQUAPARK with slides guarantees fun and relax for the whole family.

Camping Las Dunas
17130 L'Escala (Girona)
Tel. +34 972 521 717
info@campinglasdunas.com

www.campinglasdunas.com

Your UK Agent: Derek & Jessica Callaway
Tel. 01205 366856 - callaway@campinglasdunas.com

165 accommodations
371 pitches
GPS: 41.836312, 3.08711
Post Code: E-17250

Girona, Cataluña-Catalunya

Camping Treumal

www.alanrogers.com/es81400
info@campingtreumal.com
972 651 095
www.campingtreumal.com/en

Open (Touring Pitches):
23 March - 30 September

This very attractive terraced site has been developed on a hillside around the beautiful gardens of a large, spectacular estate house which is close to the sea. The house is the focus of the site's excellent facilities, including a superb restaurant with terraces overlooking two tranquil beaches, protected in pretty coves. The site has 542 pitches on well shaded terraces. Of these, 371 are accessible to touring units and there are some 50 pitches on flat ground alongside the sea – the views are stunning and you wake to the sound of the waves. Electricity (6/10/16A) is available in all parts. Cars must be left on car parks or the site roads.

Four well maintained sanitary blocks have free hot water in the washbasins (with some private cabins) and controllable showers, and a tap to draw from for the sinks. No facilities for disabled visitors. New beach block. Washing machines. Motorcaravan services. Gas supplies. Supermarket, bar and takeaway (all season). Restaurant (15/6-15/9). Beach bar. Fishing. Play area. Sports area. Games room. Bicycle hire. Satellite TV. Internet access and WiFi (charged). ATM. Safes. Dogs are not accepted.

Ideal For...

 Beach

 Fishing

 Watersports

 Walking

 Golf

 Play Area

Scan me for more information.

Costa Brava landscape near Calonge

49 accommodations
400 pitches
GPS: 42.26558, 3.1025
Post Code: E-17486

Girona, Cataluña-Catalunya

Camping Mas Nou

www.alanrogers.com/es80120
info@campingmasnou.com
972 454 175
www.campingmasnou.com

Open (Touring Pitches):
24 March - 30 September

Some two kilometres from the sea on the Costa Brava, this is a pristine and surprisingly tranquil site in two parts, split by the access road. One part contains the pitches and toilet blocks, the other houses the impressive leisure complex. There are 450 neat, level and marked pitches on grass, a minimum of 70 sq.m. but most are 80-100 sq.m, and 300 with electricity (10A). The leisure complex is across the road from reception and features a huge L-shaped swimming pool with a children's area. A formal restaurant has an adjoining bar/café, pleasant terrace and rôtisserie under palms.

Three absolutely excellent, fully equipped sanitary blocks include baby baths, good facilities for disabled visitors. Washing machines. Motorcaravan services. Supermarket and other shops. Baker in season. Bar/restaurant, rotisserie and takeaway. Swimming pool with lifeguard (1/5-25/9). Floodlit tennis and basketball. Minigolf. Miniclub (July/Aug). Play areas. Electronic games. Bicycle hire. Internet access and free WiFi over site. Car wash.

Ideal For...

 Beach

 Dogs

 Fishing

 Watersports

 Golf

 Play Area

Scan me for more information.

32 accommodations
1109 pitches
GPS: 42.206077, 3.10389
Post Code: E-17486

Girona, Cataluña-Catalunya

Camping Nautic Almata

www.alanrogers.com/es80300
info@almata.com
972 454 477
www.almata.com

Open (Touring Pitches):
18 May - 16 September

In the Bay of Roses, south of Empuriabrava and beside the Parc Natural dels Aiguamolls de l'Empordà, this is a high quality site of particular interest to nature lovers (especially birdwatchers). A large site, there are 1,109 well kept, large, numbered pitches, all with electricity and on flat, sandy ground. Beautifully laid out, it is arranged around the river and waterways, so will suit those who like to be close to water or who enjoy watersports and boating. It is also a superb beachside site.

Sanitary blocks of a very high standard include some en-suite showers with washbasins. Good facilities for disabled visitors. Washing machines. Gas supplies. Excellent supermarket. Restaurants, pizzeria and bar. Two separate bars and snack bar by beach where discos are held in main season. Sailing, diving and windsurfing schools. 300 sq.m. swimming pool. Tennis courts. Badminton. Paddle tennis. Minigolf. Games room. Children's play park and miniclub. Fishing (licence required). Car, motorcycle and bicycle hire. Hairdresser. Internet access and WiFi over site (charged). ATM. Torches are useful near beach.

Ideal For...

 Beach

 Dogs

 Fishing

 Watersports

 Play Area

 Disabled Facilities

Scan me for more information.

138 accommodations
650 pitches
GPS: 42.001130, 3.193800
Post Code: E-17256

Girona, Cataluña-Catalunya

Camping Playa Brava

www.alanrogers.com/es81010
info@playabrava.com
972 636 894
www.playabrava.com

Open (Touring Pitches):
19 May - 9 September

This is an attractive and efficiently run site with an open feel, having direct access to an excellent soft sand beach and a freshwater lagoon. The ground is level and grassy with shade provided for many of the 650 spacious touring pitches by a mixture of conifer and broadleaf trees. All the pitches have 10A electricity and 238 have water and drainage. The large swimming pool has an extensive grass sunbathing area and is overlooked by the terrace of the restaurant and bar. This is a clean, secure and pleasant family site, suitable for sightseeing and for those who enjoy beach and water activities.

Five modern, fully equipped toilet blocks include facilities for disabled visitors. Washing machines and dryers. Motorcaravan services. Supermarket. Bar/restaurant. Takeaway. Swimming pool. Pétanque. Tennis. Minigolf. Beach volleyball. Play area. Bicycle hire. Watersports on beach. Stage show. Internet. WiFi over site (charged). Satellite TV. Gas supplies. Dogs are not accepted.

Ideal For...

 Beach

 Fishing

 Watersports

 Golf

 Play Area

 Disabled Facilities

Scan me for more information.

431 accommodations
343 pitches
GPS: 41.23237, 1.69092
Post Code: E-08800

Barcelona, Cataluña-Catalunya

www.alanrogers.com/es83900
info@vilanovapark.com
938 933 402
www.vilanovapark.com

Vilanova Park

Open (Touring Pitches):
All year.

Sitting on the terrace in front of the restaurant – a beautifully converted Catalan farmhouse dating from 1908 – it is difficult to believe that in 1982 this was still a farm with few trees and known as Mas Roque (Rock Farm). Since then, imaginative planting has led to there being literally thousands of trees and gloriously colourful shrubs making this large campsite most attractive. It has an impressive range of high quality amenities and facilities open all year. There are 343 marked pitches for touring units in separate areas, all with 6/10A electricity, 168 larger pitches also have water and, in some cases, drainage. They are on hard surfaces, on gently sloping ground and with plenty of shade. A further 1,000 or so pitches are mostly occupied by chalets to rent, and by tour operators.

Excellent toilet blocks can be heated and have controllable showers and many washbasins in cabins. Baby rooms. Units for disabled visitors. Serviced and self-service laundry. Motorcaravan services. Supermarket. Souvenir shop. Restaurants. Bar with simple meals and tapas. Outdoor pools (1/4-15/10), indoor pool (all year, charged). Wellness centre including sauna, jacuzzi and gym. Play areas. Sports field. Games room. Excursions. Activity and entertainment programme for all ages. Bicycle hire. Tennis. ATM and exchange facilities. WiFi throughout (charged). Caravan storage.

Ideal For...

 Kids

 Beach

 Dogs

 Year Round Camping

 Fishing

 Watersports

Scan me for more information.

87 accommodations
300 pitches
GPS: 40.97723, 0.90093
Post Code: E-43890

Tarragona, Cataluña-Catalunya

Naturista El Templo del Sol

www.alanrogers.com/es85370
info@eltemplodelsol.com
977 823 434
www.eltemplodelsol.com

Open (Touring Pitches):
15 March - 31 October.

El Templo del Sol is a large, luxurious, terraced naturist site with a distinctly Arabesque feel and superb buildings in Moorish style. The owner has designed the magnificent main turreted building at the entrance with fountains and elaborate Moorish arches. The site has over 387 pitches of two different sizes, some with car parking alongside and 118 with full services. There is shade and the pitches are on terraces giving rewarding views over the sea. Attractive steps give ready access to the sandy beach. There is some daytime rail noise especially in the lower areas of the site where the larger pitches are located.

The sanitary blocks are amongst the best providing everything you could require. Extensive facilities for disabled campers. Washing machines. Well stocked supermarket. Health shop. Souvenir shop. Bars. Restaurant, snack bar, swimming pools (all open all season). Jacuzzi. Cinema. Games area. Boules. Separate children's pool and play area. Miniclub. Library. Entertainment. Hairdresser. Bicycle hire. ATM. Dogs are not accepted. No jet skis. WiFi over site (charged).

Ideal For...

 Naturist

 Beach

 Fishing

 Watersports

 Golf

 Play Area

Scan me for more information.

Hospitalet de l'Infant - By LimoWreck - CC BY-SA 3.0

259 accommodations
990 pitches
GPS: 41.03345, 0.96921
Post Code: E-43300

Tarragona, Cataluña-Catalunya

Playa Montroig Camping Resort

www.alanrogers.com/es85300
info@playamontroig.com
977 810 637
www.playamontroig.com

Open (Touring Pitches):
23 March - 28 October

What a superb site! Playa Montroig is about 30 kilometres beyond Tarragona, set in its own tropical gardens with direct access to a very long, narrow, soft sand beach. The main part of the site lies between the sea, road and railway (as at other sites on this coast, occasional train noise on some pitches) with a huge underpass. The site is divided into spacious, marked pitches with excellent shade provided by a variety of lush vegetation including very impressive palms set in wide avenues. There are 990 pitches, all with electricity (10A) and 661 with water and drainage. Some 47 pitches are directly alongside the beach. A member of Leading Campings group.

Very good quality sanitary buildings with washbasins in private cabins and separate WCs. Facilities for babies and disabled campers. Several launderettes. Motorcaravan services. Gas. Good shopping centre. Restaurants and bars. Fitness suite. Hairdresser. TV lounges. Beach bar. Playground. Jogging track. Sports area. Tennis. Minigolf. Organised activities including pottery. Pedalo hire. Boat mooring. Bicycle hire. WiFi over site. Dogs are not accepted.

Ideal For...

 Kids

 Beach

 Fishing

 Watersports

 Golf

 Play Area

Scan me for more information.

Cala dels Vienesos beach nr. Mont-roig del Camp

417 accommodations
976 pitches
GPS: 41.07546, 1.11651
Post Code: E-43840

Tarragona, Cataluña-Catalunya

Camping Resort Sanguli Salou

www.alanrogers.com/es84800
mail@sangulisalou.com
977 381 641
www.sangulisalou.com

Open (Touring Pitches):
23 March - 4 November

Camping Resort Sanguli Salou is a superb site boasting excellent pools and entertainment. Owned, developed and managed by a local Spanish family, it has something for all the family with everything open when the site is open. There are 976 pitches of varying sizes (75-120 sq.m) all with electricity (7.5-10A). Mobile homes occupy 58 pitches and there are fully equipped bungalows on 147. A wonderful selection of trees, palms and shrubs provide natural shade and an ideal space for children to play. The good sandy beach is little more than 50 metres across the coast road and a small railway crossing. Although large, Sanguli has a pleasant, open feel and maintains a quality family atmosphere due to the efforts of the very keen and efficient staff.

The six sanitary blocks are constantly cleaned and are always exceptional, including many individual cabins with en-suite facilities. Improvements are made each year. Some blocks have excellent facilities for babies. Launderette with service. Motorcaravan services. Car wash (charged). Gas supplies. Snack bars. Indoor and outdoor restaurants with takeaway. Swimming pools. Fitness centre. Sports complex. Bicycle hire. Fitness room (charged). Playgrounds including adventure play area. Miniclub. Minigolf. Free WiFi throughout. Security bracelets. Medical centre.

Ideal For...

Kids

Beach

Dogs

Fishing

Watersports

Golf

Scan me for more information.

CAMPING & RESORT
Sangulí Salou
BEST
2018

JOURNEY TO THE WILD AFRICAN SAVANNAH

+34) 977 38 16 41
WWW.SANGULISALOU.COM
LAMPING GENERATION
2017
CERTIFICATE of
EXCELLENCE
tripadvisor

230 accommodations
700 pitches
GPS: 41.03707, 0.97478
Post Code: E-43300

Tarragona, Cataluña-Catalunya

www.alanrogers.com/es85400
info@latorredelsol.com
977 810 486
www.latorredelsol.com

Open (Touring Pitches):
15 March - 31 October.

Camping La Torre del Sol

A pleasant tree-lined approach road gives way to avenues of palms as you arrive at Torre del Sol. This large, well designed site occupies a good position in southern Catalunya with direct access to a 800m. long soft sand beach. The site is exceptionally well maintained. There is good shade on a high proportion of the 1,500 individual, numbered pitches, all of which have electricity (700 for touring.) The site boasts three attractive pools with two jacuzzis in the bar and restaurant area. A seawater jacuzzi and Turkish sauna opened in 2012. Occasional train noise on some pitches.

Five very well maintained, fully equipped, toilet blocks include units for disabled visitors, babies & children. Washing machines. Gas supplies. Large supermarket, bakery and souvenir shops at the entrance. Full restaurant. Takeaway. Bar with large terrace with entertainment. Beach bar, coffee bar and ice-cream bar. Pizzeria. Open-roof cinema with permanent seating for 520. 3 TV lounges. Soundproofed disco. Swimming pools (two heated). Solarium. Sauna. Two large jacuzzis. Sports areas. Tennis. Squash. Language school (Spanish). Minigolf. Sub-aqua diving. Bicycle hire. Fishing. Windsurfing school. Sailboards and pedaloes for hire. Playground and crèche. Fridge hire. Library. Hairdresser. Business centre. WiFi. Car repair and car wash. No animals permitted. No jet skis accepted.

Ideal For...

 Beach

 Fishing

 Watersports

 Golf

 Play Area

 Disabled Facilities

Scan me for more information.

119 accommodations
193 pitches
GPS: 41.05789, 1.02669
Post Code: E-43850

Tarragona, Cataluña-Catalunya

Camping Joan

www.alanrogers.com/es84780
info@campingjoan.com
977 364 604
www.campingjoan.com

Open (Touring Pitches):
15 January - 16 December

Camping Joan is a very friendly, family run site to the south of the popular village of Cambrils and with direct access to a fine sandy beach. There are 193 touring pitches, most between 50-70 sq.m. and all with 5A electrical connections. There is good shade. Access can be a little tight and large outfits are not accepted. There are 119 accommodations to rent and separate areas are devoted to seasonal caravans. This is a lively site in high season with a varied and comprehensive programme of entertainment and activities for adults and children. The Palmera bar/restaurant serves authentic Spanish food including tapas and 'platos combinados.' A second bar/restaurant (Xiringuito Restaurant del Mar) with amazing sea views serves similar fare, and alongside is a well stocked shop.

Three sanitary blocks serve the touring pitches, the central one refurbished to a high standard. Controllable showers and open style washbasins. Baby rooms and unit for disabled visitors. Motorcaravan services. Bar, restaurant and takeaway service, supermarket, and small swimming and paddling pools (check the updated schedules for opening dates). Playground. Entertainment programme and club for children (high season). Bicycle and beach services hire. WiFi over site (charged). Direct access to beach, coastal footpath and cycleway. Discounted tickets for PortAventura theme park and other tourist information.

Ideal For...

 Beach

 Dogs

 Fishing

 Watersports

 Golf

 Play Area

Scan me for more information.

Red lighthouse in Cambrils harbour

3 accommodations
144 pitches
GPS: 40.12107, 0.15827
Post Code: E-12594

Castelló, Comunidad Valenciana

Camping Didota

www.alanrogers.com/es85790
info@campingdidota.es
964 319 551
www.campingdidota.es

Open (Touring Pitches):
All Year

Didota is a family campsite located on the Costa Azahar, slightly to the north of Oropesa del Mar. It is in a holiday area of apartments and campsites, and development of the area continues. The site is next to a sandy and pebbly beach which slopes to the sea. It is small and basic but friendly, with 144 well shaded pitches (90-100 sq.m) with electricity (10/16A), and bungalows to rent. There is an attractive swimming pool with two terraces alongside a restaurant and bar, plus a small, heated, indoor pool. Bicycle and kayak hire are available and there is an outdoor fitness suite, a computer room with satellite TV and a cinema room.

One modern, heated toilet block has controllable showers in cubicles and open style washbasins. Facilities for disabled visitors. Washing machine and dryer. Shop for basics. Bar/restaurant and terraces. Takeaway. Heated, indoor swimming pool and outdoor pool. Jacuzzi. Play areas. Fitness suite. Computer room. Activity and entertainment programmes for adults and children. Bicycle hire. Canoe hire. Bungalows to rent.

Ideal For...

 Beach

 Dogs

Year Round Camping

 Fishing

 Play Area

 Disabled Facilities

Scan me for more information.

1 accommodations
87 pitches
GPS: 39.32296, -0.30957
Post Code: E-46012

Valencia, Comunidad Valenciana

Devesa Gardens

www.alanrogers.com/es86240
contacto@devesagardens.com
961 611 136
www.devesagardens.com

Open (Touring Pitches):
All year.

This campsite has recently been acquired by the La Marina Group, and the huge investment made is now starting to show as the comprehensive renovation programme gets underway. It is situated between the Albufera lake and the sea, with rice fields on both sides. The 87 level touring pitches are on sand and gravel, all with 16A electricity hook-ups (2-pin sockets). There are no water connections on pitches at the moment. They are separated by fir hedges and young trees, but there is shade from more mature trees. A modern amenities complex is at the heart of the site and includes a swimming pool, extensive play facilities for children and a large auditorium. Bungalows for rent are located in a separate area from the touring pitches.

Three heated sanitary blocks, one modern, two old and requiring updating. Facilities for disabled visitors and families. Washing machine and dryer. Bar. Restaurant and takeaway. Outdoor swimming pool (lifeguard in Apr-Oct, open to public). Riding school. Bullring. Tennis courts. Play area with bouncy castle. Children's club and entertainment. Mini farm. Boat trips. Bicycle hire. WiFi throughout (free).

Ideal For...

 Beach

 Dogs

Year Round Camping

 Fishing

 Watersports

 Golf

Scan me for more information.

180 pitches
GPS: 38.9316, -0.0968
Post Code: E-46780

Valencia, Comunidad Valenciana

Kiko Park Oliva

www.alanrogers.com/es86150
kikopark@kikopark.com
962 850 905
www.kikopark.com

Open (Touring Pitches):
All year.

Kiko Park is a smart site nestling behind protective sand dunes alongside a Blue Flag beach. There are sets of attractively tiled steps over the dunes or a long boardwalk near the beach bar (good for prams and wheelchairs) to take you to the fine white sandy beach and the sea. From the central reception point (where good English is spoken), flat, fine gravel pitches and access roads are divided to the left and right. Backing onto one another, the 180 large pitches all have electricity and the aim is to progressively upgrade all these with full services. There are plenty of flowers, hedging and trees adding shade, privacy and colour.

Four mature, heated sanitary blocks (one currently closed for renovation) include facilities for babies and for disabled visitors (who will find this site flat and convenient). Laundry facilities. Motorcaravan services. Gas supplies. Supermarket (all year, closed Sun). Restaurant. Bar with TV (high season). Beach-side bar and restaurant (lunchtimes only in low season). Swimming pools. Spa with treatments and beauty programmes (charged). Playground. Watersports facilities. Diving school in high season (from mid June). Entertainment for children (from mid June). Pétanque. WiFi (charged). Bicycle hire.

Ideal For...

 Beach

 Dogs

Year Round Camping

 Fishing

 Watersports

 Golf

Scan me for more information.

24 accommodations
298 pitches
GPS: 38.905, -0.066
Post Code: E-46780

Valencia, Comunidad Valenciana

Euro Camping Oliva Beach

www.alanrogers.com/es86120
info@eurocamping-es.com
962 854 098
www.eurocamping-es.com

Open (Touring Pitches):
All year.

Approached through a new urbanisation and situated by Oliva beach with its fine golden sand, Euro Camping is a well maintained, British owned site. Spacious and flat, it is set amidst many high trees, mainly eucalyptus, so ensuring shade in summer, but plenty of sunny spaces in winter. From reception, with its helpful English-speaking staff and interesting aviary opposite, wide tarmac or paved roads lead to 298 gravel-based pitches (70-120 sq.m) which are either marked or hedged (most are for touring units). The main site road leads down to a beachside restaurant with superb views and a supermarket.

One newly built and two mature sanitary blocks are well maintained. British type WCs, preset hot water in the showers. Toilet facilities for disabled campers. Facilities for babies. Washing machines and dryer. Motorcaravan services. Well stocked supermarket and roast chicken takeaway. Restaurant/bar. Fridge hire. Entertainment in high season. Gas. Playground. Bicycle hire. Communal barbecue. WiFi over site (charged).

Ideal For...

 Beach

 Dogs

Year Round Camping

 Fishing

 Golf

 Play Area

Scan me for more information.

36 accommodations
465 pitches
GPS: 38.129649, -0.649575
Post Code: E-03194

Alacant, Comunidad Valenciana

Camping La Marina

www.alanrogers.com/es87420
info@campinglamarina.com
965 419 200
www.campinglamarina.com

Open (Touring Pitches):
All year.

Very efficiently run by a friendly Belgian family, Camping Internacional La Marina has 465 touring pitches of three different types and sizes ranging from 50 sq.m. to 150 sq.m. with electricity (10/16A), TV, water and drainage. Artificial shade is provided and the pitches are well maintained on level, well drained ground with a special area allocated for tents in a small orchard. The lagoon swimming pool complex is fabulous and has something for everyone (with lifeguards). William Le Metayer, the owner, is passionate about La Marina and it shows in his search for perfection. A magnificent new, modern building which uses the latest architectural technology, houses many superb extra amenities. A member of Leading Campings group.

The sanitary blocks offer modern facilities and are regularly cleaned. Heated in winter, they include private cabins and facilities for disabled visitors & babies. Laundry facilities. Motorcaravan services. Gas. Supermarket. Bars. Restaurant and café. Ice cream kiosk. Swimming pools (seasonal). Indoor pool. Fitness centre. Sauna. Solarium. Jacuzzi. Play rooms. Extensive activity and entertainment programme including barbecues and swimming nights. Sports area. Tennis. Huge playgrounds. Hairdresser. Bicycle hire. Road train to beach. Exclusive area for dogs. Internet café (charged) and free WiFi.

Ideal For...

 Kids

 Beach

 Dogs

Year Round Camping

 Fishing

 Watersports

Scan me for more information.

14 accommodations
193 pitches
GPS: 38.78333, 0.16983
Post Code: E-03730

Alacant, Comunidad Valenciana

Camping Jávea

www.alanrogers.com/es87540
info@camping-javea.com
965 791 070
www.camping-javea.com

Open (Touring Pitches):
All year.

The final approach to this site emerges from the bustle of the town and is decorated with palm, orange and pine trees, the latter playing host to a colony of parakeets. English is spoken at reception. The neat, boxed hedges and palms within the site and its backdrop of hills dotted with villas presents an attractive setting. Three hectares provide space for 214 numbered pitches with 193 for touring units. Flat, level and rectangular in shape, the pitches vary in size (60-80 sq.m). All pitches have a granite chip surface and 8A electricity. The restaurant provides great food, way above normal campsite standards.

Two very clean, fully equipped, sanitary blocks include two children's toilets plus a baby bath. Separate facilities for disabled campers. Two washing machines. Fridge hire. Extensive bar and restaurant with terraces where in high season you purchase bread and milk. Large swimming pool with lifeguard and sunbathing lawns. Play area. Boules. Electronic barriers (deposit for card). Caravan storage. Post. Safes. Five-a-side football. Basketball. Tennis. WiFi (free in restaurant). Car rental.

Ideal For...

 Beach

 Dogs

Year Round Camping

 Fishing

 Watersports

 Golf

Scan me for more information.

56 accommodations
1200 pitches
GPS: 38.177901, -0.809504
Post Code: E-03330

Alacant, Comunidad Valenciana

Camping Marjal Costa Blanca

www.alanrogers.com/es87435
camping@marjalcostablanca.com
965 484 945
www.marjalcostablanca.com

Open (Touring Pitches):
All year.

Marjal Costa Blanca is a fully equipped site situated 15 km. inland on the southern Alicante coast, close to the towns of Crevillente and Catral, and the Parque Natural de El Hondo. The 1,200 hardstanding pitches range in size from 90-95 sq.m, and all have electricity (16A), water, drainage, TV and high speed internet connections (charged). On-site amenities include a tropical themed swimming pool complex and a state-of-the-art wellness centre. There is full disabled access, including at the swimming pool and staffed gym. There is accommodation to rent, including 46 Balinese-style bungalows adapted for disabled visitors. The site is ideal for both family holidays in summer and for winter sun-seekers.

Six modern, spotlessly clean toilet blocks have washbasins and free showers in cabins. Facilities for children, babies & disabled visitors. Well equipped shop. Bar, restaurant and takeaway (all year). Swimming pool complex with outdoor pool (Mar-Sept), heated indoor pool (all year), sauna and Hammam. Fully equipped gym. Wellness centre. Hairdresser. Play areas. Games rooms. Library. Multisports courts. Minigolf. Tennis. Football. Entertainment and activity programme (incl Spanish lessons). Kids club. Business centre. Bicycle hire. Car hire service. Doctor and vet. Free WiFi areas, high speed internet on pitches (charged). Mobile homes and chalets to rent.

Ideal For...

Kids

Beach

Dogs

Year Round Camping

Fishing

Watersports

Scan me for more information.

Altamira Castle in Elche - By José Manuel Pérez - Public Domain

26 accommodations
303 pitches
GPS: 38.538, -0.119
Post Code: E-03503

Alacant, Comunidad Valenciana

Camping Villasol

www.alanrogers.com/es86810
info@camping-villasol.com
965 850 422
www.camping-villasol.com

Open (Touring Pitches):
All Year

Benidorm is increasingly popular for winter stays and Villasol is a genuinely good, purpose built modern site. Many of the 303 well separated pitches are arranged on wide terraces which afford views of the mountains surrounding Benidorm. All pitches (80-85 sq.m) have electricity and satellite TV connections, with 160 with full services for seasonal use. Shade is mainly artificial. Reservations are only accepted for winter stays of over three months (from 1 October). There is a small indoor pool, heated for winter use, and a very attractive, large outdoor pool complex (summer only) overlooked by the bar/restaurant and attractive, elevated restaurant terrace.

Modern toilet blocks provide free, controllable hot water to showers and washbasins and British WCs. Good facilities for disabled visitors. Laundry facilities. Good value restaurant. Bar. Shop. Swimming pools, outdoor and indoor. Satellite TV. Playground. Evening entertainment programme. Safes. Dogs are not accepted. No charcoal barbecues.

Ideal For...

 Beach

Year Round Camping

 Fishing

 Watersports

 Golf

 Play Area

Scan me for more information.

Sunset over Benidorm - By Maksim Ivanov - CC BY-SA 4.0

248 pitches
GPS: 38.64444, 0.059989
Post Code: 03710

Alacant, Comunidad Valenciana

www.alanrogers.com/es86795
reservas@ar-hotels.com
965 832 618
www.campingsoldecalpe.com/en

Open (Touring Pitches):
All Year

Sol de Calpe

Sol de Calpe is in the heart of the Costa Blanca on the shores of the Mediterranean. Surrounded by beaches and coves with crystal clear waters and crowned by the 332m high rock called Peñón de Ifach, the site features a total of 248 pitches over two areas within metres of each other, with all the home from home facilities you should need. The site is exclusively for caravans, campervans and motorhomes, there are no tent pitches. Sizes of pitch vary from 55 sq.m to 120 sq.m, all with a gravel surface, electricity (10A), water and drain and Satellite TV connection, and some pitches have been adapted for disabled guest access. There are two swimming pools, one for adults and one for children, a children's play area and a bar/restaurant which serves a variety of cuisines. During high season there is an animation programme for children including sports, games, classes and performances as well as live music on summer evenings. Calpe is on the edge of a National Park giving ample opportunity for walking, communing with nature and seeing local wildlife.

Washing facilities include showers, toilets and basins. Disabled facilities. Restaurant/bar/cafe. Terrace and picnic area. Two swimming pools. Child's play area. Sports field. Social club with animation/kids' club. Library. Mini market. Carwash. WiFi. Dogs welcome.

Ideal For...

 Beach

 Dogs

 Fishing

 Watersports

 Walking

 Play Area

Scan me for more information.

Caravaning La Manga

This is a very large, well equipped, holiday-style site with its own beach and both indoor and outdoor pools. With a good number of typical Spanish long stay units, the length of the site is impressive (1 km) and a bicycle is very helpful for getting about. The 800 regularly laid out, gravel touring pitches (100 or 110 sq.m) are generally separated by hedges which provide some privacy but very little shade. Each has a 10A electricity supply, water and the possibility of satellite TV reception. This site's excellent facilities are ideally suited for holidays in the winter when the weather is very pleasantly warm. Daytime temperatures in November usually exceed 20 degrees.

Nine clean toilet blocks of standard design, well spaced around the site, include washbasins (all with hot water). Laundry. Gas supplies. Large well stocked supermarket. Restaurant. Bar. Snack bar. Swimming pool complex (April-Sept). Indoor pool, gymnasium (April-Oct), sauna, jacuzzi and massage service. Outdoor fitness course for adults. Open-air family cinema (July/ Aug). Tennis. Pétanque. Minigolf. Play area. Watersports school. Internet café (also WiFi). Winter activities including Spanish classes. Pet washing area.

50 accommodations
800 pitches
GPS: 37.62445, -0.74442
Post Code: E-30386

La Manga del Mar Menor, Murcia

www.alanrogers.com/es87530
lamanga@caravaning.es
968 563 014
www.caravaning.es

Open (Touring Pitches):
All year.

Ideal For...

 Beach

 Dogs

 Year Round Camping

 Fishing

 Watersports

 Golf

Scan me for more information.

7 accommodations
250 pitches
GPS: 36.808159, -2.232159
Post Code: E-04150

Almería, Andalucia

Camping Cabo de Gata

www.alanrogers.com/es87630
info@campingcabodegata.com
950 160 443
www.campingcabodegata.com

Open (Touring Pitches):
All year.

Cabo de Gata, situated on the Gulf of Almería, is a pleasant, all-year campsite offering facilities to a good standard. Popular with British visitors through the winter, and within the Cabo de Gata-Nijar Nature Park, set amongst fruit farms, it is only a 1 km. walk to a fine sandy beach. The 250 gravel pitches are level and of a reasonable size, with 6/16A electricity and limited shade from maturing trees or canopies. There are specific areas for very large units with very high canopies for shade and seven chalets for rent.

Two, well maintained, clean toilet blocks provide all the necessary sanitary facilities, including British type WCs, washbasins and free hot showers. Facilities for disabled campers. Restaurant, bar and shop (all year). Swimming pool. Football. Pétanque. Tennis. Small playground. Library. Bicycle hire. English spoken. Entertainment programme. Internet access (charged). WiFi (free by reception).

Ideal For...

 Beach

 Dogs

 Year Round Camping

 Fishing

 Watersports

 Golf

Scan me for more information.

65 accommodations
250 pitches
GPS: 36.49350, -4.74383
Post Code: E-29604

Málaga, Andalucia

www.alanrogers.com/es88020
info@campingcabopino.com
952 834 373
www.campingcabopino.com

Open (Touring Pitches):
All year.

Camping Cabopino

This large, mature site is alongside the main N340/A7 Costa del Sol coast road, 12 km. east of Marbella and 15 km. from Fuengirola. The Costa del Sol is also known as the Costa del Golf and fittingly there is a major golf course alongside the site. The site is set amongst tall pine trees which provide shade for the pitches (there are some huge areas for large units). The 250 touring pitches, a mix of level and sloping (chocks advisable), all have electricity (10A), but long leads may be required for some. There is a separate area on the western side for groups of younger guests.

Five mature sanitary blocks provide hot water throughout (may be under pressure at peak times). Facilities for disabled visitors in one block. Washing machines. Bar/restaurant and takeaway (all year). Shop. Outdoor pool (1/5-15/9) and indoor pool (all year). Play area. Adult exercise equipment. Some evening entertainment. Excursions can be booked. ATM. Bicycle hire. Torches necessary in the more remote parts of the site. Only gas or electric barbecues are permitted. WiFi (charged).

Ideal For...

 Beach

 Dogs

Year Round Camping

 Watersports

 Golf

 Play Area

Scan me for more information.

47 accommodations
290 pitches
GPS: 36.739245, -3.949713
Post Code: E-29793

Málaga, Andalucia

Camping El Pino

www.alanrogers.com/es87810
info@campingelpino.com
952 530 006
www.campingelpino.com

Open (Touring Pitches):
All year.

El Pino is in the Axarquia region of the Costa del Sol, east of Malaga and is surrounded by avocado groves. The old but well maintained site enjoys some fine views of the surrounding countryside. There are now 382 pitches here, mostly well shaded, and a further 47 mobile homes and chalets to rent. Most pitches have electrical connections and vary in size from 60-100 sq.m. The site is open all year and has some good facilities including a swimming pool, supermarket and bar/ restaurant. The nearest beach is 800 m. distant – a bus service runs there from the site.

Four toilet blocks with hot showers and individual cabins. Facilities for disabled visitors. Laundry facilities. Bar, restaurant and shop (all year). Takeaway. Swimming pool with new children's pool (1/6-15/9). Play area. Games room. Pétanque. Children's club. WiFi throughout (free). Mobile homes and chalets to rent. Communal barbecue - only gas or electric barbecues permitted on pitches.

Ideal For...

 Beach

 Dogs

Year Round Camping

 Fishing

 Watersports

 Golf

Scan me for more information.

55 accommodations
335 pitches
GPS: 36.29317, -6.09547
Post Code: E-11140

Cádiz, Andalucia

Camping la Rosaleda

www.alanrogers.com/es88580
info@campinglarosaleda.com
956 443 327
www.campinglarosaleda.com

Open (Touring Pitches):
All year.

This excellent site was opened in 1999. Its owner has many years of experience and has listened to what campers want and has then delivered. Much money has been spent and will continue to be spent to make this an even better site. Great care has been taken with the planning to ensure campers have an enjoyable holiday, with many top class facilities and a first class service. There are 335 well kept pitches of three different sizes (70-120 sq.m), the smallest just for tents, the largest with electricity (10A) and water. This is an ideal place to experience the sunshine and culture of Spain.

Four modern, fully equipped sanitary blocks include facilities for campers with disabilities and were spotless when seen. Motorcaravan services. Gas supplies. Excellent supermarket (all year). Bar/restaurant (all year). Swimming pool complex (large with stunning views). Large play area. Bicycle hire. Massage, sauna, gym, yoga room, hairdressing. Wooden bungalows with good facilities and own gardens. Free WiFi over site. No barbecues on pitches 15/6-15/10. Fridge hire. Dogs are not accepted in high season.

Ideal For...

 Beach

 Dogs

 Year Round Camping

 Fishing

 Golf

 Play Area

Scan me for more information.

120 accommodations
288 pitches
GPS: 42.4352, 0.13618
Post Code: E-22360

Huesca, Aragon

www.alanrogers.com/es90600
info@penamontanesa.com
974 500 032
www.penamontanesa.com

Open (Touring Pitches):
All year.

Camping Peña Montañesa

A large site situated in the Pyrenees near the Ordesa National Park, Peña Montañesa is easily accessible from Ainsa or from France via the Bielsa Tunnel (steep sections on the French side). The site is essentially divided into three sections opening progressively throughout the season and all have shade. The 288 pitches on fairly level grass are of about 75 sq.m. and 6/10A electricity is available on virtually all (no charge is made for upgrade). Grouped near the entrance are the facilities that make the site so attractive, including an outdoor pool and a heated (out of season), glass covered indoor pool with jacuzzi and sauna. Here too is an attractive bar/restaurant with an open fire and a terrace; a supermarket and takeaway are opposite.

A newer toilet block, heated when necessary, has free hot showers but cold water to open plan washbasins. Facilities for disabled visitors. Small baby room. An older block in the original area has similar provision. Washing machine and dryer. Bar, restaurant, takeaway and supermarket (all 1/1-31/12). Outdoor swimming pool (1/4-31/10). Indoor pool, sauna and jacuzzi (all year). Outdoor social area with large TV screen and stage. Multisports court. Tennis. Playground. Boules. Only gas barbecues are permitted. WiFi in bar area (free).

Ideal For...

 Beach

 Dogs

 Year Round Camping

 Fishing

 Walking

 Play Area

Scan me for more information.

29 accommodations
272 pitches
GPS: 38.93717, -2.84744
Post Code: E-02611

Albacete, Castilla-La-Mancha

Camping Los Batanes

www.alanrogers.com/es90970
camping@losbatanes.com
926 699 076
www.losbatanes.com

Open (Touring Pitches):
All year.

This large campsite is in a lovely setting at the side of one of the many lakes in this area. The route to get here is beautiful and it is well worth the trip, but careful driving was necessary in parts with our large motorcaravan. A smaller, older part of the campsite houses reception, a small shop and a bar/restaurant. Here are medium sized pitches, shaded by pine trees with a small river running through. By the entrance are 18 new, fully serviced, hardstanding pitches. Over a wooden bridge is the main, newer part of the site with over 200 level, gravel and sand pitches of mixed sizes, shaded again by pine trees. Electricity is 6A on most pitches.

Three modern toilet blocks have hot showers, washbasins in cabins and facilities for disabled visitors. Small shop. Simple restaurant, snacks and bar. Swimming and paddling pools (15/6-10/9). Play area. Children's activities (4-12 yrs, July/Aug).

Ideal For...

 Dogs

 Year Round Camping

 Disabled Facilities

 Pets Accepted

 Bar on Site

Scan me for more information.

18 accommodations
44 pitches
GPS: 39.3219, -4.6495
Post Code: E-13110

Ciudad Real, Castilla-La-Mancha

www.alanrogers.com/es90960
info@campingcabaneros.com
926 775 439
www.campingcabaneros.com

Open (Touring Pitches):
All year.

El Mirador de Cabañeros

With panoramic views all around of the Sierra de Valdefuertes mountains, Camping El Mirador de Cabañeros is set in the Cabañeros National Park. This is a well cared for, landscaped site with 44 terraced pitches on gravel, all with 6A electricity. Although pitches are level once sited, the approach is via a steep slope which may cause difficulties for larger units. Run by a very helpful and friendly family, this site is in a very peaceful location where you can just sit and relax or visit the many attractions that the National Park has to offer. It is an ideal base for walking and birdwatching.

One spotlessly clean central toilet block with solar heating includes open washbasins and cubicle showers. Facilities for disabled visitors and babies. Laundry. Motorcaravan services. No shop but basics from reception. Bar and restaurant (15/6-15/9, w/ends in low season). Covered swimming pool (all year). Games room. Play areas. Outside fitness area.

Ideal For...

 Dogs

Year Round Camping

 Fishing

 Play Area

 Disabled Facilities

 Pets Accepted

Scan me for more information.

23 accommodations
162 pitches
GPS: 40.04218, -3.59947
Post Code: E-28300

Aranjuez, Madrid

www.alanrogers.com/es90910
info@campingaranjuez.com
918 911 395
www.campingaranjuez.com

Open (Touring Pitches):
All year.

Camping Aranjuez

Aranjuez, supposedly Spain's version of Versailles, is worthy of a visit with its beautiful palaces, leafy squares, avenues and gardens. This useful, popular and unusually well equipped site is therefore excellent for enjoying the unusual attractions or for an en route stop. It is 47 km. south of Madrid and 46 km. from Toledo. The site is alongside the River Tajo in a park-like situation with mature trees. There are 162 touring pitches, all with electricity (16A), set on flat grass amid tall trees. The site is owned by the owners of la Marina (ES87420) who have worked hard to improve the pitches and the site in general.

Two of the three modern sanitary blocks are heated and all are well equipped with some washbasins in cabins. Laundry facilities. Gas supplies. Shop, bar and restaurant (all year) with attractive riverside patio (also open to the public). Takeaway. TV in bar. Swimming and paddling pools, (1/5-15/10). Tennis courts. Central play area. Pétanque. Bicycle hire. Canoe hire. Activities for children (high season). WiFi over site (charged).

Ideal For...

Beach

Dogs

Year Round Camping

Fishing

Watersports

Golf

Scan me for more information.

107 accommodations
470 pitches
GPS: 40.62400, -4.099
Post Code: E-28280

El Escorial, Madrid

Caravanning El Escorial

www.alanrogers.com/es92000
info@campingelescorial.com
902 014 900
www.campingelescorial.com

Open (Touring Pitches):
All year.

El Escorial is very large and everything on site is on a grand scale - indeed a bicycle is very useful for getting around. There are 1,358 individual pitches of which 470 are for touring units, with the remainder used for permanent or seasonal units, but situated to one side of the site. The pitches are shaded (ask for a pitch without a low tree canopy if you have a 3 m. high motorcaravan). An attractive area of five hectares is set aside for 'wild camping' in tents on open fields with good shade from mature trees (long cables may be necessary for electricity). The general amenities are comprehensive and good, and include three swimming pools (unheated), plus a paddling pool.

One large toilet block for the touring pitches, plus small blocks for the 'wild' camping area, are all fully equipped with some washbasins in cabins. Facilities for babies and disabled campers. The blocks can be heated. Large supermarket (all year). Restaurant/bar and snack bar with takeaway (w/ends and B.Hs only in low season). Meeting rooms. Disco-bar. Swimming pools (15/5-15/9). Multisports areas. Family activities (high season, weekends in low season). Two well equipped playgrounds on sand. Bicycle hire. ATM. Car wash. WiFi in some areas (free).

Ideal For...

 Dogs

 Year Round Camping

 Golf

 Play Area

 Disabled Facilities

 Pets Accepted

Scan me for more information.

17 accommodations
90 pitches
GPS: 42.62423, -1.84259
Post Code: E-31150

Mendigorria, Navarra

El Molino de Mendigorria

www.alanrogers.com/es90430
info@campingelmolino.com
948 340 604
www.campingelmolino.com

Open (Touring Pitches):
All year (excl. 23 December - 4 January).

This is an extensive site set by an attractive weir near the town of Mendigorria, alongside the River Arga. It takes its name from an old disused water mill (molino) close by. The site is split into separate permanent and touring sections. The touring area is a new development with 90 good sized flat pitches with electricity and water for touring units, and a separate area for tents. Many trees have been planted around the site but there is still only minimal shade. The friendly owner, Anna Beriain, will give you a warm welcome.

The well equipped toilet block is very clean and well maintained, with cold water to washbasins. Facilities for children and disabled visitors. Washing machine. Large restaurant, pleasant bar. Supermarket. Superb new swimming pools for adults and children (1/6-15/9). Bicycle hire. Riverside bar. Weekly entertainment programme (July/Aug) and many sporting activities. Squash courts. River walk. Torches useful. Gas barbecues only. WiFi on part of site (charged).

Ideal For...

 Beach

 Dogs

 Fishing

 Watersports

 Golf

 Play Area

Scan me for more information.

20 accommodations
125 pitches
GPS: 42.57894, -2.85157
Post Code: E-26200

Haro, La Rioja

www.alanrogers.com/es90400
campingdeharo@fer.es
941 312 737
www.campingdeharo.com

Open (Touring Pitches):
All year excl. 9 December - 19 January.

Camping de Haro

This quiet riverside site is on the outskirts of the old town of Haro, the commercial centre for the renowned Rioja wines. It is a family run site with pleasant pools (open 15/6-15/9). Staff in the modern reception are helpful and you may well get a cheery welcome from Carlos, the owner's son, who speaks excellent English. All 236 pitches are on level ground and of reasonable size, including some open pitches. Around 50% are occupied on a seasonal and weekend basis. Most of the touring pitches have some shade, a few have a great deal. Electricity connections (6A, Europlug) are provided throughout the site.

Two toilet blocks, one heated in winter, the other with facilities for disabled campers and children. Laundry. Bar/restaurant and snack bar with small counter selling basic provisions (high seasons and w/ends). Swimming pool (15/6-15/9). Multisports area. Play area. Bicycle hire. Entertainment for children in high season. WiFi throughout (charged). Charcoal barbecues are not permitted.

Ideal For...

 Dogs

 Fishing

 Watersports

 Golf

 Play Area

 Disabled Facilities

Scan me for more information.

6 accommodations
100 pitches
GPS: 42.52911, -2.92243
Post Code: E-26240

Castañares de Rioja, La Rioja

Camping de La Rioja

www.alanrogers.com/es92250
info@campingdelarioja.es
941 300 174
www.campingdelarioja.es

Open (Touring Pitches):
1 January - 9 December.

This site is situated just beyond the town of Castañares de Rioja. This is a very busy site during the peak season with a huge sporting and play area and a predominantly Spanish clientele. In low season it is quieter, with limited facilities available. There are 100 touring pitches, 6 bungalows for hire and around 400 private accommodations on this five-hectare site. These are separated by hedges and trees allowing privacy. Each has their own water, drainage and electricity connection. There is one very large sanitary block. To the rear of the site is the Oja river and there are views of the Obarenes mountains in the distance. Some noise from the main road is possible.

The central sanitary facilities are old and traditional in style but clean. Open style washbasins and controllable showers. Laundry facilities. Shop (w/ends only in low season). Bar, restaurant, takeaway (on request). Outdoor swimming pool (20/6-20/9} supervised. Multisports court. Football. Tennis. River fishing. Children's cycle circuit. Play area. Electric or gas barbecues only.

Ideal For...

 Dogs

 Fishing

 Play Area

 Pets Accepted

 Bar on Site

Scan me for more information.

11 accommodations
133 pitches
GPS: 41.495305, -5.005222
Post Code: E-47100

Valladolid, Castilla Y Leon

Campingred El Astral

www.alanrogers.com/es90290
info@campingelastral.es
983 770 953
www.campingelastral.es

Open (Touring Pitches):
All year.

The site is in a prime position alongside the wide River Duero (safely fenced). It is homely and run by a charming man, Eduardo Gutierrez, who speaks excellent English and is ably assisted by brother Gustavo and sister Lola. The site is generally flat with 140 pitches separated by thin hedges. The 133 touring pitches, 132 with electricity (6/10A), six with 10A electricity, water and waste water, vary in size from 60-200 sq.m. with mature trees providing shade. The toilet block has been designed with environmental sustainability in mind, including solar heated water. This is a friendly site, ideal for exploring the area and historic Tordesillas.

One attractive sanitary block with fully equipped, modern facilities designed to include energy-saving measures and to be easily cleaned. Showers for children and baby room. Facilities for disabled visitors. Washing machines. Motorcaravan services. Supermarket. Bar and restaurant, frequented by locals, plus a takeaway service all 1/4-30/9. Swimming pool with new disability lift, plus paddling pools (1/6-15/9). Playground. Tennis (high season). Minigolf. No charcoal barbecues (July-Sept). WiFi throughout (charged).

Ideal For...

 Beach

 Dogs

 Year Round Camping

 Fishing

 Golf

 Play Area

Scan me for more information.

24 accommodations
129 pitches
GPS: 40.9471, -5.614
Post Code: E-37900

Salamanca, Castilla Y Leon

Camping Regio

www.alanrogers.com/es90250
recepcion@campingregio.com
923 138 888
www.campingregio.com

Open (Touring Pitches):
All year.

Salamanca is one of Europe's oldest university cities, and this beautiful old sandstone city has to be visited. This is also a useful staging post en route to the south of Spain or central Portugal. The site is 7 km. outside the city on the old road to Madrid, behind the Hôtel Regio where campers can take advantage of the hotel facilities. The 129 pitches (with two large areas for tents without electricity) are clearly marked on uneven and sloping ground, with some shade in parts and 10A electricity. Access to those pitches not on the wide central road can be difficult for caravans.

Very large, fully equipped sanitary block is in need of some repair and upgrading. Facilities for disabled campers and babies. Washing machine and dryer. Gas supplies. Motorcaravan services. Bar. Cafeteria. Shop (1/6-30/9). The hotel restaurant, cafeteria, pool and wellness centre may be used by campers (discounts available). Play area. Tennis. Car wash. Bicycle hire. Internet and WiFi within hotel area. WiFi on site (free). English is spoken.

Ideal For...

 Dogs

Year Round Camping

 Fishing

 Golf

 Play Area

 Disabled Facilities

Scan me for more information.

12 accommodations
102 pitches
GPS: 43.22594, -4.29034
Post Code: E-39510

Cabuérniga, Cantabria

www.alanrogers.com/es89640
cmcabuerniga@campingcabuerniga.com
942 706 259
www.campingcabuerniga.com

Open (Touring Pitches):
All year.

El Molino de Cabuérniga

Located in a peaceful valley with magnificent views of the mountains, beside the Saja river and only a short walk from the picturesque and unspoiled village of Sopeña, this gem of a site is on an open, level, grassy meadow with trees. Wonderful stone buildings and artefacts are a feature of this unique site. There are 102 marked pitches, all with 6A electricity, although long leads may be needed in places. This comfortable site is very good value and ideal for a few nights (or you may well choose to stay longer once there) whilst you explore the Cabuérniga Valley which forms part of the Reserva Nacional del Saja.

A superb, spotless sanitary block provides spacious, controllable showers and hot and cold water to washbasins. Washing machines and free ironing. Unit for disabled campers. Baby and toddler room. Bar serving breakfasts and 'bocadillos' (sandwiches) includes small shop section. Wonderful playground in rustic setting - supervision recommended. Fishing. Bicycle hire. Attractive stone cottages and apartments to rent. No electric barbecues. WiFi throughout.

Ideal For...

 Beach

 Dogs

Year Round Camping

 Fishing

 Golf

 Play Area

Scan me for more information.

50 accommodations
120 pitches
GPS: 43.385268, -4.33814
Post Code: E-39547

San Vicente de la Barquera,
Cantabria

Camping Oyambre

www.alanrogers.com/es89710
camping@oyambre.com
942 711 461
www.oyambre.com

Open (Touring Pitches):
6 March - 31 October.

This exceptionally well managed site is ideally positioned to use as a base to visit the spectacular Picos de Europa or one of the many sandy beaches along this northern coast. Despite its name, it is a kilometre from the beach on foot. The 120 touring pitches all have 10A electricity (long leads needed in places), ten are fully serviced. The fairly flat central area is allocated to tents while caravans are mainly sited on wide terraces (access to some could be a little tight for larger units) and there is some shade. There may be some traffic noise on the lower terraces.

Good, clean sanitary facilities are in one well kept block. Facilities for babies and disabled visitors. Washing machines. Motorcaravan services. Shop in bar. Restaurant. Takeaway. Swimming pools with lifeguard. Playground. Bicycle hire. Free WiFi over site.

Ideal For...

 Beach

 Dogs

 Fishing

 Watersports

 Golf

 Play Area

Scan me for more information.

156 pitches
GPS: 43.391608, -4.575709
Post Code: E-33590

Ribadedeva, Asturias

Camping Las Hortensias

www.alanrogers.com/es89570
info@campinglashortensias.com
985 412 442
www.campinglashortensias.com

Open (Touring Pitches):
1 June - 21 September.

Open for just four months from June to September, Las Hortensias is a friendly site located on the Cantabrian coast of northern Spain. The site enjoys a fine setting on a sheltered sandy beach, adjacent to the Mirador Hotel. There are 156 pitches connected by well lit tarmac roads. Each pitch has 6-10A electricity and there are water points throughout. After a day on the beach or exploring the nearby rock pools, the bar terrace is a great spot to enjoy the sunset. Many pitches are well shaded by pine trees, in pleasant, peaceful locations.

Two adequate sanitary blocks, one with WCs only, the other with open plan washbasins and showers. Washing machine and dryer. Basic motorcaravan services. Small supermarket. Bar with terrace overlooking beach. Basic restaurant (campers can use the hotel restaurant with 10% discount), snack bar and takeaway. TV in bar. Play area. Gas and charcoal barbecues only. WiFi.

Ideal For...

 Beach

 Dogs

 Play Area

 Pets Accepted

 Bar on Site

Scan me for more information.

12 accommodations
113 pitches
GPS: 42.88939, -8.52418
Post Code: E-15704

A Coruña, Galicia

Camping As Cancelas

www.alanrogers.com/es90240
info@campingascancelas.com
981 580 476
www.campingascancelas.com

Open (Touring Pitches):
All year.

The beautiful city of Santiago has been the destination for European Christian pilgrims for centuries and they now follow ancient routes to this unique city, the whole of which is a national monument. The As Cancelas campsite is excellent for sharing the experiences of these pilgrims in the city and around the magnificent cathedral. It has 113 marked pitches (60-90 sq.m), arranged in terraces and divided by trees and shrubs. On a hillside overlooking the city, the views are very pleasant. The site has a steep approach road.

Two modern toilet blocks are fully equipped, with ramped access for disabled visitors. The quality and cleanliness of the fittings and tiling is good. Laundry with service wash for a small fee. Small shop. Restaurant. Bar with TV. Well kept, unsupervised swimming pool and children's pool. Small playground. Internet access. WiFi throughout.

Ideal For...

 Beach

 Dogs

 Year Round Camping

 Fishing

 Watersports

 Golf

Scan me for more information.

SWITZERLAND

A small, wealthy country best known for its outstanding mountainous scenery, fine cheeses, delicious chocolates, Swiss bank accounts and enviable lifestyles. Centrally situated in Europe, it shares its borders with four countries: France, Austria, Germany and Italy, each one having its own cultural influence on Switzerland. Switzerland boasts a picture postcard landscape of mountains, valleys, waterfalls and glaciers.

The Bernese Oberland with its snowy peaks and rolling hills is the most popular area, Gstaad is a favourite haunt of wealthy skiers, while the mild climate and breezy conditions around Lake Thun are perfect for watersports and other outdoor activities.

German-speaking Zurich is a multicultural metropolis with over 50 museums, shops and festivals set against a breathtaking backdrop.

Geneva, Montreux and Lausanne on the northern shores of Lake Geneva make up the bulk of French Switzerland, with vineyards that border the lakes and medieval towns. The southernmost canton, Ticino, is home to the Italian-speaking Swiss, with the Mediterranean style lakeside resorts of Lugano and Locarno.

Language: German in central and eastern areas, French in the west and Italian in the south. Raeto-Romansch is spoken in the south east. English is spoken by many.
Capital: Bern
Currency: Swiss Franc (Fr)
Time Zone: Central European Time (GMT/UTC plus one hour)
Telephone Country Code: 00 41
Tourist Office: www.myswitzerland.com

Public Holidays
New Year; Good Fri; Easter Mon; Ascension; Whit Mon; National Day 1 Aug; Christmas 25 Dec. Other holidays are observed in individual Cantons.

Motoring
The road network is comprehensive and well planned. An annual road tax is levied on all cars using Swiss motorways and the 'Vignette' windscreen sticker must be purchased at the border (credit cards not accepted), or in advance from the Swiss National Tourist Office, plus a separate one for a towed caravan or trailer.

10 accommodations
90 pitches
GPS: 46.68605, 7.830633
Post Code: CH-3800

Bern, Central

Camping Lazy Rancho 4

www.alanrogers.com/ch9430
info@lazyrancho.ch
033 822 8716
www.lazyrancho.ch

Open (Touring Pitches):
25 April - 25 October.

This popular site is in a quiet location with fantastic views of the dramatic mountains of Eiger, Monch and Jungfrau. Neat, orderly and well maintained, the site is situated in a wide valley just 1 km. from Lake Thun and 1.5 km. from the centre of Interlaken. The English speaking owners, Stephane and Alina Blatter, lovingly care for the site and will endeavour to make you feel very welcome. Connected by gravel roads, the 155 pitches, of which 90 are for touring units, are on well tended level grass (seven with hardstanding, all with 10A electricity). There are also 30 pitches with water and waste water drainage.

Two good sanitary blocks are both heated with free hot showers, good facilities for disabled campers and a baby room. Laundry. Campers' kitchen with microwave, cooker, fridge and utensils. Motorcaravan services. Well stocked shop. TV and games room. Play area. Small swimming pool, sauna and hot tub (all season). Wooden igloo pods and bungalows for rent. Internet/laptop room. WiFi throughout (free).

Ideal For...

 Beach

 Dogs

 Fishing

 Watersports

 Walking

 Golf

Scan me for more information.

24 accommodations
180 pitches
GPS: 46.7483, 8.04871
Post Code: CH-3855

Bern, Central

Camping Aaregg

www.alanrogers.com/ch9510
mail@aaregg.ch
033 951 1843
www.aaregg.ch

Open (Touring Pitches):
1 April - 31 October.

Brienz, in the Bernese Oberland, is a delightful little town on the lake of the same name and the centre of the Swiss wood carving industry. Camping Aaregg is an excellent site of the highest quality situated at the eastern end of the lake with breathtaking views across the water to the surrounding mountains. Cabins to rent and seasonal pitches occupy part of the site with 180 available for touring, all with electricity (10/16A). Of these, eight lakeside pitches have been newly upgraded with full services and 18 have hardstandings, water and drainage. The trees, flowers and well tended grass make an attractive and peaceful environment.

New, very attractive sanitary facilities built and maintained to first class standards. Showers with washbasins. Washbasins (open style and in cubicles). Children's section. Family shower rooms. Baby room. Facilities for disabled visitors. Laundry facilities. Motorcaravan services. Pleasant restaurant with café/bar and shop. Guest lounge with TV. Play area. Fishing. Bicycle hire. Boat launching. Lake swimming in clear water (unsupervised). English is spoken. WiFi in reception area. New camping pods and mini chalets for hire.

Ideal For...

 Beach

 Dogs

 Fishing

 Watersports

Play Area

 Disabled Facilities

Scan me for more information.

14 accommodations
94 pitches
GPS: 46.88390, 8.24413
Post Code: CH-6060

Unterwalden, Central

Camping Seefeld Sarnen

www.alanrogers.com/ch9540
welcome@seefeldpark.ch
041 666 5788
www.seefeldpark.ch

Open (Touring Pitches):
All year.

One of the finest sites we have seen, Camping Seefeld Sarnen was completely rebuilt with all the features demanded by discerning campers and reopened in 2011. The location alongside Lake Sarnen is breathtaking, with views across the water to lush meadows, wooded hills and mountains topped with snow for most of the year. The seasonal pitches are immaculately maintained on their own area. There are 94 touring pitches arranged on almost level grass, each with 13A electricity and its own water tap. There is some shade from young trees which will increase as time goes on. The site not only offers active family holidays on land and on the water, but is ideally placed for exploring this beautiful part of Switzerland.

Heated sanitary facilities are in the main building supplemented by unheated facilities in the central block. Baby room and cubicles for children. Facilities for disabled visitors. Washing machines and dryers. Shop, bar and restaurant with large terrace (Easter-Oct). Campers' lounge with kitchen, TV/DVD, tables and chairs. Two swimming pools with lifeguards (20/4-15/9). Two playgrounds. Watersports. Tennis. Bicycle hire. Dog bath; dogs not accepted in high season. WiFi throughout (free).

Ideal For...

 Beach

 Dogs

Year Round Camping

 Fishing

 Watersports

 Golf

Scan me for more information.

3 accommodations
100 pitches
GPS: 46.67999, 7.81728
Post Code: CH-3800

Bern, Central

Camping Alpenblick

www.alanrogers.com/ch9425
info@camping-alpenblick.ch
033 822 7757
www.camping-alpenblick.ch

Open (Touring Pitches):
All year.

Alpenblick is an all-year site, located at the heart of the Bernese Oberland just 100 m. from Lake Thun. Susanne Knecht and George Zehntner took over the site in 2006 and have made many improvements, including an excellent new toilet block. The old reception building has been replaced with a new Swiss chalet housing reception, a bar, restaurant and shop. There are 100 touring pitches and a further 80 residential pitches. The touring pitches all have 10/16A electrical connections and 18 good hardstanding pitches are available for motorcaravans. Three teepees are available for rent. A larger teepee, complete with bar and indoor barbecue, is used for socialising in the evening and is very popular with campers and local residents.

Sanitary block with hot showers, some washbasins in cubicles and a family shower room. Facilities for disabled visitors. Laundry facilities. Shop (1/4-20/10) with daily delivery of bread. Bar, restaurant and takeaway (all year). Teepee with bar and barbecue for socialising and events. Playground. Boules. Basketball. Teepees for rent. WiFi throughout (charged).

Ideal For...

Beach

Dogs

Year Round Camping

Fishing

Watersports

Golf

Scan me for more information.

250 pitches
GPS: 46.58807, 7.91077
Post Code: CH-3822

Bern, Central

Camping Jungfrau

www.alanrogers.com/ch9460
info@camping-jungfrau.ch
033 856 2010
www.campingjungfrau.swiss

Open (Touring Pitches):
All year.

This friendly and ever popular site has a very imposing and dramatic situation in a steep valley with a fine view of the Jungfrau at the end. It is a busy site and, although you should usually find space, in season do not arrive too late. A fairly extensive area is made up of grass pitches and hardcore access roads. All 391 pitches (250 for touring) have shade in parts, electrical connections (13A) and 50 have water and drainage also. Over 35% of the pitches are taken by seasonal caravans, chalets to rent and two tour operators. Family owned and run by Herr and Frau Fuchs, you can be sure of a warm welcome and English is spoken. You can laze here amid real mountain scenery, though it does lose the sun a little early.

Three fully equipped modern sanitary blocks can be heated in winter and one provides facilities for disabled visitors. Baby baths. Laundry facilities. Motorcaravan services. Well equipped campers' kitchen. Excellent shop. Self-service restaurant with takeaway (all year). General room with tables and chairs, TV, drinks machines, amusements. Playgrounds and covered play area. Excursions and some entertainment in high season. Mountain bike hire. ATM. Drying room. Ski store. Free shuttle bus in winter. Internet point. WiFi throughout (free).

Ideal For...

 Dogs

 Year Round Camping

 Fishing

 Walking

 Play Area

 Disabled Facilities

Scan me for more information.

13 accommodations
125 pitches
GPS: 46.20583, 7.27867
Post Code: CH-1963

Valais, South

www.alanrogers.com/ch9520
info@botza.ch
027 346 1940
www.botza.ch

Open (Touring Pitches):
All year.

Camping du Botza

Situated in the Rhône Valley just off the autoroute, this is a pleasant site with views of the surrounding mountains. It is set in a peaceful wooded location, although there is occasional aircraft noise. There are 125 individual touring pitches, ranging in size from 60 to 155 sq.m. all with 4A electricity, many with some shade and 25 with water and drainage. Pitches are priced according to size and facilities. The reception, office, lounge, shop and restaurant have all been completely rebuilt. The conservatory-style restaurant overlooks the pool and the entertainment area. Both are open to the public but free to campers. A warm welcome is assured from the enthusiastic English-speaking owner. A new barrier has been installed.

New sanitary block and another completely renovated. Some private cabins in the heated sanitary block. Washing machines and dryers. Shop. Brand new restaurant (closed Jan) and terrace. Bar. Bakery. Ice cream kiosk. Takeaway. Heated swimming pool with slides and diving board (15/5-31/8). Playground. Table football and electronic games. Tennis. Basketball. TV room with Internet corner. Entertainment stage. Multi-lingual library, board games and tourist information. WiFi on part of site (free).

Ideal For...

Dogs

Year Round Camping

Fishing

Golf

Play Area

Scan me for more information.

86 accommodations
610 pitches
GPS: 46.16895, 8.85592
Post Code: CH-6598

Ticino, South

Camping Campofelice

www.alanrogers.com/ch9890
camping@campofelice.ch
091 745 1417
www.campofelice.ch

Open (Touring Pitches):
27 March - 31 October.

Considered by many to be the best family campsite in Switzerland, Campofelice is bordered on the front by Lake Maggiore and on one side by the Verzasca estuary, where the site has its own marina. It is divided into rows, with 610 generously sized touring pitches on flat grass on either side of hard access roads. Mostly well shaded, all pitches have electricity connections (10-13A, 360 Europlug) and 410 also have water, drainage and TV connections. Pitches near the lake cost more (these are not available for motorcaravans until September) and a special area is reserved for small tents. A little more expensive than other sites in the area, but excellent value for the range and quality of the facilities.

The six toilet blocks (three heated) are of exemplary quality. Washing machines and dryers. Motorcaravan services. Gas supplies. Supermarket, restaurant, bar and takeaway (all season). Snack kiosk at beach. Lifeguards on duty. Tennis. Minigolf. Bicycle hire. Canoe and pedalo hire. Boat launching. Playgrounds. Doctor calls. Dogs are not accepted. New chalet for disabled visitors. Camping accessories shop. Car hire. Car wash. WiFi (charged).

Ideal For...

 Kids

 Beach

 Fishing

 Watersports

 Golf

Play Area

Scan me for more information.

1 accommodations
65 pitches
GPS: 46.29781, 7.65937
Post Code: CH-3952

Valais, South

Camping Gemmi Agarn

www.alanrogers.com/ch9730
info@campgemmi.ch
027 473 1154
www.campgemmi.ch

Open (Touring Pitches):
Easter - mid October.

The Rhône Valley is a popular through route to Italy via the Simplon Pass and a holiday region in its own right. Gemmi is a delightful small, friendly site in a scenic location with 65 level touring pitches, all with 16A electricity, on grass amidst a variety of trees, some of which offer shade. There are 41 pitches with water, 26 with drainage as well. Some pitches have TV connections. Always well maintained, the grounds have been greatly improved by the enthusiastic new owners. Seven seasonal pitches remain, with one unit to rent. This site will be enjoyed by campers of all ages. Enjoying some of the best climatic conditions in Switzerland, this valley, between two mountain regions, has less rainfall and more hours of sunshine than most of the country.

A modern sanitary block, partly heated, is kept very clean. It includes some washbasins in cabins. Eight private bathrooms for hire on a weekly basis. Washing machines and dryers. Motorcaravan services. Gas supplies. Well stocked shop. Small bar/restaurant where snacks and a limited range of local specialities are served. Terrace bar and snack restaurant. Play area. TV room. Small library. WiFi throughout (charged).

Ideal For...

 Beach

 Dogs

 Fishing

 Golf

 Play Area

 Disabled Facilities

Scan me for more information.

4 accommodations
220 pitches
GPS: 45.93347, 7.09367
Post Code: CH-1944

Valais, South

Camping des Glaciers

www.alanrogers.com/ch9660
info@camping-glaciers.ch
027 783 1826
www.camping-glaciers.ch

Open (Touring Pitches):
15 May - 30 September.

Camping des Glaciers is set amidst magnificent mountain scenery in a peaceful location in the beautiful Ferret Valley, almost 5,000 feet above sea level. The site offers generous pitches in an open, undulating meadow and the rest are level, individual plots of varying sizes in small clearings, between bushes and shrubs or under tall pines. Most of the 220 pitches have 10A electricity (long leads useful). M. Alain Darbellay has meticulously maintained the family's determination to keep the site unspoilt and in keeping with its mountain environment. He intends to maintain the strong family interest and friendships built up over the years. Additional land has been added to increase the number of pitches available.

Three sanitary units of exceptional quality are heated when necessary. The newest unit has super facilities for children and wide access for disabled visitors. Hot water is free in all washbasins (some in cabins), showers and sinks. British style WCs. Washing machines and dryers in each block, one block has a drying room, another a baby room. Gas supplies. Motorcaravan services. Small shop for basics. Bread and cakes to order daily. Recreation room with TV. Playground. Mountain bike hire. Communal fire pit. WiFi (free). Torches useful.

Ideal For...

 Dogs

 Fishing

 Walking

 Play Area

 Disabled Facilities

 Pets Accepted

Scan me for more information.

3 accommodations
160 pitches
GPS: 46.29808, 7.87271
Post Code: CH-3930

Valais, South

www.alanrogers.com/ch9775
info@camping-visp.ch
027 946 2084
www.camping-visp.ch

Open (Touring Pitches):
25 March - 31 October.

Camping Mühleye

Camping Schwimmbad Mühleye is a popular family site located in the Valais near the busy centre of Visp. The site has 199 grassy pitches, 160 for touring units with 18A electricity, ranging in size from 80-150 sq.m, including 20 very large (150 sq.m) pitches (with electricity, water and drainage). Although the pitches are marked and numbered, the site has a relaxed informal appearance with plenty of space between units. The valley and mountain views are typically Swiss. The town of Visp is a 15 minute walk away, from where it is easy to explore the area by bus and train. Saas Fee, Zermatt and the Matterhorn are all within reach.

New central sanitary block is modern and spacious. Facilities for disabled visitors. Washing machines and dryers. Free use of fridges and freezers. Motorcaravan services. Two children's play areas and an indoor play room if wet. Large covered sitting area with tables and chairs. Extensive information for walking, hiking and mountain biking. Internet access. WiFi throughout (free).

Ideal For...

 Beach

 Dogs

 Fishing

 Watersports

 Golf

 Play Area

Scan me for more information.

4 accommodations
160 pitches
GPS: 47.05254, 7.06978
Post Code: CH-2525

Neuchâtel, West

Camping des Pêches

www.alanrogers.com/ch9040
info@camping-lelanderon.ch
032 751 2900
www.camping-lelanderon.ch

Open (Touring Pitches):
1 April - 15 October.

This relatively recently constructed, touring campsite is on the side of Lake Biel and the river Thielle, close to the old town of Le Landeron. The site is divided into two sections, on the lake side of the road are residential seasonal caravans, and on the other is the modern campsite for tourers. The 160 touring pitches are all on level grass, numbered but not separated; a few have shade, all have 13A electricity and many conveniently placed water points. All the facilities are well maintained and in good condition. A short walk brings you to the historic old town.

The spacious, modern sanitary block contains all the usual facilities including a food preparation area with six cooking rings, a large freezer and refrigerator. Payment for showers is by card (1 CHF/min). Baby room. Facilities for disabled visitors. Laundry. Motorcaravan services. Community room and small café in reception building. Shop, restaurant and takeaway (all season). Playground. Bicycle hire. TV and general room. WiFi throughout.

Ideal For...

 Beach

 Dogs

 Fishing

 Watersports

 Golf

 Play Area

Scan me for more information.

84 pitches
GPS: 46.743845, 9.779297
Post Code: CH-7277

Graubünden, East

Camping RinerLodge

www.alanrogers.com/ch9842
rinerlodge@davosklosters.ch
081 417 0033
www.davosklosters.ch

Open (Touring Pitches):
13 December - 6 April, 17 May - 20 October.

Camping RinerLodge forms part of a holiday complex that has been developed at Glaris, 5 km. south of the important resort of Davos. The complex consists of a small campsite and an adjacent hotel and restaurant. The campsite offers 84 pitches, all equipped with 16A electricity. They are grassy and many have fine mountain views. A number of footpaths and cycle trails pass close to the site. The hotel restaurant is very good, and specialises in regional cuisine. There is no toilet block on site but there are ample facilities within the hotel for use by all campers.

Play area. Hotel restaurant and bar adjacent. Fishing. Skiing. Shop. Wifi (partial). Cycling and walking routes form the campsite. Games room. TV.

Ideal For...

 Dogs

 Fishing

 Golf

 Play Area

 Pets Accepted

 Bar on Site

Scan me for more information.

INDEX

LOCATION